THE LITERARY SITUATION

The
LITERARY SITUATION

by
MALCOLM COWLEY

New York

THE VIKING PRESS

COMPASS BOOKS EDITION
ISSUED IN 1958 BY THE VIKING PRESS, INC.
625 MADISON AVENUE, NEW YORK, N.Y. 10022.

DISTRIBUTED IN CANADA BY
THE MACMILLAN COMPANY OF CANADA LIMITED

FOURTH PRINTING APRIL 1966

Grateful acknowledgment is made to the editors of
the following, in which portions of this book
originally appeared: *Harper's Magazine, New Republic, New World Writing, New York Herald
Tribune Book Review, The New York Times Book
Review, The Times* (London) *Literary Supplement,
Perspectives USA, The Reporter, Saturday Review,*
and *Chicago.*

Library of Congress catalog card number: 54-7984

PRINTED IN THE U.S.A. BY THE COLONIAL PRESS INC.

FOR ROB AND HIS FRIENDS

—who asked the questions

CONTENTS

FOREWORD

This isn't a collection of critical essays. It isn't a collection, it isn't intended to be critical, and it doesn't, or I hope it doesn't, consist of separate essays. Recent criticism has been best when dealing with single books or authors and the reasons why they should be read with attention. Here I am dealing with whole categories of books—war novels, the "new" fiction, and the new criticism among others—and with the qualities that books in each group have in common. As a result I am sometimes unfair to the authors as individuals; an author's best qualities are his own, not those he shares with a group. I like and admire criticism "in depth," but there are occasions when one should stand back to survey the situation in breadth, from a perspective in space or time. Although I lack the perspective in space, since it is many years since I lived abroad, I have been watching the literary situation for a longer time than one likes to think about, so that I can compare what is happening in the 1950s with my memories of what happened after another world war. I thought of the book as a social history of literature in our times, or, let us say, as the report and observations of a stay-at-home traveler.

In a sense I have been writing it all my life, but it started to take shape in the autumn of 1952. At that time I was editing an issue of *Perspectives USA* for distribution in Europe. The issue—which appeared a year later, after more than the customary delay—was supposed to be prefaced by an editorial, and this, I thought, might try to explain for European readers what was happening in American literature. I found myself writing a great deal more than would go into any editorial, even a leader in the *New York Times*. I wrote about the "new" fiction, and that became an article for *Harper's*. I wrote about the effect of critical slogans on the younger novelists, and that became an article for the *Saturday Review*. In the midst of these excursions I found the editorial I was looking for, together with a title, "The Literary Situation," but then I began working on a new subject, connected with the others; it was living and working conditions in the writing profession.

As the book continued to grow—for by that time it was clearly a book—I saw that some earlier pieces also belonged in it, though never in exactly the shape in which they had appeared in magazines. Everything was changed and expanded as I went along. The survey of the writing profession, which I called "A Natural History of the American Writer," was intended to be one chapter, but it grew into four and might have been a book in itself. I planned a chapter, and wrote two, on the publishing business, which is now in a period of transition, though I couldn't say to what. The changes in publishing will have an effect on the types of fiction and poetry that are presented—or sometimes aren't presented—to the reading public. I wrote a final chapter describing some changes in the intimate life of Americans that are likely to produce a somewhat different literature in the future; and I offered a few hesitant prophecies about the directions this future literature might follow. The chapter also discussed the new generation of writers, who aren't "beat" or broken and certainly aren't silent, but who seem a little uncertain about where they are going.

I hate to write and love to revise, and this book is the most extensive work of revision I have undertaken. It starts with the first paragraph of the editorial in *Perspectives USA* (revised), and ends with the last paragraph of the editorial (also revised), but at first there were three thousand words between them and now there are a hundred thousand. A great many persons have contributed information or ideas that went into the book, often without knowing that they were doing so. Among them I should like to mention, alphabetically, Conrad Aiken, Benjamin Appel, Nathan Asch, Marshall A. Best, Van Wyck Brooks, Kenneth Burke, Pascal Covici, Muriel and Robert Cowley, Reuel Denney, William Faulkner, Hartley Grattan, Harold K. Guinzburg, Ernest Hemingway, Randall Jarrell, John Kerouac, Robert N. Linscott, Arabel Porter, Dr. William H. Resnik (of Stamford), David Riesman, Alvin A. Rolfs (of Purdue University), Diarmuid Russell, Philip H. Smith, James Thurber, Thornton Wilder, and Louis Zara. I owe special thanks to the Newberry Library of Chicago and its librarian, Dr. Stanley Pargellis, for giving me a fellowship that enabled me to write, or revise, part of the book in comfortable circumstances, in a city that won't let one's mind be idle. I hope the book will be of some value to writers, old, new, and beginning, and of interest to general readers with that American passion for taking things apart to see how they work.

M.C.

THE LITERARY SITUATION

I.

THE NEW AGE

OF THE RHETORICIANS

1.

One has to be skeptical of phrases like "the advance of the novel" and "the progress of poetry," yet there have been times when the novel did advance, for example in firmness of structure or in understanding of persons and groups of persons. Alternating with periods of decline there have been times when poetry did make progress, both technically and as a social institution, one that loosely unites a guild of poets with an attentive body of readers. In the United States today the institution has a flickering sort of life and poetry seems to be retreating, while fiction seems to be standing still. Partly that is only an appearance, caused by a diversity of movements in opposite directions that threaten to cancel out. Partly there has been an actual halt or withdrawal while novelists and poets tried to consolidate positions already reached by the more daring of their predecessors; forces are shifted about or drilled and strengthened, but without much change in the map of the battlefront.

These are years of armistice in which, for all the appearance of inactivity, we are entering a new literary period, and one that bears little resemblance to the immediate past. Sometimes we hear that the 1920s have been revived or reborn; the truth is that they have become a sort of excavated ruin, a subject for historical studies and critical arguments. Unlike the present age, the 1920s were a time of experiment in all the creative arts, including poetry, fiction, and hot jazz. Criticism was not then widely admired or practiced, though some of it was influential; the best of it was written by experimental poets like Eliot and Pound who were defending their own ventures or trying to give directions to those who followed them. There were further experiments in the 1930s, but most of them were concerned with problems of subject and purpose more than they were with forms or methods. In those years literature had come to be regarded as an instrument of social change, and the catchwords were "social realism" in fiction, "social symbolism" in poetry, and "art in the service of the revolution."

Then, at the end of the decade, there was an abrupt loss of interest in social themes, but without much indication of what would take their place. Everybody felt that literature after the war would be "different." Nobody had clear grounds for prophesying what the new writers would say, since most of the younger men—and soon the younger women too—were in uniform or were occupied by wartime activities that left them little time for literary work. Some prophecies were made and soon confuted by events. There was, for example, no such outburst of lyric poetry as there had been in England during World War I. There was not much topical writing that reached a literary level. After the war there was more than the expected number of novels about the armed services, and they were interesting for the mood they shared as well as for their subject matter, but they did not reveal many changes in the art of writing fiction.

Unexpectedly, most of the really new developments since 1940 have been in the field of criticism. Even the new creative writing shows a high degree of critical consciousness—so much of it that the novels and poems of the new age sometimes read like themes written to illustrate the best critical principles. Criticism has come to occupy such a central place in the literary world that it is hard to find historical parallels for the situation. Certainly there is none in American history, and one thinks of China under the Ming dynasty or, better still, of the Roman Empire during and after the age of the Antonines, which was also the great age of the rhetoricians. In those days politics had ceased to be a career open to talents; philosophy was stagnant and imaginative writing was regarded as something that belonged to the past. The central study in the schools was rhetoric, and this had ceased to be merely the art of persuasion; it had developed into a study of literary structure and texture that resembled much of our contemporary criticism. Teachers of rhetoric occupied an even more commanding position than American critics, most of whom are also teachers. Says the eleventh edition of the *Britannica*:

The public teacher of rhetoric was called "sophist," which was now an academic title, similar to "professor" or "doctor." . . . The Rhetorical school [at Athens] had two chairs, one for "sophistic," the other for "political" rhetoric. By "sophistic" was meant the academic teaching of rhetoric as an art, in distinction to its "political" application to the law-courts. The "sophistical" chair was superior to the "political" in dignity as in emolument, and its occupant was invested with a jurisdiction over the youth of Athens similar to that of a vice-chancellor in a modern university.

Some of the rhetoricians excelled in the critical analysis of texts. Longinus, for example, was famous for his commentaries on Homer, and it is interesting to note that the treatise *On the Sublime*, attributed to him, is once again being widely quoted. But the parallel can be carried too far, and I am inclined to doubt that the present age of criticism results from any such prolonged cultural process as that which produced the reign of the rhetoricians; we are not late Romans yet, or sixteenth-century Chinese scholars; there are too many creative forces at work in our society. Rather the situation seems to be one of the temporary sequels of the Second World War.

Every postwar generation, whether it is Romantic or Lost or Silent, feels that it has been asked to share in too many public emotions. After the fighting stops it leaves the fate of the world to professional politicians—most of whom are conservatives in such periods—and concerns itself with the questions it regards as personal and immediate, or eternal. Every big war or revolution since 1800 has been followed by a period of reaction in the countries that did the fighting; in its political sense the word "reaction" is almost a synonym for public apathy or discouragement. The Russian revolution of 1917 is an apparent exception only because the new ruling group fought against the popular mood—and in so doing fell into a more confusing and ominous type of reaction.

In the literary world every big war of our time has been followed by a movement away from socially oriented writing toward abstract or subjective literature, toward pure poetry, dream fiction, or dogged scholarship. After World War I what happened to American writers was largely a repetition in different terms of what was happening in

England and Germany (as witness the Bright Young People and the German Expressionists) and of what had happened in France after 1848 and 1870, in Russia after 1905—and even after 1917, when Russian poetry was dominated for a time by the Futurists and Russian painting by the Abstractionists. I remember a delegation of young Russian writers who visited Paris in 1923 and made speeches in their own language—but I could recognize one word they used, the word *abstrakt* repeated over and over, as if they were all determined to be *abstrakt* at any cost. In a few years abstractionism and even mere formalism—that is, an "undue" interest in the technical side of writing—would be punished as crimes against the Russian workers. The radical (or reactionary) politicians had triumphed over radicalism in the arts.

In this country after World War II one might have expected a similar movement of artists away from politics; in fact the movement started before the war and shows no signs of halting. One also might have expected a period of literary experiment. There has been such a period in painting, with American abstractionists warring against American subjectivists or surrealists, but the writers found themselves in a different situation from that which prevailed in the other arts. Literary experiment had been carried so far in the hundred years since Poe and Baudelaire that there seemed to be hardly anything experimental for writers to do that hadn't been done already —if they thought, for example, of writing a whole novel about the dreams of one night, that was what Joyce had done in *Finnegans Wake* and they couldn't hope to do it better; or if they merely thought of copying a list of names from the telephone book and publishing the list as a poem and a gesture of defiance, well, Tristan Tzara had published such a list and there was no use imitating the Dadaists. At such a time as this it seemed more fruitful to review and reconsider the whole modernist movement and to define its permanent achievements as a basis for future work; in other words it seemed more fruitful for novelists and poets to transform themselves into critics.

But besides this postwar mood, with the special turn it had taken in the literary world, there were other developments that help to explain the popularity of criticism. There was the practical circumstance that more young writers than ever before were postgraduate students or teachers in the universities. Writing criticism was more helpful to an academic career and grew out of it more naturally than the writing of poetry or fiction. The question of personal leadership cannot be disregarded. Several men of great personal authority had chosen to be critics, and their example was effective in persuading others to follow them; also they had developed new methods of interpretation that made the critical field more attractive to young men who wanted to be explorers and discoverers. Finally there was the simple matter of fashion, which has always played an important part on this continent where everything goes by extremes, heat, cold, sunshine, rainfall, even popular moods and systems of belief. Everything produced by society or nature is produced to excess, whether it is salmon that choke the rivers, carrier pigeons that blacken the sky, or stock salesmen, flappers, and literary revolutionists. Nothing appears but it increases; nothing increases but it teems, pullulates—and suddenly is gone. One might picture another literary situation in which new critics had become as rare as proletarian novelists, New Humanists, technocrats, muckrakers, single taxers, transcendentalists, or bison on the prairies.

But that is a mere speculation, not a prophecy, and critics are in fashion today. One hears it maintained that this is an age of criticism in the special sense that the Elizabethan period was the age of the poetic drama and the Victorian period the age of the novel. That is not the opinion of the wider public, which still reads novels (preferably those reprinted in soft covers and sold on the newsstands) when it doesn't read personal narratives or inspirational books. The mass-circulation magazines like *Life* and *Reader's Digest* and the *Saturday Evening Post* don't publish criticism, and newspapers confine it to the book-review section or the editorial page. The best of it appears in books with a limited sale and magazines with a small body of readers. But the critics today have power and status; there are more of them than ever before, including more writers of original talent, and they are listened to with greater attention, because they speak with more authority than most of the novelists or poets.

2.

Only an unobservant reader could fail to be impressed by the growing quantity and generally higher quality of writing in the critical field. Reviews of current books—to start with a humble corner of the field—are better written and better informed than they were thirty years ago. Too many of them used to be dashed off by boys just out of college—I was one of them—or by suburban housewives who had once shown promise and were trying to keep a foothold in literature. The principal virtue of the reviews was to reveal the writers' opinions in all their innocence. Now the reviewers are much older on the average, they are paid at somewhat higher rates, and they seem to feel that they will be additionally rewarded for brilliant work: that they will be admired by their friends and will earn better positions in the literary, publishing, or academic worlds. Accordingly they express themselves with care and their reviews have acquired a professional quality, in a field that used to be pre-empted by amateurs.

Criticism proper, as distinguished from book reviewing, is also finding opportunities for development. One notes the growing number of quarterly reviews devoted largely to critical writing, like *Kenyon*, *Sewanee*, *Hudson*, *Western*, and at least a dozen others, generically described as "little magazines." The term is an old one and leads to confusion, since nothing like these quarterlies existed thirty years ago—not even *Sewanee Review*, which did exist but was directed chiefly to scholars. The little magazines of the 1920s really deserved the name. They were smaller in size, smaller in circulation, shorter-lived (if we except the *Little Review* and *transition*); they were usually edited by very young men, and their tone was informal, even irresponsible. The literary quarterlies of the 1950s are mature, solid, academic. Some of the best are partly subsidized by colleges or universities (*Sewanee*, *Kenyon*, *Western*) and most of the others are edited on campuses, with some help from members of the teaching staff. Even those published by non-academic groups (like *Partisan Review*, which resembles the quarterlies but appears six times a year) have a high proportion of junior professors among their contributors, and some of their editors compile anthologies that are used in college courses as collateral reading.

The little magazines of the 1920s had no such academic connections. They were published as much for fun—today the youngsters would say "for kicks"—as for any other motive. Most of them were printed in Europe at a very low cost; I remember one issue of *Secession* for which I paid the Viennese printer in full with a twenty-dollar bill. Editors earned a little prestige in lieu of salary, and contributors, in most cases, earned nothing at all, not even thanks. Many of the new quarterlies have salaried staffs, and most of them make at least token payments for what they print. A few have been given grants by foundations and pay contributors at a respectable rate. Other expenses are high, and publishing a literary magazine in the 1950s is a costly venture, one that requires plans, conferences, and long-continued efforts, with the result that even the smaller quarterlies are becoming institutionalized. One might define an institution as a joint undertaking that has acquired a life of its own and does not mirror the personality of any member of the staff. Early in the history of a quarterly review the founder and editor-in-chief will find himself explaining that he admires a certain manuscript and agrees with almost everything it says, but still it can't be printed because it runs counter to the policy of the magazine. He means— if he is telling the truth—that the magazine has partly escaped from his direction and has acquired a life and character of its own; already it has become an institution.

The little magazines were seldom institutional, and indeed they tried to stand outside the social system as a whole, where the quarterlies are involved in it. The professor who writes for the quarterlies is more respected, in many academic circles, than his colleague who reads a scholarly paper to the Modern Language Association, and as a reward for his writing he has as good a claim as the colleague to academic advancement. He feels a burden of responsibility to his wife and children. He can safely attack novelists or poets or other critics—and does attack them, time and again— but I suspect him of hesitating a little before exposing the blunders of Professor X——, whom he meets every day at the Faculty Club, or questioning the wisdom of Dean Y—— of a sister university, who might some day offer him a better job. Contributors to little magazines felt no such need to be reticent.

But the principal difference between the two types of publication is in their contents. The little magazines printed manifestoes, a few tributes or appreciations, and many blasts against recognized writers, but they seldom printed a formal literary essay. Chiefly they consisted of stories, poems, and what might be classified as fragments of experimental writing. There is little such writing in the quarterlies. In each issue we are likely to find one or two rather long and carefully written stories, and a long poem or a group of shorter ones, but at least two-thirds of the magazine will be devoted to criticism. Recently I examined the four 1952 issues of the useful and generally distinguished *Sewanee Review*; together they contained 741 pages

of text. There were 90 pages of fiction, or four stories, and 53 pages
of poetry, so that creative writing provided a little more than 19
per cent of the year's harvest. Everything else was criticism, including 198 pages of commentaries and book reviews. There were five
critical essays in each issue, as against one story, and the essays
occupied exactly 400 pages during the year, or more than half
the text.

Almost all the essays are of a type that hardly existed in the
1920s. They are usually about six thousand words in length, or
the equivalent of a forty-five-minute college lecture, and they give
very close attention to a narrowly defined subject. Often the critic
writes fifteen or twenty pages about one lyric poem, or even one
stanza of a poem, or about a single theme chosen from other themes
in one of William Faulkner's novels. This close attention is the
mark of the newer critics; perhaps it is their trade secret. Primarily
they are studious, intelligent, and imaginative—sometimes too
imaginative—readers. They have discovered that every literary
work is much more complicated and meaningful than it seems to
those who read with less care, and they have set themselves the task
of explaining or—as many of them prefer to say—"explicating" the
work in all its complexity.

"Explicate" is an old and respectable English word, but during
the first half of this century it had been almost completely abandoned
for "explain," which comes from a Latin verb that means to spread
out or make smooth. Most of the older critics tried to make a smooth
path for the reader. The newer critics explicate—or unfold, to give
the word its etymological sense—and often they leave the creases
showing, so that reading their work may be like deciphering a sheet
of crumpled vellum. Most of them are not afraid of being difficult
and some are fond of using technical language; it is as if they regarded criticism as one of the learned disciplines, almost like
biometrics or paleontology. They seem to feel that "explicate" has
the right technical sound, and there is another reason, too, why some
of them like to use it: the word reveals their kinship with French
academic critics (and students) and their *explications de texte*.
There is no doubt that the newer criticism in this country is partly
derived from French nineteenth-century sources. There is also no
doubt that in certain directions it has outdistanced the sources and
entered new territory.

I say "outdistanced" without making any judgment of quality.

Perhaps in failing to make it I reveal, and share, a weakness of present-day American critics as a class: that they hesitate to make broad judgments, that they sometimes discuss a poem or a novel for twenty pages and still leave us in doubt whether it is good or bad or whether it justifies their prolonged attention. Outside of the professional book reviewers, who are a contentious race, there are only a few critics like Edmund Wilson and Allen Tate who clearly put forward their opinions about an author and their reasons for holding them. The others explicate their chosen texts and sometimes in making the explication—or exegesis—they forget what the author was consciously trying to say, to what sort of audience, and whether it was worth saying. Yet in certain directions—let us say in subtlety of interpretation, in finding different levels of meaning, in revealing the mechanism of literary effects—I think that some of them go beyond any other critics writing today.

There is Kenneth Burke, for example, with his "dramatistic" method, as he calls it, of studying literary works as symbolic actions. His critical essays—sometimes difficult, always new and stimulating —are incidental to a broader series of speculations based on his definition of man as "specifically the symbol-using animal." Edmund Wilson is a critic by popular request and almost in spite of himself—that is, in spite of his expeditions into poetry, fiction, and drama, which have never been so widely admired as his criticism. Nobody is better at interpreting the general drift and meaning of a work, but Wilson is also interested in the author's personality as affected by the historical background, and in that respect he belongs partly to the tradition of Taine, partly to that of Sainte-Beuve.

Allen Tate and Yvor Winters are distinguished by their sense of literary values, which is so strongly developed that it has become a moral and almost a religious feeling. As a matter of fact Tate is a Catholic convert, while Winters is a sometimes wrong-headed and always independent puritan. Richard Blackmur has a special feeling for patterns of language, one that casts a new light on any poem he studies. Cleanth Brooks is skilled in discovering hidden ironies and in unraveling the complicated series of meanings that a poet may attach to apparently simple words. Like Blackmur he is essentially a *rhetor*, in the late Greek application of the word to a subtle student of linguistics. I. A. Richards, who teaches at Harvard, is one of several writers born in England and educated at Cambridge who have played an important part in American criticism.[1] Two of his interests are the science of communication and the psychology of the reader. R. S. Crane, Elder Olson, and others of the Chicago school are trying to revive and modernize the principles of criticism first enounced by Aristotle. William Troy puts his emphasis on myths and rituals as embodied in great works of literature, and there are many younger critics, including Joseph Campbell, Richard Chase, and Leslie Fiedler, who are working in the same direction.

I mention these names chiefly to show the diversity of critical writing, and I might have chosen others instead: Morton Zabel, Francis Fergusson, Newton Arvin, Lionel Trilling, W. K. Wimsatt, Jr., Katherine Anne Porter, F. O. Matthiessen (who died in 1951), Robert Penn Warren, Austin Warren, Mark Schorer, Alfred Kazin, Randall Jarrell, and John Crowe Ransom, an older critic who taught some of the others and provided an example to most of them. It was Ransom who published a book of essays called *The New Criticism* (1941), and his title has been applied at one time or another to the work of all these critics except Wilson and the Chicago Aristotelians. In fact the phrase is being flung about so loosely that Ransom himself has been forced to declare, "I do not know what is meant nowadays by a 'new' critic." But Ransom once used another phrase that casts more light on a current tendency. He called for an "ontological" criticism and seemed to imply that critics should not concern themselves with the sources of a work or with its moral and social effects, but should confine their discussion to the work as a separate entity with its own laws of being. In that sense many of the newer critics might be described as ontological. They like to argue about esthetic questions, they refrain from discussing social movements, and they devote an extremely close and fruitful attention to each new work they discuss.

Reading such critics, many of whom are university professors, one half expects to enter an atmosphere of dry scholarship and meaningless disputation. Somehow the picture of widespread critical activity suggests that we are living in an Alexandrian or late-Roman age of lowered creative vigor. There are indeed clear traces of Alexandrianism in present-day critical writing, but more among the younger disciples than among the older critics I mentioned. In 1952 Ransom reviewed a volume of essays on poetry by Richard

1. Others are William Empson, who often lectures in the United States, and F. R. Leavis.

Blackmur, *Language as Gesture*. He gave the volume high and justified praise, but then made an unexpected reservation: that Blackmur treated ideas as if they had no value in themselves or in relation to life and as if their only function in the poem was to furnish a scheme of organization. The founder of ontological criticism was reproving Blackmur for being too ontological. Both Ransom and Blackmur are independent thinkers who have retained the liberty to change their minds, but their disciples have no such liberty, being disciples; they can only accept the leading ideas of the master and apply them to new subjects, or carry them to extremes that the master is realistic enough to avoid. Sometimes they are embarrassed when he contradicts himself—as when T. S. Eliot, who had always disparaged Milton, suddenly rediscovered the virtues of *Paradise Lost* in an essay that was like a stick poked into an anthill. There was a confused scurrying. Some of the younger critics protested that Eliot used to be right about Milton but was now denying his own principles, while others readjusted their scale of values and tried to convince themselves that Milton was a great poet after all.

This deference to authority is Alexandrian or scholastic and it encourages other harmful tendencies that I plan to discuss; but first I should say that an atmosphere of lowered creative vitality is not characteristic of the newer criticism. The atmosphere that still prevails is one of excitement, vigor, combativeness, as if we were reading the rival reports of pioneers who had entered an unexplored region of great promise. The best of the present-day critics have discovered new methods of research and new values in the books they criticize. The best of their long essays—I might mention Edmund Wilson on Dickens and Newton Arvin on *Moby-Dick*, among many other examples—are lasting works that give us a fresh respect for the powers of the human mind. If a central function of literature is to broaden or deepen our sense of life, not a few of these critics are performing that function, even if they must approach life through books that others have written. No law of nature decrees that one literary form is necessarily better or more constructive than another form. In some ways our critics are now performing the writer's function better than many of the new novelists and poets, whose work by comparison seems timid, formal, and correct—more critical and less creative.

And the critics have been lucky in one respect: American nineteenth-century literature furnished them with a comparatively new field for study. Every culture has to create its past as well as its future, and there was a time when the American past, in literature, was neglected and almost forgotten. That was of course before Van Wyck Brooks started to publish his five volumes on the writer in America. As late as 1920 literary journalists kept beseeching young writers to provide something that they always described as "the great American novel." The journalists did not suspect that it might have been written already. The great American novel had indeed been written, published, and reviewed, and yet in a sense it did not exist. I don't mean to speak in puzzles: the fact is that "great," in the sense in which literary journalists were using the word, is not merely a quality of the novel itself, but also describes the attitude toward it of the educated public. In 1920 there was still no American novel that was great in the sense of being greatly admired.

There is more to be said on the subject. It is possible to maintain that any great literary work, any classic, is a joint undertaking for which the author, of course, is chiefly responsible, but in which he requires a host of collaborators. A whole culture helped to fashion the work and a whole culture must learn to accept it before it acquires the charismatic quality implied by the word "great." *The Divine Comedy, Hamlet, Don Quixote, Phèdre, Faust*: all these are more than the texts bequeathed by their authors, who, for all their exceptional talents, were men of their time, not mythical heroes or demigods. Clustered round the texts, interfused with the texts, are all the values discovered in them or added to them by generations of students, critics, interpreters, and ordinary readers.

As recently as thirty years ago the United States had no national classic of this order (and when I say "of this order" I am, once more, implying no judgment of the works in their relative quality, but only of their position in various cultures). That lack has at last been supplied by a vast collaborative undertaking, by hundreds of scholars and critics sometimes making their discoveries in common, sometimes quarreling with one another or with the adherents of a different candidate for greatness, but always working toward the same goal. Perhaps the principal creative work of the last three decades in this country has not been any novel or poem or drama of our time, not even Faulkner's Yoknapatawpha saga or Hemingway's *For Whom the Bell Tolls* or Hart Crane's *The Bridge*; perhaps it has been the critical rediscovery and reinterpretation of Melville's *Moby-Dick* and its promotion, step by step, to the position of national epic.

3.

To the extent that criticism has become a central form, it exercises a sort of magnetism and attracts talents that might have expressed themselves in other fashions. Burke, for example, would certainly have been a dramatist if he had lived in another age (and he calls his critical theory "dramatism" as if to reveal his bent). Wilson is a positive and somewhat Johnsonian character who, if he had been born in the eighteenth century, would have put his essays into heroic couplets, besides writing prose satires and moral tales. Ransom, Tate, Winters, and Jarrell are distinguished poets and so is Robert Penn Warren, who is also a novelist and a dramatist, while Katherine Anne Porter is a born story-teller. All these writers first practiced criticism as a subsidiary activity that yielded them a small income, where poetry and fiction yielded less or nothing, and they understand the author's point of view because they are authors.

Many of the younger men are in the different position of having been critics and teachers from the beginning. In the quite natural attempt to put their whole personalities into their critical writing, they sometimes allow it to be deformed by a sort of thwarted creativeness. Instead of approaching any imaginative work as an object to be studied for itself and revealed in its true nature, they are tempted to regard it as subject matter for an imaginative work of their own, a critical tone poem or fantasia. The result is that the work under discussion may be transformed into something its author never intended or dreamed it would be. In the critic's interpretation, or "reading," it is seldom a "mere" poem or drama or novel, written to render a mood or present a situation or tell a story; instead it is a myth based on Jung's theory of the collective unconscious, or a Freudian revelation of the author's repressed homosexuality, or a complicated exercise in linguistics—or again it is Telemachus in search of his father, Odysseus descending into the underworld, a ritual of rebirth, a casting out of devils, a social allegory, a study in classical allusions, a theological commentary on the Fall of Man, or even—as one critic reinterpreted *Billy Budd*,

after stewing together a mess of Freudian and Christian symbols—
it is "castration and cannibalism, the ritual murder and eating of
the Host." [2]

We shouldn't forget that some of these critical readings or
exegeses are justified by the text and succeed in giving it a new
dimension. In particular the search for mythical patterns is a fruitful
study and helps to reveal the connection between literature and the
popular mind at any given period—that is, if the critic also studies
the popular mind. But the fact remains that far too many of the
readings are more like spiritualistic séances or demonstrations of
parlor magic. When the critic utters an incantation, waving his
sorcerer's wand—presto!—everything is transformed into something else; and now bright college students are learning to be
sorcerer's apprentices. Saul Bellow gave his class at Princeton a story
to read because he thought it was a good piece of narration, and
the students kept asking him, "But what does it *mean*?"—as if they
were convinced that any story admired by an instructor must have
an allegorical meaning and must be something more and less than
a story.

Although this process of critical transformation results in magnifying literary works into scriptures and testaments, it also involves

2. Richard Chase was the critic who envisioned the worship and eating of
a castrated god. That is only one of the curious concepts put forward in his
Herman Melville, which is called "A Critical Study," but is really a long exercise in transubstantiation. Every novel by Melville is explained, in Chase's
reading, as a magic ritual, or a series of rituals. All the characters—but
especially those in *Pierre*—cease to be persons and instead become symbols
or correspondences. Thus: "Like Ahab, Pierre is the vessel of the Promethean
fire. He is 'stone,' charged 'with the fire of all divineness'; he is the human
clay, transfigured into a Titan. . . . Isabel, or Bell, as she is also called,
is Darkness. . . . Lucy is light in more than name. . . . Isabel . . . is the
'clog from Chaos' who drags the world back into the womb of Old Night."
Turning a few pages, we find that Chase has finished with his fire-day-night
correspondences and is now explaining *Pierre* in terms of the Apocalypse of
St. John. "Pierre is Christ," he says. ". . . Glen is Antichrist. Pierre's mother
is History or Society, the old established, conventional, unredeemed Jewish
church. The Reverend Mr. Falsgrave is the Laodicean church. Lucy is the
New Jerusalem. Isabel is Babylon." And so for page after page until we
reach the statement that "Perhaps at less conscious levels"—were all these
other transformations consciously present in Melville's mind? —"there are
other relationships. . . . Lucy may be the silver cord, Isabel the golden
bowl, Mrs. Glendinning the pitcher, the cycles of history the wheel, Pierre
the body which contains these symbolic organs"—namely, cords, bowls,
pitchers, and wheels. Not being a person—in Chase's reading—but merely
a system of correspondences, Pierre can get along with purely symbolic
organs, in the absence of heart and stomach, liver and lungs.

a subtle disparagement of their authors. Somehow the man writing fades out of the picture and all that remains is the sacred text with its oneiric or anagogic meaning—and, of course, the perceptive critic who first discovered the meaning. "See!" the critic seems to be saying, "this poor fellow didn't know what he was doing when he produced the sacred text. He was merely the instrument of his subliminal drives, or of his social prejudices, or of the collective instinct for creating myths. He spoke in riddles and vaticinated like the Delphic priestess, drunk on charcoal fumes, but the critic interprets his riddles, as did the high priest of Apollo's shrine." In modern terms the author is like the patient on a couch, retelling his dreams, while the critic plays the part of wise psychiatrist. And will there be a cure? Unfortunately the author is dead, or is too confirmed in authorship to be helped by therapeutic measures, but there is always the reader who can profit from his example and perhaps can be inducted into the state of critical awareness that is "beyond" fiction and drama and poetry.

So the critic might defend his procedure, but others might ask whether these critical reinterpretations really help the reader—that is, the sort of highly educated reader who subscribes to the quarterlies and tries to follow what the critics are saying. Sometimes, of course, the critical reading makes one conscious of depths and subtleties where at first one had seen only the smooth surface of the work. At other times I suspect that the reading has a different sort of effect: it frightens other readers away from a masterpiece by making it seem impossibly difficult and by suggesting that before it can be "read" in the critical sense one must consult a shelf of books and then puzzle over the ironies and allusions hidden in every phrase of the work. I also suspect that many readers are tempted to substitute the critic's fable for what the author really said. In that case, Jacob has stolen Esau's birthright, and the too creative critic has not only taken the author's place but has driven him into the wilderness.

It is easy to overemphasize these and other faults of the younger critics, while forgetting the really new and valuable work that some of them have performed. They are powerful, if not as individuals, then as a group or tendency, and therefore they have powerful enemies. The enemies bring charges against them, some true, some exaggerated. I think the frequent charge that they are a reactionary influence in politics is more exaggerated than some of the others.

It is true that some of the youngest critics talk about liberals as contemptuously as the Communists used to do, while they celebrate tradition, orthodoxy, and authority almost as if they were ruined noblemen plotting to crown a king in Washington—or would it be Rome?—and institute an Established Church. But their language is more extreme than their program, which appears to be nonpolitical, and their rebellion is confined to the two fields of literary standards and private morals, where a counter revolution might be justified.

But the political case against them might be examined from a broader point of view. Earlier I suggested that a political reaction is a period of apathy or discouragement about public matters; it is also a period when the important decisions are made by a comparatively small number of politicians and military leaders, partly because the popular will is undecided or ill informed or haltingly expressed. If we are now living in such a period, that is the result of wars and threatened wars, not of books or essays in the quarterly magazines. The work of the younger critics, so far as it reveals conservative sentiments, might be treated as a symptom of the times rather than as one of the forces that are shaping them; certainly the critics are not to blame for Hitler, Stalin, or the atom bomb. There is one respect, however, in which their work might be charged with having a reactionary influence. Most of it is so divorced from politics and even from the notion that the books they discuss might have been affected by different political situations; most of it is so confined to discussing literature as if it were completely separate from public life, and indeed from any life, that their work might well strengthen the mood of political apathy that already exists among their readers.

Sometimes they write as if authors, readers, and critics all existed on the island of Laputa, which floated in the sky and was protected from the field of terrestrial gravity. Captain Lemuel Gulliver, after his visit to the island, reported that the Laputan nobles had no share in the ordinary concerns of ordinary people. They were immersed in high problems of ontology, epistemology, and esthetics to such a point that they could hardly carry on conversations with their friends; after a few words they would fall back into a silent daze of abstraction. They all had attendants, called "flappers," whose duty it was to bring them back to their senses by flapping them on the cheeks with a bladder containing a few dried peas. The critics need flappers too, not to make them talk, but to make them see and hear and feel the world outside of books, the world from which all books come and into which good books will return, while the others are forgotten.

4.

A striking example, or result, I hardly know which, of this divorce from life and retreat into libraries is the craze for writing essays and books about T. S. Eliot. No other living poet has been discussed at such inordinate length. At the turn of the century Browning had even more critics and commentators, but that was after his death in 1889 at the age of seventy-seven. Eliot is still in his early sixties and is rapidly catching up with his absent rival. Already there have been a dozen full-length books about his work, and more than four hundred critical essays, and the number increases with each new issue of the literary quarterlies.

So much has been written about his poems that apparently there is nothing left to say, except a few of the simplest things. So much has been written that the poet's rather slender production—which has been collected in one not very large or closely printed volume —seems to be buried deep under an accumulated mass of commentaries, glosses, readings, exegeses, and explications. More interesting than any new essay on Eliot that followed the established lines would be a psychological and sociological study of Eliot's critics; at some universities they include almost every member of the English department who hasn't written or planned a book on Herman Melville.

Instead of writing such a study I might indicate some of the lines that a future student should follow. He should begin, I think, with the obvious notation that Eliot's poems are excessively dense or difficult and that every line is packed with meanings and allusions. He should next observe that the difficulty in itself has been a challenge to some of our ablest critics, who have discovered that deciphering the meanings and tracking down the allusions are pursuits more exciting than the attempt to solve a mysterious crime. Some of the longer essays on Eliot are masterpieces of detection that rank with "The Gold Bug" and "The Purloined Letter." There are, however, comparatively few studies that reach this high level of ratiocinative thinking, and our future student might note that most of the Eliot material published since World War II has been on the conventional or Ph. D. level of plodding scholarship. The next step would be for him to inquire why Eliot has been making such a strong appeal to academic critics, including many of the less original or venturesome type.

I think the answer lies in the poet's extreme bookishness. That is not Eliot's central quality, of course; for thirty years he has been a practical man of affairs, and his plays and his essays on public questions, more than his poems, contain a great deal of worldly wisdom; he is urbane where his critics are pedantic; but he is also the modern poet who has made the widest and most elaborate use of his reading. All his poems are full of phrases from older authors, and he has written—we might better say, put together—whole passages that are mosaics of quotations. A famous example is the last eight lines of *The Waste Land*, which contain eight quotations in five languages, including Provençal and Sanskrit, besides a line and a half that Eliot himself wrote in English. The passage has always interested scholars, who are still arguing at length about the exact shade of hope or despair that Eliot intended to convey by each of the quoted phrases. Other scholars avoid the passage as a hackneyed subject and instead try to discover new literary allusions in *Four Quartets*, where they also abound, but where most of them are taken from rather obscure devotional works.

This search in Eliot's books for references to other books has proved to be a fascinating pastime for doctors of philosophy. It is challengingly difficult, it allows them to exercise their special skills, and it involves no untidy connections with life, nor does it force them to express unpopular opinions. The fact is that it never tempts them to step outside the library. Everything comes from books; everything is noted down, compared, systematized; and the result of their labor goes back into other books.

> O books, books, books. They all go into the books,
> The vacant interlinear spaces, the vacant into the vacant,

one might say, paraphrasing Eliot's lines about men going into the dark.

I am not thinking about the best of the Eliot critics, writers like F. O. Matthiessen, Cleanth Brooks, Richard Blackmur, James Johnson Sweeney, and Helen L. Gardner, to mention a few of those who follow their own lines of research and try to present independent judgments. I am thinking here of the "pure" scholars who are interested chiefly in a search through books for hidden meanings and allusions. When they find Eliot's sources in Dante or the *Upanishads* or *The Hound of the Baskervilles*—for he once borrowed a phrase from Conan Doyle—the scholars' search is ended. They publish their findings in the literary reviews and hope for better faculty posts next autumn.

But Eliot himself is a critic—one more likely to deal with general questions, less concerned with the meaning of separate phrases than any of those who explicate his work—and his own practice suggests that most of the Eliot students have performed only part of their critical function. After answering the question, What does this poem mean? they should go on to ask and answer other questions—for example, Which of his poems are best? How do they compare with the best work of other poets, living and dead? Much of the recent Eliot criticism simply avoids judgments. Much of it makes the wrong judgments, as a result of the critic's preoccupation with sources and allusions. After puzzling for a week or a month over a short passage and finally deciphering it like a rebus, he can hardly fail to decide that it is a great passage; otherwise his time would be wasted.

A good example of this critical overestimation is Eliot's last book of poetry, *Four Quartets*. It is his longest, most elaborate work, with an intricate thematic pattern, and certainly it is the hardest to grasp in all its implications. Critics have been forced to spend even more time on it than on *The Waste Land*, and most of them have concluded that it is a correspondingly greater poem. One critic says that it contains "some of the most moving poetry that English literature has known." Another, a disciple of Jung, finds that it embodies the symbols of many religions, including Tibetan Buddhism, and therefore seems inclined to place it somewhere between Dante and the angels. Younger poets speak well of it too, but I note that few if any of them have paid it the sincere flattery of letting their own poems be influenced by it, as thousands of poems were influenced by Prufrock and Sweeney and *The Waste Land*. Some of them say that the verse seems bleak and tired, as if Eliot had been so exhausted by the intolerable wrestle with words and meanings and recurring themes that he hadn't the vigor left to write phrases that echo in other poets' minds. *Four Quartets* is a great book—there isn't much doubt of that, considering the care and skill and bitter experience that have gone into it—but why didn't some of the critics ask whether it wasn't a great devotional or liturgical work rather than anything that the future is likely to recognize as a great poem?

This failure to ask the right questions and this inability to pass judgments—unless the judgments are supported by a consensus of critical opinion, in which case they might be thunderingly wrong —are not confined to the explicators of Eliot. Critical attention is in itself a form of judgment, and the newer critics—with a few notable exceptions—are timid in their choice of subjects to discuss. Most often they write about the works of authors who are generally admired by other new critics; they explicate and admire, but they don't try to discover new objects of admiration. It is as if their critical apparatus had become so complicated and difficult to operate that, like some of the big Hollywood cameras, it was too expensive to be used for experimental subjects; they all must have been tested in advance for audience reaction.

There is, moreover, a surprisingly small number of these tested subjects. Most of the newer critics—when they don't write about other critics, incestuously—have been devoting themselves to authors in one of three groups: they deal with American classics, with American poets and novelists of the 1920s, or else with European authors in the subjective or symbolist tradition. Names like those of Melville, Hawthorne, Henry James, Henry Adams, and Stephen Crane in the first group; like those of Pound, Faulkner, Fitzgerald, Hart Crane, and Hemingway in the second; like those of Yeats, Eliot, Joyce, Hopkins, Rimbaud, Rilke, Proust, Gide, Kafka, and Garcia Lorca, appear time and again in the titles of critical essays, almost to the exclusion of other names. All these authors are distinguished, and most of them have the added charm of being difficult. For years they have provided rich fields for critical investigation, but there are signs that the fields are beginning to be exhausted —"corned out," as they say in Kentucky of river-bottom land where one crop of field corn has followed another. The fiftieth book on Herman Melville will either repeat and expand the first forty-nine or else, in the effort to be original and express the critic's creative impulse, it will become fictitious and grotesque. What the critics need today is what the late Roman rhetoricians needed and lacked —that is, new novels, new poems, new dramas of sufficient intensity and distinction to justify the sort of close and prolonged analysis for which they are trained. Criticism has not become autonomous, for all the efforts to make it so, and its future still depends on that of the other literary arts.

II

WAR NOVELS: AFTER TWO WARS

I.

There is one category of recent fiction that seems to be little affected by the standards of the newer critics: it consists of novels about World War II. Almost all of these are based on the wartime experience of their authors. The experience calls urgently to be retold and, much more than civilian life, it takes the shape of stories with a beginning, a middle, and an end. The hero enlists, has adventures, and at last comes home; or he goes into action, suffers, and is killed; or again there may be a collective hero, a platoon or a ship's company that is brought together, becomes a living unity, and then is dissolved at the end of a campaign.

In other words, the form of the novel is largely determined by the subject—which is always Americans at war, no matter where they fight—and the same formal structure may be used in stories about different types of combat service on different sides of the globe. The authors as a group haven't shown much interest in discovering new forms. That explains why American critics, with their specialized interest in structure and texture, have paid little attention to the novels of World War II. I can remember only three— *The Gallery, The Naked and the Dead*, and *From Here to Eternity* —that have been discussed at any length in the critical reviews. On the other hand, war novels as a class have been reaching an extremely wide public that doesn't listen to what the critics say.

It is time now for a long second look at the novels as a group.

It is time to ask what they reveal about the behavior, the anxieties, and the aspirations of Americans in the Second World War. It is also time for one more attempt to answer the old question, how the novels compare with those written after 1920 by American veterans of another war.

1.

I have read some fifty of the novels, most of them as printed books, but others as manuscripts in search of a publisher. Taken together, they cover a wide range of human experience and more than half of the terraqueous globe. They include stories laid in peacetime barracks, in training camps, at bomber fields in England, on Navy vessels patrolling all the oceans, and in combat units fighting in Africa, Europe, Asia, and Oceania—not to mention other stories dealing with prison camps, the liberated countries, and occupation forces in Germany and Japan. They also include first-hand accounts of every major battle from Pearl Harbor to Iwo Jima, with reports of the other battle that every veteran had to fight for himself when he returned to civilian life. And the novels as a group are comprehensive in other fashions as well. Here are characters— and authors too—from every economic level and almost every racial strain in American society. Here are stories of their adventures in the three armed services and in special branches of each: infantry, artillery, engineers, paratroops, bombing and pursuit squadrons and their ground crews, ambulance sections, salvage outfits, Army Transport Service, Navy destroyers and cargo ships, War Crimes Commission, Military Government, and the psychiatric hospitals where some of the heroes were patients.

Had I looked farther I could have found other novels, published or in manuscript, about nurses, surgeons, Wacs, Waves, ski-troopers, tank crews, battle wagons, submarines, and the General Staff—in fact, about every arm and rank of all the services in every theater of operations. For having failed to read these other novels, I offer no apologies. Some of them, I am sure, are exciting or thoughtful stories, and most of them would broaden our picture of America's fighting men, but I doubt that any of them would change the general picture. And there *is* a general picture that, emerging from all these books, becomes their most impressive feature.

At this point I am thinking particularly of first novels about the

war, to the exclusion of books that were written by somewhat older
authors like Herman Wouk (*The Caine Mutiny*) and Irwin Shaw
(*The Young Lions*) and James Gould Cozzens (*Guard of Honor*,
which is a solider work than any of the novels by younger men).
For these established writers the war was a subject that they chose
like any other, but the first novelists were chosen by the subject and
wrote about the war because it was their central experience. This
immersion in the subject gives them a strong family resemblance.
Different as they are in their social backgrounds and wartime adventures, they end by presenting the same American characters,
the same conflicts of purpose, and the same message or group of
messages. Some of the novels are so much alike that dialogues and
episodes could be transposed from one to another without a change
except in names. There are a few individualists among the new
authors: notably there is James Jones, who is the only one to write
about the Army as an institution and a permanent way of life; there
is Norman Mailer, who has a political sense that is rare among
writers of his generation; and there is John Horne Burns, with the
strained but persuasive lyricism he achieved in *The Gallery* and
never achieved again; but these and a few others are exceptions.
Most of the young novelists might as well have been commissioned
and trained in advance to write each his separate volume in a great
collaborative history of World War II as seen by the fighting men.
That is the great defect of the separate novels, but it is also a virtue
of the undertaking as a whole. Together the novels form a production of lasting value, one that may well be richer and more complete
than the account we possess of any nation's part in any other recent
war.

To some extent the nature of this joint report is determined by
the nature of its authors as observers and story-tellers. War novelists
are not sociologists or historians, and neither are they average
soldiers. The special training and talent of novelists lead them to
express rather special moods. They are usually critical in temper
and often they are self-critical to the point of being burdened with
feelings of guilt. They are sensitive—about themselves in the beginning; but if they have imagination (and they need it) they learn
to be sensitive for others, including the conquered peoples among
whom American soldiers were forced to live. In military service
many future writers were men of whom their comrades said that
they were "always goofing off by themselves." They suffered more

than others from the enforced promiscuity of Army and shipboard life. Most of them were rebels against discipline when they thought it was illogical—which they usually did—and rebels against the system that divides officers from enlisted men. Rather more than half of the novelists served in the ranks. The others were commissioned, but, being young, they seldom rose above the grade of Army captain or Navy lieutenant and they formed a lasting resentment toward senior officers. Politically most of them were indifferent or vaguely liberal without belonging to any party.

All these characteristics lend a special color to their joint report, which, before being accepted as historical fact, would have to be compared with reports by others having different temperaments and different types of specialized training. Yet the war novelists were trying hard to be accurate observers and to tell the true story of what they saw. When we find them in substantial agreement on a number of topics, we should listen attentively to what they say.

2.

A first point on which almost all the novelists agree is that Americans in the mass remained a most unwarlike people, even when they were drilled, armed, and set to fighting all over the globe. *From Here to Eternity* is the only novel that presents a group of professional soldiers, thirty-year men, with sympathy and understanding. The other books are written from the standpoint of uniformed civilians, men for whom the war, although it lasted four years, was merely an interruption in their civilian lives. In the armed services they adopted an interim code of morality. Uncertain of the future, the soldiers depicted in the novels had ceased to judge any action by its distant effects. Most of their efforts were directed toward momentary gratifications—getting cash, getting drunk, getting laid —or simply toward keeping alive and out of trouble.

With a few exceptions they didn't know or couldn't say why they were fighting. "American soldiers rarely go in for ideological discussion and that kind of thing," says the hero of *The Gesture*, by John Cobb, a novel about bomber crews in England. Nevertheless the question was discussed in orientation lectures and sometimes by the men themselves, though it made them feel uncomfortably solemn. Almost all of them agreed that Hitler and the Japanese had to be stopped, but they couldn't understand why somebody else than they, individually, shouldn't have done the stopping. The exceptions among them were either radicals and bleeding hearts or else Polish and Jewish refugees, and both types are presented in the novels with a sort of distant incomprehension. In *The Gesture* a lieutenant colonel who understands and hates fascism nearly ruins the bombing squadron because he doesn't understand his fellow Americans. In *Point of Honor*, by M. L. Kadish—a thoughtful novel about the fighting in Italy—there is a Jewish soldier who had once served in the German army and now wants to destroy it. His fighting zeal makes him so unpopular with his American comrades that he ends by going insane.

This indifference about larger issues had some effect on morale, to judge by the novels, but less than might have been expected. Morale was good in some outfits, bad in others. The novels report that it was excellent in the Marines and the paratroops (see *Battle Cry*, by Leon M. Uris, and *Those Devils in Baggy Pants*, by Ross S. Carter), generally good in the Navy, except on small vessels commanded by incompetent officers (see *Mr. Roberts*, by Thomas Heggen), and mixed in the Army, where it was worst in battalions kept too long at the front (see *Day without End*, by Van Van Praag) and in segregated detachments of Negroes. Among aviators it was good in the air, bad on the ground (see *The Gesture*). Most men in all services accepted the war as they might have accepted an earthquake and tried to do their best in the circumstances.

To judge by their reported conversations, Americans in World War II were tougher and more sophisticated than their fathers in 1918. They were less ashamed of their vices, less religious (except for devout Catholics), and less affected by political propaganda. Often they proved refractory to discipline, and several novelists tell us that in the South Pacific they killed most of their prisoners. Although they were good fighting troops and highly skilled, if reckless and wasteful, in handling their superb mechanical equipment, they proved irresponsible and corrupt as garrison forces in conquered territory.

It is this last characteristic of Americans as soldiers that left the deepest impression on many of the novelists. Alfred Hayes and John Horne Burns writing about Italy, Lionel Shapiro about Germany, Robert Shaplen about ports on the China Sea, and Elliott Chaze about Japan all make it clear that the early occupation forces were leaving bitter memories behind them. In *The Stainless Steel*

Kimono, a novel about seven tough paratroopers, Chaze tries to explain why the soldiers acted as they did. "The reaction of most occupation troops in Japan," he says, "is that of a person suddenly handed a brimming bedpan and told to guard its contents carefully. It comes as a shock to the average American to find himself custodian of such a smelly and strange country." In *A Corner of the World*, Robert Shaplen finds almost nothing but corruption in postwar Shanghai, Saigon, Manila, and Macao. The one truly honest man in his book, a German Jew, is murdered by the Macao police for his honesty. Alfred Hayes, in *All Thy Conquests*, quotes the Italians on their conquerors. "We have been liberated," they say. "We have been liberated from cigarettes, shoes, meat, gasoline, and our women." Lionel Shapiro's book, *The Sealed Verdict*, is a picture of demoralization in the American zone of Germany. Although the style is close to that of slick-paper magazines, some of the descriptions are hard to forget:

A Red Cross club for enlisted men occupied the most important building still standing in the street, the former Palast Kino. Just beyond the lights that brightened the entrance to the club, each dark doorway of the boarded, fire-gutted shops was populated by one or two girls. They were mostly children of thirteen or fourteen, and the rouge that was lumpily applied to their cheeks made them look like Halloween pranksters rather than apprentices on the dreary night watch of the camp follower. . . . A little man with sunken cheeks appeared at Lashley's elbow and walked with them briefly, whispering, "What got to sell? *Zigaretten*? *Amerikanische* dollars?" He fell away in the darkness and a boy, perhaps ten, took his place. "Want girl? Pretty girl. Young. No sick." He too slunk away. As they crossed in front of the Red Cross Club, two MP's saluted briskly.

The briskly saluted conquerors were themselves affected by the demoralization around them and helped to make it worse by profiteering at the expense of the conquered. "I don't know why," says Burns in *The Gallery*, "but most Americans had a blanket hatred of all Italians. They figured it this way: these Ginsoes have made war on us, so it doesn't matter what we do to them, boost their prices, shatter their economy, and shack up with their women. . . . I saw that we could mouth democratic catchwords and yet give the Neapolitans a huge black market. I saw that we could prate of the evils of fascism, yet be just as ruthless as Fascists with people who'd already been pushed around."

As a rule the soldiers made little distinction among the occupied, the liberated, and the Allied countries, since the people in all of them were foreigners—that is, frogs, limeys, heinies, ginsoes, yellow bastards, wogs, flips, or gooks. Yet the Americans themselves belonged to many racial strains, and this created a problem of discrimination that is a major or minor theme in many novels. A favorite device is to present a squad or platoon composed of different racial elements. There will be a Jew and an Italian (one of them from Brooklyn), a Texan, a farm boy (always from Iowa), a hillbilly, a Mexican, and an Anglo-Saxon from an Ivy League college —these are the required characters—and sometimes there will also be a Boston Irishman, an Indian from Arizona, a Pole from the Midwestern steel mills, and a Swedish lumberjack from Puget Sound. The Texan or the Irishman creates dissension by his racial prejudice, but the Jew and the Mexican turn out to be heroes, the Texan is killed or converted, and the squad becomes a family of blood brothers. Sometimes the squad stands for the whole nation, as we learn from one of the later novels, *Mask of Glory*, by Dan Levin. The book tells how Glenn Manson, born Kasimir Minkiewicz, enlists in the Marines and is accepted by his comrades. By dying on Iwo Jima he enables his Polish family in Cleveland to feel at home and proud in their adopted country.

Although the novelists are always opposed to racial discrimination, some of them are also opposed to the zealots who try to impose racial equality without sufficient preparation. In *The Gesture* —as also in *Guard of Honor*, by James Gould Cozzens—a liberal-minded officer tries to introduce Negro troops into an area reserved for whites, and the result comes close to being a military disaster. In *Last of the Conquerors*, by William Gardner Smith, we learn what the Negroes themselves were thinking. After a year in Germany, the author tells us, not one of them wanted to be sent home. "You know what the hell I learned?" one of them says on his last night in Berlin. "That a nigger ain't no different from nobody else. . . . I hadda come over here and let the Nazis teach me that. They don't teach that stuff back in the land of the free."

Almost all the novels have a great deal to say about the sexual behavior of the human male, and in many respects they support Dr. Kinsey's conclusions. On two points, however, they present so much opposing evidence that they make you wonder whether Kinsey's statistics are accurate. His first book says at some length that there were no significant changes in the male sexual pattern during the period of twenty-two years covered by his researches. "There is not even evidence," he says, "that patterns of sexual behavior are materially altered among men in the armed forces during a period of war." The novelists do not argue with these two statements, but they describe American soldiers as acting with vastly more freedom in sexual matters than any novelist, even Hemingway, described them in World War I. Moreover, the novelists show by many examples that Americans learned new patterns of behavior during their wartime service in Europe or Asia or the South Seas.

There is more sex than love in the novels, and the usual explanation is simply the stress of war. "Overseas," says John Cobb, "love, like everything else, is a form of direct action." Some of the authors hint that romantic love is difficult for self-centered and self-conscious Americans to achieve. Says John Horne Burns, who is given to making direct statements, "In America I remember a tension between the sexes. Human love is a disease for the isolation ward, not at all nice. Thus love in America is often divided into the classifications of Having Sex and Getting Married. Neither has much to do with love." He depicts several of his characters as learning naturalness and self-forgetfulness from the Neapolitan women. In *The Wolf That Fed Us*, Robert Lowry's soldiers are renewed and restored by Roman women, as if these were the she-wolf that suckled Romulus and Remus.

Few American women appear in the novels, and there are fewer still whom the authors seem to admire; many of the others are cold, selfish, even malignant. For some reason the prejudice against American women seems to be strongest in novels published shortly after the war.[1] I counted the romantic or tragic love stories in ten of these earlier books. Of the affairs that go beyond the category of merely Having Sex, there are four with Italians, two with Germans (including the love affair of the young Negro in *Last of the Conquerors*), two with Frenchwomen (of whom one is half Javanese), one with a Tonkinese, one with a New Zealander, and one with a Japanese "just like Madame Buttercup in the movies." Only two of the soldiers portrayed at length fall in love with American girls. One of these affairs ends in frustration and the other (in *All*

1. But later we find the case against American women stated at length, and classically, by James M. Michener in *Sayonara* (1954).

Thy Conquests) is presented with cold disgust, like a dead mouse held out in a dustpan.

Rather more than half the novels, as I said, are written from the standpoint of enlisted men, and the others from that of commissioned officers—except for books like *The Naked and the Dead*, which try to include both standpoints by presenting all the ranks involved in a separate action or a minor campaign. Almost all the authors agree, however, that a gulf exists between the two military castes. Most of them show that there is sullen resentment on one side and uneasiness on the other. Often the men complain of special privileges granted to officers in respect to food, liquor, and liberty. Some of the more sensitive officers, but only a few, are depicted as being ashamed to enjoy the privileges, while the effect on others is to make them feel that they are living in an unreal world. "What am I doing with bars on me?" a captain asks his American mistress in *All Thy Conquests*. "I look in the mirror and I don't believe it. We're an army of phonies, baby, that's what we are. An army of jerks playing soldier."

The novels reveal a special conflict over the superior sexual opportunities enjoyed by officers. Apparently it was worst in the South Pacific; there the only white women in the advanced areas were nurses, who ranked as lieutenants and weren't allowed to associate with enlisted men. Michener, writing his *Tales of the South Pacific* from the naval officer's point of view, gives a pretty lurid picture of the situation. "There were," he says, "many other attacks or near attacks on nurses in the islands. They were grim, hushed-up affairs. Nobody ever knew exactly what had happened. Just rumor and surmises. But in time every nurse knew that she lived in danger. She could see in the baleful looks of enlisted men that they considered her little more than a plaything brought out to amuse the officers. With thousands of men for every white woman, with enlisted men forbidden to date the nurses, it was to be expected that vague and terrible things would occur."

Michener writes almost like a Southern planter in the Black Belt, living in fear that his womenfolk will be outraged by a sullen peasantry. Once when he paid a visit to the enlisted men in their quarters he was surprised to find that most of them were friendly. There was one man, however, who looked at him "with that grim stare which officers see so often and which always means: 'What the hell

are you doing here?' " Norman Mailer describes the rivalry between
Lieutenant Hearn and his platoon sergeant, who deliberately leads
him into a Japanese ambush. After Hearn's death one of the men
blurts out, "The Lootenant was a good guy." Another swears, "They
ain't a ——— one of those officers is worth a goddam." "I wouldn't
spit on the best one of them," a third man says furiously. "I ain't
afraid of saying what I think. They're all bastards."

The war novels published after 1950 are less rancorous as a
group, and some of them present a new hero who bridges the gulf
between enlisted men and officers; he is a sergeant commanding a
squad or a lieutenant commanding a platoon. In either case he is
trusted by his superiors, while he serves as a father image to the
soldiers, who follow him like children. Sometimes at the end of the
book (see *Walk on the Water*, by Ralph Leveridge) he becomes a
Christ who gives his life to save them. In *Victory Also Ends*, by
Fred W. Booth, the father figure is a captain, but that is the highest
rank he reaches in any war novel I have read. Majors continue to
be represented as pompous fools, lieutenant colonels as butchers,
generals as heartless villains—"And they're all bastards," most of
the novelists might be saying.

Michener is almost the only author who accepts the caste system.
The epauleted heroes of his *Tales of the South Pacific* come from
wealthy homes, and more than once he celebrates "those graces of
behavior which mark the true naval officer and distinguish him
from men of the other services." One suspects him of ranking Army
colonels with boatswains in the Navy. All the other novelists make
it clear that they favor more democracy in the armed forces, and
Norman Mailer offers an indirect but persuasive plea for democracy
by allowing General Cummings, the villain of the novel, to state the
arguments against it. Cummings' notion is that Americans, because
of their high living standards, are naturally the worst soldiers in the
world. "What you've got to do," he says, "is break them down.
Every time an enlisted man sees an officer get an extra privilege, it
breaks him down a little more. . . . The Army functions best
when you're frightened of the man above you, and contemptuous of
your subordinates."

A feeling present as an overtone in some novels is the fear that
the military hierarchy will become the model and furnish the leaders
for an American fascism. In *The Naked and the Dead* the feeling is
discussed in a series of conversations between Hearn, the liberal-

minded lieutenant, and the odious General Cummings. "The machine techniques of this century demand consolidation," Cummings says, "and with that you've got to have fear, because the majority of men must be subservient to the machine, and it's not a business they instinctively enjoy." Later he says, dotting the i's, "There are countries which have latent powers, latent resources, they are full of potential energy, so to speak. And there are great concepts which can unlock that, express it. As kinetic energy a country is organization, coordinated effort, your epithet, fascism. . . . Historically the purpose of this war is to translate America's potential into kinetic energy." The general explains that we are about to take over the German dream. "You can consider the Army," he concludes, "as a preview of the future."

It would be wrong, however, to end on this political theme, since it appears in a minority of the novels and since Mailer has stronger political convictions than any of his colleagues. A note or at least an undertone to be heard more often is a sort of distrust for all human institutions larger than a squad or at most a platoon, and with it a feeling that goodness is to be found only in separate individuals. While describing horrors on the battlefield, bureaucracy at headquarters, and corruption in the occupied countries, the authors keep finding separate men who are not only heroes but martyrs and saints. Never have I read a group of novels that contained so many truly good persons—simple souls like Joey Goldstein, the Brooklyn mechanic, and his friend Ridges, the sharecropper, in *The Naked and the Dead*; champions of the oppressed like Noah Ackerman in *The Young Lions*; Christs of a new dispensation like Sergeant Hervey in *Walk on the Water* (as Christ walked) and Lieutenant Shulman in *The Gallery*; and there are even saintly women, provided they are foreigners, like Carla in *All Thy Conquests*, Thémis Delisle in *The Sealed Verdict*, and the New Zealand widow in *Battle Cry*. The novelists are like the two angels who looked for virtue in Sodom that the city might be saved, and, luckier than the angels, each has come forward with a righteous few.

3.

All this will serve as a partial answer to the first question, what the new writers have been saying about the war. There is still the second question, how the combat novels of this period compare with those written after 1920 by young veterans of the other war. The question must be simple to ask, since we have heard it on every side, but it isn't simple to answer. It calls for a series of explanations, some of which lead us into a curious borderland between literary history and military tactics. Besides a discussion of the novels themselves, in terms of method and purpose, it also involves a comparison between two wars fought in different fashions and leaving behind them different memories.

A few points, fortunately, are now beyond dispute. There is no longer any doubt that many more novels have been written about World War II than about World War I, that more of them reach a certain level of competence or merit, and that, as a group, they compose a sounder body of work. Writers of the second wartime generation have been quick to master the tools of their craft. On the average, their books are not only more smoothly and skillfully written than most war novels of the 1920s but are also better as reporting of "what really happened in action," to borrow a phrase from Ernest Hemingway.

Speaking of his early years, Hemingway said, "I was trying to write then and I found the greatest difficulty, aside from knowing truly what you really felt, rather than what you were supposed to feel, and had been taught to feel, was to put down what really happened in action." Most adventure-story writers had talked about the hero's emotion—that is, the fear or wonder or blind fury aroused in him by the events in which he was taking part. Hemingway wanted to arouse the same emotion in his readers instead of merely telling them how the hero had felt. He was trying to put down, so he said, "the actual things which produced the emotion that you experienced . . . the sequence of motion and fact which made the emotion and which would be as valid in a year or in ten years or, with luck and if you stated it purely enough, always."

Because his eyes were fixed on "actual things," Hemingway's battle scenes had a force and clarity that impressed the novelists who came after him. His method has become an accepted part of their technical equipment and it has led to a change in war fiction that I can illustrate by quoting some paragraphs written twenty-five years apart. The first is from Thomas Boyd's *Through the Wheat* (1923) and describes the taking of a village near Soissons:

Bullets flew in every direction. Men toppled down from the windows of houses. Others raced up the steps of dwellings. Men ran through the streets, wild and tumultuous. They returned to the pavement, guarding their captives. Men poured the hate of their beings upon the town. They wept and cursed like lost souls in limbo. All of their fear, all of their anxiety, all of the restraint which had been forced upon them during the morning when they lay like animals in a slaughter-house and their brains numbed with apprehension, came out in an ugly fury.

Boyd is stressing the anxiety and rage of the Marines who took the village, rather than the events that produced those emotions. He is writing honestly, but awkwardly and in the fog of war, so that all his violence is dim and distant. He is also using elegant synonyms— if he writes "houses" in one sentence he has to write "dwellings" in the next—and fancy phrases like "hate of their beings" and "lost souls in limbo." A very few novelists of the Second World War still render combat scenes in this old-fashioned prose. Ralph Leveridge, in *Walk on the Water,* writes as if all his models for imitation had been selected from the ten-cent counter of a second-hand bookstore. Here is a typical paragraph:

Men swore and raved. Men sweated with exquisite apprehension. They raised their fists, and their mouths slobbering, they wildly, incoherently jabbered obscenities, heaped every curse they knew upon the civilians back home, their government, their mothers who had conceived them, and sometimes, upon the Japs.

Except for the one word "Japs," that might have been written by Thomas Boyd in 1923. It is, however, by no means typical of the second-war novelists, most of whom practice the new method of writing combat scenes, using the simplest language to set down "what really happened in action." Here, for example, is a paragraph by Norman Mailer describing a Japanese attack across a jungle river:

"Shit." Croft's hand found the flare box, and he loaded the gun again. He was beginning to see in the darkness, and he hesitated. But something moved on the river and he fired the flare. As it burst, a few Japanese soldiers were caught motionless in the water. Croft pivoted his gun on them and fired. One of the soldiers remained standing for an incredible time. There was no expression on his face; he looked vacant and surprised even as the bullets struck him in the chest.

The paragraph begins with a formerly unprintable expletive. That sort of beginning is a habit of many novelists in this second postwar period, and Mailer is more addicted to it than most of his colleagues. But the chief feature of the paragraph, from the technical point of view, is the absence of terms like "fear," "hate," "fury," and "exquisite apprehension." Instead of stating the emotion of his characters, Mailer gives us "the sequence of motion and fact which made the emotion." He follows the method that Hemingway had discovered twenty-four years before him; and the fact is that Mailer's paragraph is reminiscent of one that Hemingway included in his second booklet, *in our time*, which was privately printed in Paris in 1924, a year before his book of stories with the same title was published in New York. The earlier paragraph reads:

We were in a garden in Mons. Young Buckley came in with his patrol from across the river. The first German I saw climbed up over the garden wall. We waited till he got one leg over and then potted him. He had so much equipment on and looked awfully surprised and fell down into the garden. Then three more came over further down the wall. We shot them. They all came just like that.

It happens that among the second-war novelists Mailer reveals less kinship with Hemingway than most of the others. The spirit is different, the style is different, the characters are seen with different eyes. If Mailer has clearly contracted a literary debt it is rather to James T. Farrell, so that his first novel has been described as the Studs Lonigan boys in the South Pacific. Yet even Mailer depends on the Hemingway method when he describes men in battle, and his dying Japanese "looked vacant and surprised," almost exactly like the German climbing over the garden wall in Mons. The truth is that Hemingway discovered what has so far proved to be the most effective method of rendering a battle scene. It can be learned from his books or studied in college courses, and most of the younger war novelists have followed it instinctively.

They are good technicians, good reporters, and I should judge that they are also good historians. Perhaps the most serious criticism of their work is that the group of books is more impressive than the separate works of fiction. These are on a higher level of competence than almost all the first-war novels, but what they form is a tableland, not a chain of mountains. I may be speaking as a prejudiced witness, proud of his long memory, but it seems to me that none of the authors, not even Norman Mailer and James Jones, has had the separate impact for these times that Dos Passos and Cummings and Hemingway had in the early 1920s.

4.

Partly the lack of impact may be the fault of their readers more than that of the writers. The American public has become so familiar with horrors recounted from life that it is no longer much impressed with those described in novels, even if the novels are also based on life. Although the slaughter of Japanese prisoners in *The Naked and the Dead* is more shocking than any battle scene in the first-war novels, it produced no such public outcry. In *Three Soldiers* (1922) Dos Passos described an Army stockade for American prisoners, the one commanded in life by Captain "Hardboiled" Smith. Congressmen debated his charges of cruelty, and I seem to remember that the Army promised reforms. There is a still worse stockade in *From Here to Eternity*, described from more intimate experience, but it has produced no public protests. In the matter of horror the novelists are always a step behind reality, and the public is too stunned by reality to demand action. Even the novelists have developed an attitude of acquiescence in horror, and some of them— not James Jones—have lost the capacity for indignation; their books contribute to the general picture of a situation which they do not attempt to change.

The earlier group of postwar writers, those of the 1920s, were often described as being "disillusioned," but I have always felt that the adjective was badly chosen. They were something quite different: rebels in life and art. To be a rebel implies faith in one's ability to do things better than those in power. Young writers of the 1920s had that faith, which was sometimes close to being an illusion; they believed that a world in which their standards prevailed would be gayer, more tolerant, and more natural than the world of their elders. It would have no armies. Never again—and this is what they kept saying in novel after novel—must there be such a pointless sacrifice of lives as in the battles on the Western Front.

Even a professional soldier would now admit that their rebellion was based on a valid complaint, since the Western battles of World War I were most of them useless and stupid from the military point of view. Until 1918 the commanding generals on both sides had no real military objectives. Their imaginations were deadened by the sheer quantity of manpower and material at their disposal. They planned their massive offensives merely to gain terrain, when yield-

ing it might have been the wiser strategy, or merely to inflict losses
on the enemy. Verdun is the archetypical example. The battle was
started by the Germans in the hope—as General von Falkenhayn
confessed in his memoirs—that the French would "bleed to death."
It lasted five months without interruption and was several times
renewed; it killed a million men, including as many Germans as
Frenchmen, and ended with both sides almost exactly where they
began.

In that same year the British attacked on the Somme and lost
sixty thousand men on the first day without gaining any ground
whatever. The war continued on the same premises, behind the
same barbed-wire entanglements that were like climbproof factory
fences; it was death on the production line. Death, not victory, was
in the air and the two most famous poems of the war were "In
Flanders Fields"—about poppies in the mass graveyards—and "I
Have a Rendezvous with Death." Even Blackjack Pershing caught
the contagion. When he offered his men to Foch after the German
break-through of March 1918, he said, not "We are here to win,"
but "We are here to be killed." This background has to be kept in
mind when we are judging the books that grew out of World War I.
The military leaders of the time, and most of the politicians too, had
shown their inability to think except in quantities of material and
numbers of corpses. The young men who wrote the books were in
revolt because their elders had betrayed them and slaughtered their
friends and because they believed that the world would be better if
all the principles of the elders were set aside. They said, and deeply
felt, "The war was wrong," then rushed on to a broader conclusion:
"All wars are evil, like the munitions makers who foment them for
dividends and like the governments that order young men to be
killed."

Today their broad conclusion seems wrong-headed or simple-
minded, but it gave emotional force and a broad perspective to the
novels that some of them wrote. There is no such conclusion to be
found in the novels of World War II. Emotionally it would be less
justified, because the new war wasn't fought in the same blindly
stupid and life-destructive fashion. Civilians died pointlessly by the
hundreds of thousands, but this time the leaders were not so eager
to have our soldiers die. The war included battles where the losses
were on the same scale as in 1914–18, not to mention separate actions like Tarawa and Iwo Jima where they were proportionately

higher, but these were not useless sacrifices like Verdun for the Germans or Passchendaele for the British, and they usually ended in clear-cut victories or defeats. If the soldiers didn't know why they, individually, were fighting, they still accepted the war as a fact of nature and could usually see the military logic of the campaigns in which they were engaged.

All this helps to explain why novels about the Second World War have no such message of simple pacifism as we find in many books of the 1920s. There are still rebellions, but they are on a smaller scale and have limited objects of attack: racial prejudice among soldiers, the military caste system, and the self-centeredness of American women. Many of the novels—especially those written after 1950, under the shadow of another world conflict—are not rebellious at all; instead they are celebrations of squad-room comradeship, Navy traditions, or the fighting Marines.

The novelists write as if they were wholly immersed in the war and as if, instead of being an exterior event to describe, it had become an inner condition of their lives. Sergeant Holloway, one of the two principal characters in *Point of Honor*, goes into action with a battery of howitzers. As the guns fire, "Holloway eases into a kind of peace. Now he lives compact within the space of action. He can eye the present the way he saw a small snake eye a bird's nest once before the war." Many of the novels give us just such a narrow-focused, intent, and snake's-eye picture of the fighting. Even when they soar over the battlefront, the picture remains narrow. Lieutenant Evans, the other hero of the same novel, is an artillery observer in a Piper Cub who muses as the battle unrolls beneath him. "Had he thought once that the war had an issue? Anti-fascism, perhaps? Under aerial observation, war shed issues. War was Fact, Thing-in-Itself, Existence sheer beyond argument; it spoke from the Rapido and beyond. 'I AM THAT I AM,' it declared to you. 'I AM MY OWN JUSTIFICATION.' "

In general the new novelists do not presume to judge the war. They do not suggest that it was foolish in its aims or that, given the temper of the people, it might have been avoided by wiser statesmanship. They are not in revolt against the war itself so much as they are disappointed by the fruits of victory, and more than disappointed: some of them are heartbroken at the contrast between our aims and efforts on one hand and our achievements on the other; between soldiers dying in the jungle and soldiers drunk in Japanese houses of prostitution; between the delirious joy with which our men were greeted as they marched into a liberated city and the despair of the inhabitants when they learned that we could be—to quote from John Horne Burns—"just as ruthless as Fascists with people who'd been pushed around already. That," he says, "was why my heart broke in Naples in August 1944."

Many of the novelists have begun to question the whole idea of progress through collective effort. It was the idea that dominated the 1930s, both in the democracies and in the totalitarian countries, but now the novelists are asking what can come of such an effort, except more cruelty and more corruption. They have even begun to question themselves and are not at all sure that they could have done better in the circumstances than our actual leaders. In a word, many of the novelists are really disillusioned this time, instead of being rebellious, and the disillusion lends a more conservative tone to their writing.

Their conservatism, or conservative liberalism, is also expressed in their literary technique. Here they offer a contrast with many novelists of the First War, who were always trying experiments and hoping to make discoveries on the order of Hemingway's method for describing battle scenes. Novelists of this later group are apparently more concerned with using and perfecting discoveries already made by their predecessors.

Many war novelists of the 1920s were deeply influenced by French literature and especially by the French Symbolist tradition. Speaking in the broadest terms, one can say that Flaubert was their model, either directly or else as his ideals were refracted through the work of James Joyce and others in the same line. Like Flaubert they wanted to achieve the qualities of precision, economy, and formal balance in hard, new books that shocked the middle classes —books in which, as Edmund Wilson said, "every word, every cadence, every detail, should perform a definite function in producing an intense effect." That was a European ideal, or so it seemed at the time, but the young writers also wanted to use American subject matter and a new literary idiom developed from American speech. They were determined to write truly what they really felt, as Hemingway said, "rather than what you were supposed to feel, and had been taught to feel." The result was that their novels, when they finally appeared, were so different from anything in the past that no French critic could recognize the source of their inspiration. They illustrated an old rule of comparative literature, that the same methods translated from one culture into another are likely to produce radically different results. They may even produce a literary renaissance, and that, in a modest way, was what happened during the 1920s.

In the novels of the Second War I can find very few signs that their authors have been reading French, German, or even English books. There is a touch of Joseph Conrad in *The Gesture* and a few other novels; a touch of Graham Greene in some of the stories about occupied Germany; a suggestion of Kipling's atmosphere in Michener's *Tales of the South Pacific*. Although Kafka, Gide, and Sartre were the Continental authors in fashion during the 1940s, and although they influenced many novels about civilian life, they had no effect on the war novels I have been reading—unless there is a hint of Gide in *The Gallery*, and of that one can't be sure. American influences, on the other hand, are easy to recognize. They even form a sort of pattern that was evident as early as John Hersey's *A Bell for Adano*, published in 1944. One might say that a great many novels of the Second War are based on Dos Passos for structure, since they have collective heroes, in the Dos Passos fashion, and since he invented a series of structural devices for dealing with such heroes in unified works of fiction. At the same time they are based on Scott Fitzgerald for mood, on Steinbeck for humor, and on Hemingway for action and dialogue.

From Here to Eternity was more directly influenced by Thomas Wolfe, and I have already remarked that *The Naked and the Dead* is written in the mood of James T. Farrell. Sometimes—though not in these two cases—the relation of a new writer with an older one is close enough to make the reader uncomfortable; for example, *Mr. Roberts*—the novel, not the play—is Steinbeck's *Cannery Row* towed out to sea. *All Thy Conquests*, by Alfred Hayes, and his later war novel, *The Girl on the Via Flaminia*, are convincing stories that would have been better still if the author hadn't adopted Hemingway's point of view along with his style, so that he seems to be looking at Rome through borrowed spectacles. In most of the books, however, the influence of older American novelists is a little less evident on the surface, though just as pervasive, and it suggests a conclusion about the two periods in fiction. During the 1920s writers were trying to create a new tradition in American literature because the older one had broken down or couldn't be accepted. Now, in the middle of the century, most American writers are trying to develop a tradition that already exists. Some of them, as we shall see, are entirely too faithful to the tradition as expounded by the newer critics.

III.

THE "NEW" FICTION:
A TIDY ROOM IN BEDLAM

Besides combat fiction, I have been reading a great many novels, also by younger writers, that belong to another category. They are not pictures of a great common experience and they are not intended for a wide audience—though some of them have found the audience as if by stumbling into it. Some of the authors are known by name to everyone who follows the book-review sections of Sunday newspapers: they are men and women like Frederick Buechner, Robie Macauley, Jean Stafford, Truman Capote, Paul Bowles. There are a few talented older novelists—for example, Eudora Welty and Caroline Gordon—who write in somewhat the same manner, and I suspect that their books have served as models for many younger members of the group, although their best qualities are hard to copy.

Some of the youngsters have published one or more novels without attracting much attention, and others haven't succeeded in getting their books accepted. No matter: they are all "serious" new writers, they are trying to produce works of art in accordance with the best literary standards, and they would like to be admired by the critics who write for *Kenyon, Sewanee, Hudson,* and other quarterly reviews. I have read many scores of their novels, published or in manuscript, and have heard about scores of others. Together these books compose a separate literary genus: they are the "new" fiction that corresponds to the new criticism and the new poetry.

Many of the better-known novels by new authors since World War II are not in the least new-fictional. Strictly defined, the genus doesn't include *The Naked and the Dead* or *From Here to Eternity* or in fact any books about the armed forces. It doesn't include *The Man with the Golden Arm*, by Nelson Algren, or *The Invisible Man*, by Ralph Ellison, both of which won the National Book Award. It doesn't include another novel that won the award—*The Adventures of Augie March*, by Saul Bellow—even though the author had written two earlier books that might have been called new-fictional for their sparseness of incident. Bellow's third book is too rich and disorderly, it takes too many chances, and it is old-fashioned enough to have a social background. All the novels mentioned in this paragraph are "about" something—Americans in uniform, the Chicago slums, the rebellion of an educated Negro, or the uncommitted man of our times—and any novel with a social or general subject is described by many of the newer critics as "naturalistic," a word that now carries a derogatory meaning. If the subject is of current interest, the novel is not only naturalistic but is exposed to the last term of contempt: it is "sheer journalism."

The new fiction avoids the taint of journalism by being aggressively non-social and non-political. But it is negative in other fashions too: for example, it is non-historical, since it doesn't deal with the past as past or with the changing nature of the present; it makes an effort to be timeless. It is non-intellectual in the sense that the authors try not to express their own ideas, and also in the sense that the characters drift on their streams of consciousness without ever really thinking. One might conclude that the novels had little to do with present-day American life, and yet they depend on it; indeed they are among its most elaborate by-products. They might be interesting to describe, not from the standpoint of a literary critic, for they have received such attention already; not to praise or ridicule the authors, though often the praise would be deserved and sometimes ridicule is hard to avoid; but objectively, in the spirit of a foreign sociologist, say a cultivated Hindu, reading the novels for the first time and trying to decide whether they cast any light on our amazing postwar society.

1.

The new fiction can be recognized in the bookstores without reading a page of the text. Almost always it consists of thin books about the size of printed plays and hardly thicker than volumes of poetry. Fat novels are either naturalistic or else they are historical romances.

On the back of the dust wrapper there is a posed cabinet-size photograph of the author, who usually wears an intent and other-worldly look around the eyes. Beneath the photograph—if it doesn't fill the page, like the famous picture of Truman Capote brooding on a couch—there are critical comments, often calling attention to the depth or inwardness of the novel, its graceful irony, its meanings "on different levels," and its effective use of symbols. Naturalistic novels wear a different type of dressing gown. They give the blurb writer so much to talk about that there is room for only a small photograph, and the advance critical comments are supposed to be written by booksellers on order blanks.

Opening the book to the front matter, we usually find an epigraph or inscription. If it consists of a quotation from Rimbaud or Dante (in French or Italian), or from a seventeenth-century English author, or if there are several quotations, including one from T. S. Eliot, and another from a Greek or Roman classic, preferably Longinus *On the Sublime*, then we can be certain that the book is new-fictional and can go on to examine the text. Let us see what remarks are suggested by its various features, including time, setting, point of view, characters, themes, structure, and style.

The *time* of the new fiction is vaguely the present, or rather it is a recent but undated yesterday. Not much time elapses from beginning to end of the action; it may be a few days or weeks, perhaps a summer (*Wait, Son, October Is Near*), at most an academic year of two semesters. Sometimes the foreground of the novel is confined to a single day, but in that case it is rounded out with memories, so that we learn to know the principal character from birth.

The *setting* is seldom one of the centers where policy decisions are made; it is never Capitol Hill or the Pentagon or the board-room of any corporation or political London or Paris or Army head-quarters in the field. These are backgrounds for novels with public or social subjects. Preferring to deal with private lives, the new fic-

tion is likely to have a remote and peripheral scene, for example—
as I think of some recent novels—a lonely ranch in Colorado, a
village in East Texas, a small town in Georgia, various plantation
houses in Louisiana and Mississippi (all rotting into the dank loam),
a country house in Maine, a "happy rural seat" in Ontario that
haunts a house in Cleveland (don't ask how), an abandoned summer hotel, two beach resorts full of homosexuals, several fresh-
water colleges, a private asylum, the international colony in Rome,
the still more international colony in Tangier, and a caravan cross-
ing the Sahara under the sheltering sky. There is always an excuse
for assembling the characters in one of these out-of-the-way places.
Sometimes it is merely the accidents of travel; more often it is a
house party, a vacation, a deathbed, a wedding (dozens of wed-
dings), a family reunion—at any rate the device permits the novelist to present his story without any of the frayed edges that are so
irritating when we encounter them in life.

The *point of view* from which the story will be told is chosen with
extreme care so as to give an effect of depth and immediacy. The
author with X-ray eyes who could look at a scene and know what
everybody was thinking—but without penetrating deeply into anyone's mind—has practically vanished from American fiction. With
him has vanished the museum-guide type of author who kept judging his characters and explaining them to the reader. The new
author hides his personality in the background, like a dramatist.
He tries to submerge himself in one or more of the characters and
he tells the story as the character sees, hears, and feels it.

This concern with point of view is not exclusively a mark of the
new fiction, since it extends to almost all our postwar writing. The
"new" novelists, however, have devices and refinements of their
own. One device is to describe a series of events through the eyes
of a first character, then of a second, then of a third, then back to
the first again, and so to the end of the novel (which might be *The
Disguises of Love*, by Robie Macauley). Each character offers a
different picture of the situation, and the author makes no explana-
tory comments, thus leaving the reader with a much-desired effect
of irony or ambiguity, or plain confusion. Another device is for the
novelist to pretend that he is a very young or stupid person who
watches the behavior of grown-ups with an innocent eye. Very often
the young person is a pre-adolescent girl vaguely resembling Henry
James's Maisie; there are heroines of about her age in *The Member*

of the Wedding, by Carson McCullers, *The Mountain Lion*, by Jean Stafford, and *The Strange Children*, by Caroline Gordon. Again the central intelligence may be a boy, also pre-adolescent, as in Truman Capote's *Other Voices, Other Rooms* and Peter Taylor's *A Woman of Means*. The hero of *Wait, Son, October Is Near*, by John Bell Clayton, is a bright ten-year-old. In *The Caged Birds*, by Leroy Leatherman, an adult drama is rather dimly registered on the rather dim consciousness of a little boy of eight. All these books, except the last, are effectively written, and two or three of them are distinguished, but there are others in the same genre that give the effect of a country-club masquerade where busty debutantes and hairy-legged attorneys come dressed as babies.

The *characters* in the new fiction are distinguished by their lack of a functional relationship with American life. They don't sow or reap, build, mine, process, promote or sell, repair, heal, plead, administer, or legislate. In a still broader sense they don't join or belong. One widely observed feature of present-day America is that the lives of most individuals are defined by their relations with an interlocking series of institutions—for example, government bureaus, churches, schools and universities, the armed services, labor unions, chambers of commerce, farm bureaus, veterans' organizations, and, for most of us, that center of our daily activities, the office. But characters in the new fiction are exceptional persons who keep away from offices—at least for the duration of the novel—and are generally as unattached as Daniel Boone.

It is true that some of them are teachers, but they don't engage in faculty politics and seldom enter a classroom. Some are housewives who never cook or clean, and some are businessmen who have retired or are on vacation or play subordinate roles as fathers of the heroes and heroines. The characters likely to be treated at length are students of both sexes, young artists and writers, gentlemen on their travels, divorced or widowed mothers, gay boys, neurotic bitches, virtuous grandfathers, old women on their deathbeds, and preternaturally wise little girls. As compared with the population at large, the characters include an abnormally large number of persons living on inherited incomes. They also include more than the average proportion of very old people and children, with a smaller proportion of men and women in the active or money-earning ages. The women, down to the age of six, are more forceful or malignant and less inhibited than the men, most of whom are victims rather than heroes or villains. Some of the men are likely to be symbolic figures—for example, a scientist as prototype of evil, a doctor or a priest to represent spiritual wisdom, and a reformer as an object of scorn.

Instead of political or social subjects the new fiction has *themes* that are taken from individual lives. The distinction becomes clear if you ask one of the authors what is the subject of his next book. "It's hard to say," he will answer; then, after a pause, he will add brightly, "I guess it's just about people." On reading the manuscript you will find that it is about people in some private crisis or dilemma that serves as the novelist's theme and his excuse for presenting a picture of human destinies.

So far the themes considered suitable for the new fiction have proved to be limited in number, and many of them keep reappearing in one book after another. One of the most popular is the initiation of a pre-adolescent girl or boy into the knowledge of sex or evil (as in *The Mountain Lion* and *Other Voices, Other Rooms*). Another is the mad infatuation of a middle-aged man or woman with a predatory younger person (as in *The Disguises of Love*, and in *The Roman Spring of Mrs. Stone*, by Tennessee Williams). Still another is the heroine's flight from reality, involving her surrender to drugs, nymphomania, or catatonic dementia (as in Paul Bowles' *The Sheltering Sky*). Some of the novels deal with the interplay between a religiously inspired character and a group of unbelievers; some show the hero or heroine struggling toward and finally reaching maturity; others, by contradiction, exalt the innocent world of childhood and depict grown persons as dangerous hypocrites. Later I shall have more to say about the novels—there are scores of them circulating in manuscript—that describe the ruin of a sensitive and truly artistic young man by his possessive mother.

The new fiction seldom deals with the familiar American theme of social mobility. In the old fiction one expected the hero (or the heroine, if she was the central character) to rise in the world like Silas Lapham and Sister Carrie and Susan Lenox. Sometimes he surprised us by falling, like Sister Carrie's lover and Dr. Richard Diver of *Tender Is the Night*, but in any case there was a vertical movement through different layers of society. In the new fiction there is little movement of the sort. Both the hero and the heroine can be expected to stay in the same position, socially speaking, though sometimes one of them suffers a moral decline. If the other characters include a man making his fortune, he is likely to be presented as a disagreeable person. Often the novelist seems to be making a plea for social stability and inherited position.

That is not the only social or political idea implied by the new fiction. Another idea suggested in many novels, including some but not all of those with a Southern background, is the foolishness of racial prejudice. Still another is the weakness and cowardice of liberals, and a fourth, expressed in terms of character, is the selfishness of reformers. Very old men and women are often depicted admiringly, as if to demonstrate that the past, with its widely accepted values and simple code of conduct, is better than the present. It remains true, however, that most of the ideas to be deduced from the new fiction are moral rather than social or political. Usually they can be translated into statements of a highly generalized type: for example, "Evil is in the human heart," "We must have compassion," "Let us be content with our lot," "Ripeness is all," "Little children, love one another!" or simply, "Mother was to blame."

The *structure* of the novels is usually balanced, efficient, economical, and tightly joined. A reader is left with the impression—which may be false in some cases—that the author has made a complete plan for the novel before setting to work on the first chapter. That is a comparatively safe method of writing novels and it has been followed by many distinguished authors. There are others, perhaps including more of the great, who have started with characters involved in a situation and have allowed them to work out their own destinies. "I write the first sentence," said Laurence Sterne, "and trust in God for the next." Dickens and most of the famous Victorians began publishing their novels by installments before they were finished and before the novelists knew how the stories would end. Jean Giraudoux said that he liked to go to the country with a ream of paper and an empty mind; when he came back to Paris his novel would be ready for publication.

There are all sorts of middle courses for novelists, but I am trying to suggest the two extremes. The second, that of Sterne and Giraudoux, implies a great deal of self-confidence, or trust in God. Even when followed by men of talent it is likely to produce formless, wasteful, inconsistent books, but the stories will flow like rivers or music and the characters may be a continual surprise to the author as well as the reader. The other method, that of the new fictionists, involves so much planning and preparation that the characters are no longer free to develop as in life. At best the stories will have an architectural form; their music is frozen and has ceased to flow; their economical structure is balanced in repose.

As for the *style* of the new fiction, there seems to be an impression that it is precious and hard to understand. The impression is justified in the case of a very few authors. Frederick Buechner, for example, likes to use glittering phrases that seem to have been picked from a jeweler's tray with a pair of tweezers. William Goyen (*The House of Breath*) writes as if from a twilight region where extreme sensitivity is on the point of being transformed into simple hallucination. Neither of them is typical of the "new" novelists. The typical style is simple and correct; often it is the sort of language that one of the characters, chosen as observer, would use in his daily life. The story-telling character is seldom or never a foul-mouthed person, and it is safe to assume that any novel peppered with obscenities belongs to the old-fictional or naturalistic school. The tone of the new writing is decorous, subdued, in the best of taste, and every sentence is clear in itself. The difficulty for the reader lies in recognizing the symbols and what the author intends by them. or —in view of the author's aloof and ironic attitude—in finding the meaning of the story as a whole.

2.

The typical authors of the "new" novels are university men and women. They start by taking advanced courses in writing fiction, then they apply the lessons in their own books, under critical supervision, and meanwhile they support themselves by working as part-time instructors, preferably in fiction courses. If the books are published they can expect to be named assistant professors, with academic tenure. There has never been a time when so many practicing writers were attached to the staffs of American universities.

One pictures the young academic novelist as working in a study lined with books from floor to ceiling. Here are the great world classics in translation (he teaches them in his freshman course in the humanities); here are the well-thumbed English metaphysical poets; here are anthologies of the new criticism (with passages underlined and notes penciled in the margin); here is shelf after shelf of the nineteenth-century novelists who are still being praised

—Jane Austen, Stendhal, Flaubert, Melville and his critics (a double shelf), Dostoevski, Hardy, Conrad, with the New York edition of Henry James, which the novelist bought when he was a college senior (and went almost hungry for two months to pay for it). Here is Proust in French, with pages uncut, standing beside the half-read English translation, and here are all the moderns, beginning with Joyce and Pound and Eliot, the record of half a century's experiments in poetry and fiction.

As a young novelist—he reflects as he finishes his two pages for the day—there is no need for him to waste his time in experiments, since they have all been performed for him and the results are standing on his shelves. If he wants experiments in point of view he has James's prefaces to guide him; if he wants experiments in language he has Joyce and Gertrude Stein; if he wants the fantastic or allegorical he has Kafka and the surrealists; if he wants to re-member and re-create the past there is always Proust. Instead of being driven to invention and speculation he can live on inherited capital, or rather on the income from inherited capital, and find a sort of intellectual security.

He has also found economic security—though on a rather low level, he reflects as he starts to read over his notes for the lecture on "Symbolism in Henry James's Later Novels" that he will be giving at one-thirty. What a bad hour for a lecture, and how can he keep the students awake? . . . The house is quiet now that the children have been bundled off to nursery school. From the kitchen he can hear the faint sound of his wife putting dishes away. Poor girl, she hasn't been able to finish her volume of short stories, after everyone said that the first of them showed such a power of malicious observation. If the novel sells he can get her a part-time maid. If it is well reviewed in the quarterlies he is certain to be made a full professor—that is, if nobody on the board of regents happens to read that seduction scene in Chapter XII. It might be better to soften the scene, leave it a little blurred and symbolic. . . . The young novelist, now wholly a young professor, puts his lecture notes into a folder, puts the folder into his briefcase, and goes downstairs to kiss his wife before setting out for luncheon at the Faculty Club.

Not even an Illinois board of regents would be likely to find politi-cal heresies in his manuscript, or in any of its class. There is an-other group of new fictionists composed of crew-cut bohemians who

are proud of their political ignorance. Charles Rolo wrote an article
about them in which he repeated the story of a famous young poet
who asked a famous young novelist, "What is Latvia?" Any of
the academics could have answered him. They know that Latvia is
next to Estonia, know that both were annexed by Russia, and are
properly exercised by the Soviet menace. In domestic politics they
are, with some exceptions, mildly liberal, and in 1952 almost all
of them voted for Stevenson, but they try to keep their opinions
out of their fiction—not from caution, or not consciously so, but
rather from a feeling that opinions change with the years and have
no place in art, which is permanent.

"We're not going to be fooled," I have heard more than one of
them saying. "A great many of the prewar novelists were trying
to save the world, and see where their efforts led them, straight into
the arms of Stalin and into writing books that seem foolish today. We
detest communism, but we're not going to be fooled into becoming
professional anti-Communists—or anti-anti-Communists, or anti-
anti-anti-Communists, or whatever the fashionable stance may be.
We're going to attend to our proper business, which is writing about
human beings in permanent human situations."

"What sort of situations?"

The novelist has been speaking in low tones, so as not to be overheard and misunderstood by student waiters at the Faculty Club.
Now the dining room has emptied and his voice becomes more
confident. "Moral dilemmas," he answers, "caused by the human
weakness of the characters and their incurable propensity for evil.
We have learned that society isn't responsible for our faults, and
therefore naturalism is dead. Social realism is also dead, and we'd
like to be moral realists. You might say that we are trying to produce
pure fiction."

There is a great deal to be admired in this confession of faith, but
it contains two phrases that suggest important reservations. "Moral
realists" is the first of these.[1] The novelists seldom deal with any

---

1. The phrase was rendered popular by Lionel Trilling, who gives it a narrower and more accurate meaning than it has since acquired. He defines
moral realism as "the perception of the dangers of the moral life itself,"
in other words, the perception that when we strike moral attitudes we may
really be parading our vanity and aggressiveness. The man who wants to
save the world by imposing his own beliefs on it is often incapable of loving
his neighbors, and the novelist who perceives this fact is, in Trilling's scheme,
a moral realist. In the same essay, "Manners, Morals, and the Novel" (in *The*

human institution larger than the separate family. How can they be morally realistic without presenting the full background of moral decisions? In American life today that background is partly institutional. One's hope of advancement, the opinion of one's colleagues (and of student waiters), the wisdom of resisting institutional pressures, the best interests of the firm (or university or government bureau)—all these elements are involved in the decisions that most of us are called upon to make. I don't mean to imply that novels in the 1950s should deal primarily with institutions. They should deal primarily with persons, as always. But today, more than ever in the past, the intimate daily lives of Americans are being changed by institutions, which are also changing. By omitting institutions from their novels, the new writers present their characters as if silhouetted against an empty sky, and end by giving them a curious effect of thinness and partial reality.

The second phrase, "pure fiction," is one that was historically inevitable. First there was pure poetry, as discussed in France by Paul Valéry and Abbé Breuil and in England by George Moore— poetry divorced from any purpose and resembling a game of solitaire with incredibly complicated rules. Then there was pure criticism, as advocated here by René Wellek and Austin Warren in their influential book, *Theory of Literature*. Pure criticism would be divorced from history, biography, sociology, or psychology and would confine itself to explaining the intrinsic qualities of a work of art. As for pure fiction, it would develop from the principles of the pure or "ontological" critics. Having purged itself of any historical, social, or ideological elements, it would try to answer the one question: What would a group of characters do in a given situation? The characters would be studied in depth and the situation would be set apart from ordinary life, including the human institutions of its time and place.

Meanwhile some of the older men who started as pure poets or abstract painters might have told the young novelists what was likely to happen and is in fact happening today. Fiction would acquire a neoclassical purity and correctness, but would lose much of its force and its common humanity. The result would be novels like highly

---

Liberal Imagination, New York: The Viking Press, 1950), he defines the novel as "a perpetual quest for reality, the field of its research being the social world." Too much of the new fiction is a quest for reality outside the social world, in an effective vacuum.

polished *objets d'art*, not really designed to be read but rather to be displayed like framed diplomas: Know all men by these presents that this is a cultured home.

3.

Yet for all its appearance of being far from the main currents of American life, our Hindu sociologist might find that the new fiction does offer a number of interesting sidelights on American society. What it reveals by indirection is a state of mind that prevails among many others besides the new novelists.

I think the real background of their work is a sort of horror at what is happening in the world—not a specialized horror at any one development like atomic weapons, totalitarian governments, the cold war, or the restrictions on personal liberty in all countries, but rather a generalized dismay at the results of five centuries of progress and widening enlightenment. Men have outrun themselves; their technical knowledge has increased so much more rapidly than their moral judgment and self-control and simple kindness—if these have increased at all—that the knowledge might destroy them as a species. "If I could push a button and destroy the world—" romantic adolescents used to boast in their conversations late at night. Now the pushbutton is there, the technicians are busy wiring it, and we have learned from Hitler's story that great countries can be ruled by perverted adolescents.

That is our nightmare, but not the whole of it. Combined with the fear of catastrophe is the feeling that individuals are unable to prevent it—at least the sort of individuals whom young novelists know and feel justified in writing about. Perhaps the statesmen, the generals, the managers of big corporations have some power to direct events. At least they have the sort of knowledge on which decisions can be based, in these days when much of the knowledge has to be concealed from the public for reasons of military security. But their power is limited, since they must act chiefly as spokesmen for great bureaucratic institutions—and moreover they remain distant figures for the novelists, who are never likely to meet them. Teachers, scientists, artists, the writers themselves have little knowledge of government affairs and less political influence; if they support a candidate he is likely to be beaten. Their feeling of helplessness is mingled in some cases with a feeling of guilt that goes back to the prewar years. During the Roosevelt era some of them did exert a little influence, they tried to act on their ideas, and they failed—they didn't even succeed in saving the Spanish republic, let alone averting a new world war. Many of them now feel that they let themselves be used by the Communists and ended by doing more harm than good.

Their disillusionment is not merely with communism, here and in Russia, but with a broader aspiration of which communism is an extreme form. A dream has been dislodged from their minds. It is the old dream that men might control their own destinies by reasoning out and applying the laws that govern society—might cease to be victims of blind forces, and might, in Edmund Wilson's words, "impose on the events of the present a pattern of actual direction which will determine the history of the future."

That dream of reshaping history is as old as the first human tribes and their efforts to control the future by sympathetic magic. It was never so prevalent as in the 1930s. At that time it was shared in different degrees by Italian and German Fascists, by Socialists, Labourites, and New Dealers, not to mention smaller sects like Single Taxers, Social Crediters, Townsendites, Technocrats, and dozens of others, each with its own notion of what the determining pattern should be. The Communists had the clearest notion, based on the most coherent body of doctrine, which they called a science, and supported by the most disciplined body of adherents. Their effort to change the world can hardly be called a failure, in the political sense, considering that they now rule Europe east of the Elbe and Asia north of the Himalayas—almost one-fourth of the land area of the globe, with almost one-third of its total population. But the conditions of life in that area are not what Marx or Lenin planned, are not a background for the historical pattern they wished to impose, and in fact are strikingly less favorable to the arts, to freedom of inquiry, and to the general welfare than conditions in many other countries that, like our own, argued and drifted and compromised without a fixed doctrine. One after another the American intellectuals have come to feel that communism not only is a failure in terms of the dream but may lead to a worldwide disaster.

One might have expected them to keep the dream while looking for other methods of attaining it, as a scientist might do after the failure of some ambitious experiment in chemistry. They might have gone back—and some of them did go back—to the method of piecemeal reform that was advocated by the Socialists. They might have puzzled over the problem of ends and means and might have decided that when the means were brutal or dishonest, as they had been in Russia, the end would also be corrupted. Again they might have concluded that the central error in Marxian communism was a false picture of the human species: fundamentally the doctrine was based on the notion that men were reasonable creatures who would be happiest under the system of ownership that gave them the greatest economic advantages. It disregarded everything illogical or unconscious, the struggle for social distinction, and the human need for drama, ritual, and mystery. The intellectuals might have looked for more accurate pictures of man's nature, to be deduced not from economics but from other fields of study, including psychology, anthropology, education, linguistics, and comparative religion. As a matter of fact, progress was made in all those fields, even during the war, but it seemed unexciting and much too slow to offer hope of defeating the destructive forces that were progressing more rapidly. Science itself had become a destructive force. Moreover, the intellectuals were so disheartened by the results of the Communist experiment that many of them were losing faith not only in one method of realizing the dream but in the possibility of realizing it by any method available to the human intelligence.

That was the "failure of nerve" so widely discussed at the end of the war. Even more than a loss of faith in progress by logical or scientific methods, it was a loss of faith in themselves as guides to progress. The intellectuals had to admit that their own record as a class was bad in many countries. They had planned the Russian revolution and had administered the Soviet state until Stalin was firmly in power and turned against them; by a series of apparently correct decisions they had reached the wrong goal. Intellectuals of a sort had also planned the Italian corporate state and Hitler's Thousand-Year Reich. Other intellectuals had exerted some power in this country during the first eight years of the New Deal, and their record was better here, but they had quarreled disgracefully among themselves and some of them had been misled by Russian flattery. All during the 1930s Russia had been trying hard to cultivate the Western intellectuals, regarding them as a power group that might further Russian policies. The intellectuals had come to believe that those policies were identical with their own, at least in the international field: wasn't Russia opposed to fascism and bent on preserving peace? Then suddenly, after Munich, Russia decided that they were too powerless to serve as allies, got rid of their friend Litvinov, and made a pact with Hitler. The intellectuals were left bitterly divided, without support, foreign or domestic, and still worse they were left without confidence in themselves or a clear picture of what was to be done.

All that is history, now misrepresented or forgotten, and the new novelists had no share in it. What they have acquired from the experience of others is a sort of generalized distrust of the intellect as a means of improving life on this planet. Where is the progress? they might ask. Stone Age men huddled together in their firelit caves while the darkness outside was filled with hostile animals. Step by step they tamed or exterminated the animals, their own descendants overran the earth, and still later descendants set out to conquer the elements. Today men are descending to the depths of the ocean and flying above the breathable limits of the air, while their new ambitions are to abolish diseases, control the weather, and travel to other planets. At the same time they are using the intellect to create still deadlier enemies of mankind than those they subdued in the past; the new ones are poison gases, atomic clouds, microbes more virulent than any that existed in nature, and explosives that might burn the earth to a cinder. Again we must huddle together for safety in our brilliantly lighted caves, but this time the beasts that go prowling through the mind-made darkness are themselves fashioned from the human mind.

A hint of these feelings I have tried to suggest can be found in the background of the new novels. They are deep feelings, responsibly held by young men and women who for the most part—we can forget the apes of fashion—are trying to do their best in a situation for which nobody was prepared. If the feelings are seldom directly expressed in novels, that is partly because of a prevailing literary convention that fiction shouldn't deal with the sort of ideas on which the feelings are based. It is also because of a justifiable caution. In these days of investigations run wild, Americans are learning to be timid about expressing their opinions, especially if these are in the least heretical. The result is that we are now reading novels by intellectuals, for intellectuals, about supposedly intellectual or at least well-educated characters, in which not a single intelligent notion is expressed about the world in which we live.

Yet the novels do express what is essentially the reaction to a social situation. They express first of all a retreat from international and national and even sectional problems—except in the case of some Southern writers—into personal problems for which a solution can presumably be found. They express the belief that the suicidal folly of nations and classes is the magnified image of individual selfishness ("Evil is in the human heart"). Like the war novels, they express an admiration for simple goodness that is rather new in American writing; time and again we note the appearance of characters who are goodness personified. The novels do not exalt the American way of life or the American mission to save the world —in that respect they preserve a sort of artistic chastity—but they do express a new sympathy for the middle-class virtues. They also express a search for lasting beliefs in the midst of confusion, for fixed standards of good and evil; and finally they express the novelists' desire for security and order—even if the order can be achieved only in a neat and housewifely story that is like the one cleanly swept and furnished room in Bedlam.

IV.

CRITICS OVER NOVELISTS

1.

Every age has its stereotypes in fiction, its familiar stories endlessly repeated in novels by young authors, each of whom is convinced that his darling tale has never been told before. Publishers' readers are a more skeptical if always hopeful breed. After paging through hundreds of manuscripts, they have learned to recognize the stereotypes of this postwar age, which differ in an interesting fashion from those of the preceding half-century.

In the early 1900s a favorite story was about the cultured young man, apparently a weakling, who nevertheless surmounted hardships and defeated savage enemies—in the jungle, at sea, or in the frozen North—by reverting to the qualities of his Viking ancestors. It was the Darwinian or Jack Londonian novel, based on the notion that the wilderness is the test of manhood and that well-born Nordics are fittest to survive. By 1910 it was giving way to the muckraking novel, about the young reformer who single-handedly fought the corrupt politicians, besides courting the daughter of the biggest boss of all. The boss, converted by her innocent wiles, ended by proving that he could be a reformer too.

In the 1920s, that age of cynicism and moral rebellion, there was the story of the sensitive young man, the idealized Artist, oppressed and broken by the philistine World (like the hero of *Manhattan*

Transfer and the heroine of *Main Street*). There was also the story of the completely natural or Hemingway young man who suffered in monosyllables and preserved a drunken composure while women flung themselves at his neck and hell broke loose. The social rebellion of the 1930s gave us another stereotype, the strike novel, which was usually laid in a Southern cotton-spinning town. The strike was broken, its leader was killed by the bosses, but there was a second hero as well, a boy from the hills who was won over to the revolutionary faith. In the last chapter he began to organize the defeated workers for new struggles, under a sky that was red with hope.

Nobody has been writing strike novels since World War II. The other prewar stereotypes have also vanished, with two exceptions noted: (1) The early-Hemingway young man occasionally saunters or shambles into a novel about Greenwich Village, and (2) the Darwinian novel reappears from time to time as a serial in the *Saturday Evening Post*, which, conservative in everything but typography, still likes to picture the triumph of well-born Nordics over the Canadian wilderness. But these Ernestian and Darwinian heroes are living fossils, so to speak, and would be no more at home in most of the new novels than Jake Barnes in a progressive boarding school (grades 8 through 12, coeducational). What are the favorite stories today? Setting aside mystery stories, subject or problem novels, and popular romances of every type, and considering only the "serious" novels that aspire to literary distinction, I should estimate that more than half of the manuscripts now in circulation belong to one of the following six varieties:

1. There is the novel about the sensitive and so artistic young man who pities himself with good reason. His life has been ruined, not by the world—as in the case of his 1920 uncle—but simply by the blindness of his possessive mother. In the end he commits suicide or murder, or both (see *The Christmas Tree*, by Isabel Bolton), or marries and is killed by his wife, or, in a happier version of the same story, escapes from the mother and comes to New York, where he finds release in the company of other sensitive young men. This fairy-Freudian novel doesn't often reach the bookstores, but it provides a high proportion of the manuscripts that publishers reject.

2. There is the adventure story that starts in a familiar setting, realistically presented, but then becomes more and more fantastic, more confusing to the reader, until he discovers that the author is trying to find symbols, symbols, symbols for the moral chaos of

the modern world. This novel is often brilliantly written and it is sometimes accepted and printed—with a dust wrapper that mentions Kafka and Graham Greene—but it never has much sale.

3. There is the satirical and slightly surrealistic novel about the rich young man surrounded by mad bohemians. Usually the scene is Greenwich Village, but it may also be the upper East Side or the American colony in Florence or Rome. Like the symbolic adventure story, this novel is sometimes brilliantly written, but it is never published except at the author's expense. I can't explain the reason, but the Greenwich Village novels that reach the bookstores (like *Who Walk in Darkness* and *Go*) are almost always Hemingway-realistic and deadly serious.

4. There is the novel about puritans abroad. Some well-educated young Americans are traveling in Italy, Spain, or one of the Arab countries. They come in contact with peasants or bedouins who, by their fecund vitality and readiness for action, reveal the essential bloodlessness of the travelers. The novel takes one of two turns: either the Americans are morally ruined by trying to imitate the peasants or else (in memory of E. M. Forster's *A Room with a View*) the hero and the heroine are redeemed into their natural, passionate selves.

5. There is the tender, nostalgic novel about the world of childhood, usually written by authors who feel surly and cheated at being forced to grow up. They tell how boys and girls revolted against the mean hypocrisy of their elders. Often (as in Truman Capote's *The Grass Harp*) the children are aided in their revolt by old persons or Negro servants with childlike hearts.

6. There is the novel about the obsessive pursuit of some animal —fox, bear, deer, mountain lion, or very large fish—that ends by becoming an almost supernatural beast and symbolizes the indifferent or malignant forces of nature. Several of the great American stories have dealt with this theme, as witness Faulkner's *The Bear* and Hemingway's *The Old Man and the Sea*, but lately the theme has been tried by too many beginners, with the result that readers are losing patience. They finish three or four chapters of the manuscript and snarl, "Come out from behind those bushes, Moby Dick."

These are the six stereotypes most frequently encountered among the novels now circulating in manuscript, but there are others almost as common. There is, for example, the story of the good citizen who tries to track down a criminal and learn the motive for his crime, but ends by discovering that much of the guilt is in his own heart. First readers describe the manuscript as "you know, that psychomelodrama." There is the story of the pre-adolescent boy or girl who learns about sex (Tot Spies on Love Nest); there is the tragedy of the religiously inspired character among a group of un-believers; and the list of stereotypes might be continued. The point I wanted to make is that all these novels show the influence of the newer criticism. All the novelists have a double audience in mind: first there is the broader public they would like to reach without really trying, and second there are the critics they must be sure to please—the distinguished critics for the quarterlies, who write with such an air of certainty about the faults to be shunned and the virtues to be praised in American fiction.

2.

A striking feature of book reviews in the quarterlies is that they use a new set of words to indicate praise or disparagement. Today the bad words applied to fiction by a great many of the younger critics are *naturalism*, *liberalism*, *optimism* (which is either *vague* or *shallow*), *progressive* (usually put in quotation marks), *scientific*, and *sociology*. Among the good words and phrases are *tradition*, *depth* or *inwardness*, *values* (especially if they are *moral* and *perma-nent*), *irony*, *formal patterns*, *close texture*, *meanings on different levels*, *symbols*, and *myth*. Most of the bad words are self-explana-tory, or have already been explained. Some of the goods words re-quire a gloss for readers unfamiliar with the new critical language.

Of all good words in the quarterlies, "irony" is perhaps the most overworked, and it is also, in its current usage or abuse, the hardest word to define. There was a time when authors could be ironical merely by stating the opposite of what they conceived to be the truth: thus, they would say that Tony Lumpkin was the greatest hero in Christendom when they meant that he was a coward. There was also dramatic irony, defined as the quality of speeches under-stood by the audience but not grasped by speakers on the stage ("My lover is coming tonight, I'm so happy," the heroine says; but the audience knows that an ambush has been laid and that the lover will be killed if he comes tonight). Later there was the fictional irony that was a favorite device of the early naturalistic novelists. It was the effect obtained when a character set out for one destination and reached another—for example, when Henry Fleming of *The Red Badge of Courage* became a hero by running away, and when Sister Carrie Meeber became a great actress through losing her virtue.

All these devices are easy to define, but the irony that is often discovered and praised in the new fiction is a vaguer quality, and sometimes I wonder whether critics or authors could explain what they mean by it. Apparently it is present at any moment when the novelist's attitude toward the story is complicated or ambiguous. Thus, if he describes the same event from the standpoints of three different characters—as Robie Macauley does in *The Disguises of Love*—and if each of the characters interprets the event in a different fashion, while the author doesn't try to indicate which of them is right about it, then he is being ironical. He is also taking no risks and is avoiding all arguments with readers who mightn't like his opinions if they were frankly stated. This sort of irony, prevalent in the new fiction, is completely different from satire, since the satirist isn't afraid to make his own opinions clear. One would think that our present society might offer rich opportunities to satirists, but hardly anyone is seizing them.

"Symbolism" is another overworked word, not to mention its being a much-abused literary device. In this case the new critics and teachers of literature are clearly to blame for what the new novelists are doing. The critics and teachers discovered, or rediscovered, some twenty years ago that many of the classic American novels were full of objects and actions that were intended to convey a whole group of meanings "on different levels," to use the trade-marked phrase: there was the literal meaning, and beyond it the moral meaning, and, looming in the distance, there was the final or anagogic meaning that transformed the symbolic object into a spiritual truth. It became the fashion to write essays and books, to deliver lectures and whole courses, on the symbolism of Hawthorne, Melville, or Henry James. Critics tortured themselves to be more ingenious than other critics, and soon they were discovering symbols that didn't exist and that the novelist, even in his subconscious depths, had never dreamed of using.

The new novelists joined in the game. Since critics were expounding and praising the use of symbols, the novelists determined to furnish the symbols, and in God's plenty—perhaps with the hope of becoming the subjects of critical researches in the twenty-first century. The result is apparent in most of the serious novels published during the last five years, and is even more apparent in the manuscripts now being read and rejected by publishers. These last are so full of symbols that the reader feels as though he were stumbling blindfold in a room overcrowded with furniture. If an object seems out of place, you can be sure that the author intended it as a symbol. If an action seems falsely emphasized or out of keeping with the character who performs it, the author regards it as having a symbolic value.

Such aberrations are sometimes encouraged by critics and teachers, as I learned when attending a summer writers' conference. One novel I was asked to read was about the attendants and patients in a state asylum. The young author had a subject he knew at first hand—he had been employed in the asylum for a year—and he had the beginnings of an effective style; the trouble was that he had no story. His hero went to work in the asylum, met a few schizophrenics with interesting case histories, watched them for a year, and then resigned his position without being changed by the experience. I was getting ready to discuss some ways in which the book could be rearranged to give it emotional sequence when the author forestalled me.

"I know what you're going to tell me about the novel," he said. "Professor Z—— explained what was wrong with it, and I had to admit that he was right. I haven't laid enough emphasis on the symbols of the wall and the door."

When symbols are arranged in logical order they compose an allegory, something about which critics are still in doubt. Ten years ago the device was almost universally condemned, but then Hawthorne's "blasted allegories," as he called them in his later life, came back into fashion and it was discovered that similar allegories were concealed in Kafka and even in Faulkner. That restored the word to respectability, but still, like a churchgoing madam, it retains traces of a disreputable past. Today one can't be certain whether a critic means to praise or disparage a novel when he describes it as allegorical.

There is no such uncertainty about the word "myth." To say of a novel that it "has mythical qualities" or "embodies a myth" is always a compliment. New myths are continually being discovered or reported or imagined in the American classics. Richard Chase tried to demonstrate that *The Confidence Man* was Melville's myth of the sinister American liberal (it was intended, the critic seemed to say, as a foresighted pamphlet against Henry Wallace). Leslie Fiedler outdid him by proving—or perhaps that isn't the word—that *Moby-Dick* and *Huckleberry Finn* are myths of combined homosexuality and miscegenation, "splendidly counterpoised in their oceanic complexity and fluminal simplicity." [1]

The new novelists would like to oblige the critics by creating other American myths, but two difficulties have been holding them back. The first is that the word has several contradictory meanings and that nobody has defined it to anyone's satisfaction except his own. Some critics seem to hold that myths are simply erroneous beliefs. From this it would follow that the more such beliefs are expressed in a novel, the more mythical it becomes. Much as they would like their work to have a mythical quality, the novelists are not prepared to follow this easy method of achieving it, and they are also dubious about some other meanings attached to the word. Their second difficulty is that myths, however defined, have always been the expression of widely shared feelings; they are stories that embody the common hopes and fears of a tribe, a class, or a nation. Myths have a broad archetypical quality, whereas the novelists like to deal—and apparently the critics like to have them deal—with subjects that are narrow and exceptional.

It is hard to create an archetype of modern life by recounting the private experience of a few isolated individuals in some untypical setting—for example, a Back Bay mansion transformed into a brothel (as in Howard Nemerov's *The Melodramatists*), or an old plantation house five miles from a telephone (as in dozens of Deep Southern novels), or what Frederick Buechner describes as "a small colony of summer friends." The most any novelist can do in this direction is to choose some ancient myth and echo it faintly in contemporary terms, thus giving his characters a sort of retrospective magnitude. But he runs the risk of emphasizing their smallness instead—as happened in Buechner's *A Long Day's Dying*, where the legend of Philomela and Procne was presented in modern dress, on the scale of one inch to the foot, as if the ancient story of lust and revenge were being re-enacted in a doll's house. In the

1. What the critic means is not "their" complexity and simplicity, but the oceanic complexity of one and the fluvial—not "fluminal"—simplicity of the other. And the two books are "splendidly" counterpoised by whom—by Melville? By Mark Twain? No, by the critic, who splendidly rises over the ruins of English grammar and our two greatest novels.

new fiction—and elsewhere in American writing—there is a lack
of contemporary myths like those which Melville, Mark Twain,
Henry James, and Dreiser all created in their times; nobody seems
able to present a life-size hero.

One critical slogan, about the desirability of myths, has set an
ideal before the novelists, while other critical slogans have been
making it difficult or impossible for them to attain the ideal. The
solution might be to stop following slogans. Meanwhile, at the risk
of having them followed, I would suggest three anti-slogans for the
next period in American writing:

IF IT ISN'T REAL, IT ISN'T A SYMBOL.

IF IT ISN'T A STORY, IT ISN'T A MYTH.

IF A CHARACTER DOESN'T LIVE, HE CAN'T BE AN ARCHETYPE OF
AMERICAN LIFE.

3.

There is another favorite word of some critics that has to be
explained at greater length. The word is "values," a collective plural
that seems to be borrowed from the special language of sociologists.
The sociological definition of values, according to the *American
College Dictionary*, is "the things of social life (ideals, customs,
institutions, etc.) toward which the people of the group have an
affective regard. These values may be positive, as cleanliness, freedom, education, etc., or negative, as cruelty, crime, or blasphemy."
Sometimes the critics follow this definition, but at other times they
seem to be using the word "values" in a larger and looser sense.
As in the case of "irony" I am not always certain what they mean
by it, but apparently it denotes or suggests any system of moral
judgments that a novel might conceivably express, or fail to express. The novel may have more than one singular value—it may
be dramatic and unified and also accurate—but still it may be dismissed by critics as "lacking in values." Usually the critics mean
that it depicts a group of persons without fixed standards of right
and wrong, or with standards of which they disapprove.

That all the postwar novelists are lacking in values is the central
theme of a book by John W. Aldridge, *After the Lost Generation*.
Aldridge is a young critic but not a "new" one; he is not opposed
to novels with social subjects and makes a rather sparing use of
words like "myth," "symbol," and "irony." His book, published

in 1951, was the first to deal in a serious and challenging fashion with the novelists who have appeared since World War II. Among the writers discussed in it are Norman Mailer, John Horne Burns, Irwin Shaw, Alfred Hayes, Merle Miller, Gore Vidal, Paul Bowles, Frederick Buechner, and Truman Capote. Aldridge sets them against the new novelists after World War I—especially Hemingway, Fitzgerald, and Dos Passos—and concludes that the older group was doing much more important work at the same age.

A similar conclusion has been reached by others, but Aldridge combines it with a thesis about the problem of writing novels in our time. The thesis is that novelists must have a sense of values, that the values must be shared by an audience, and that such an audience can no longer be found. It could not exist, Aldridge says, without "a society based on certain stable moral assumptions, the sort of society to which, perhaps, Richardson and Smollett belonged, to which, in a different way and to a lesser extent, even Scott Fitzgerald and Ernest Hemingway belonged, but to which we obviously do not belong today." Aldridge keeps driving his thesis home. "These writers," he says of the postwar novelists, "have been constantly handicapped by the emptiness of the characters and situations about which they have been obliged to write. Since they have inherited a world without values and since they have had no choice but to find their material in that world, they have had to deal with value-lessness, and that can never form the basis of a successful literature."

By an almost mathematical demonstration he has proved—if we accept his premises—that the new generation of writers is doomed to failure, yet still he continues his attack on the times. He says that besides lacking subjects and an audience the new novelists also lack magazines willing to publish their work and critics interested in what they are trying to do. The new critics are subtle and spirited, but most of them deal only with widely admired authors. For a younger critic to analyze books that have not yet been "officially recognized, approved, classified, documented, explicated, and foot-noted by other critics would be tantamount to professional heresy and suicide. . . . Yet the state of criticism, like the failure of values and the absence of a community of art, is only a symptom of the general debility of the times as a whole. Since the end of the war there has been, in all parts of the world, a gradual dwindling of creative vitality and impulse."

At this point Aldridge's thesis seems a little sweeping for a book about a dozen contemporary novelists. Before accepting it we should ask whether this world of ours is so lacking in values as he would like to have us believe. I plan to discuss the question briefly, but first I should say that Aldridge's thesis is perhaps not the important feature of his book. For me the important feature is that he discusses new authors with the same care that others are devoting to Proust and Gide, or Fitzgerald and Faulkner. He pronounces doom on the novelists of the 1950s, but not until he has carefully scrutinized their work, and he gives them more honor by this close attention than he takes away from them by dismissing the work in theory.

One example is his treatment of *Other Voices, Other Rooms*, Truman Capote's novel about a pre-adolescent boy who sets out to find his father and ends in the nightmare world of homosexuality. Aldridge tells us that the characters and devices in the novel "do not produce a world of exterior significance. They belong eternally to the special illusion that Capote has created; outside it they do nothing and are nothing." It is a hostile decision, but Aldridge doesn't reach it until he has written a passage of twenty pages explaining the characters and devices more clearly than any other critic has even tried to do. The result of the explanation was to give one reader, at least, a new and more favorable impression of Capote's talent.

Aldridge also writes well about Norman Mailer and John Horne Burns; he sees their faults and sees their achievements. In Irwin Shaw's panoramic war novel, *The Young Lions*, he sees only faults, and his passage on the book is a long denunciation—an effective one, too, for he knows where Shaw is weakest and slickest. I don't think he is fair to Alfred Hayes's two novels about wartime Italy; he makes too much of the obvious debt to Hemingway and doesn't seem to realize that Hayes's feeling for people is his own. It is not at all certain that either Hayes or Shaw belong in the book, considering that its real subject is the new wartime generation of novelists born after 1915. These two are somewhat older men who didn't write their first novels till the end of the war, but won their early reputations in other fields during the depression years: Shaw wrote stories for the *New Yorker* and a pacifist play, while Hayes wrote proletarian poems. Both men grew up in a political age, and there is always a sense of politics in the background of their writing. Shaw knows the beliefs—or values—that are fashionable to hold; perhaps he sincerely holds them. Hayes knows that political decisions at a high level can affect the lives of very simple people; in *The Girl on the Via Flaminia* he shows how the decisions lead to bedside quarrels and kitchen brawls. In most of the novels by younger men —excepting Normal Mailer—politics is a missing element.

If Aldridge had omitted Hayes and Shaw he would have had room for more novelists from the younger group. He was writing too soon to include William Styron or James Jones, but it is hard to see why he failed to discuss Carson McCullers, Saul Bellow, or Jean Stafford, who were already more important novelists than most of those with whom he dealt at length. His choice of authors makes the work of the new generation seem poorer and less varied than it is in reality, but the fault is easy to forgive when we reflect that he was doing pioneer work. He was taking risks that others critics refused to take and was expressing his opinions in a reckless and rather appealing way. He was also offering an indispensable first draft of the critical verdict that, after many revisions, will be reached in twenty or thirty years.

But what about his complaint that it is impossible to write good novels today because we are living in a society uniquely lacking in values? It seems to me that the complaint has been made for a long time and that the first authors who made it are now buried and forgotten, or revered. They didn't use the collective plural "values," which hadn't been invented at the time; they spoke of ideals, standards, faith, belief, piety, convictions, but they meant almost the same thing. The world had changed for them, as it always changes, and with it the ideals or the sense of life of each new generation. For a century or more the change has been more rapid; we might say that the acceleration began with the French Revolution, or with the Industrial Revolution, or with the publication in 1859 of *The Origin of Species*. Many young Englishmen in the 1860s had an even more desperate sense of being lost, unguided, left without standards of judgment, than American novelists have today. It seemed to them that the moral world had collapsed with the first statement of the principle that men, instead of being specially created in God's image and guided at every step by divine providence, were descended from lower animals and subject to the indifferent laws of the physical world. Yet some of the young Englishmen wrote novels, and good ones, about a society that now seems to us remarkably stable, self-assured, and rich in values.

Darwinism as interpreted by Huxley, Tyndall, and Spencer had a destructive effect on the faith or standards of young American novelists in the 1890s. Theodore Dreiser, for example, read these authors when he was in Pittsburgh working as a young reporter on the *Dispatch*. He tells us that all of them, but especially Herbert Spencer's *First Principles*, "quite blew me, intellectually, to bits." He had rebelled against his pious father, but without quite forsaking his father's world. In the second volume of his memoirs, *Newspaper Days*, he says:

Hitherto, until I had read Huxley, I had some lingering filaments of Catholicism trailing about me, faith in the existence of Christ, the soundness of his moral and sociologic deductions, the brotherhood of man. But on reading . . . *First Principles* and discovering all I deemed substantial—man's place in nature, his importance in the universe, this too, too solid earth, man's very identity save as an infinitesimal speck of energy or a "suspended equation" drawn or blown here and there by larger forces in which he moved quite unconsciously as an atom—all questioned and dissolved into other and less understandable things, I was completely thrown down in my conceptions or non-conceptions of life.

Dreiser, had he been living today, would have said that he had been deprived of all values, yet he managed to get his novels written and found new values to express. In his last novel, *The Bulwark*, which is like an unfinished scenario for what might have been his greatest work, he almost completed the circle from alienation or rebellion to reintegration. He didn't become reconciled with his father's church, but he did try to explain, even to celebrate, the father's religious sense of life.

It would seem that every generation in turn starts with this feeling of lost values, as if it were a necessary step in education. I can remember coming down the steps of Widener Library one morning in the early spring of 1917. I looked out at the leafless elms in the hard sunlight, and the duckboards still in place along the walks, and found myself saying compulsively, "It was all lies, everything they told me at home, everything they taught me at school." I can remember too that I found comfort in the statement; it wasn't so much the wail of a little boy deserted in the night as a sort of incantation and a first step toward seeking the truth, wherever it might still be found. Later I decided that the statement wasn't so meaningful, even for myself, as it had seemed in the bleak sunlight of that New

England morning. I didn't really believe that everything taught me in school was a lie, or I would also have questioned what I was learning in college and wouldn't have continued to study hard in the hope of making A's and winning another scholarship that would allow me to study harder. What I really meant was that I couldn't any longer accept what I had been told about some important matters—such as sex, primarily, but also God, the hereafter, patriotism, right living, and the American ideal of success.

All over the country in that year boys like myself were making similar discoveries as they walked down library steps. Later they would be called the lost generation. It is true that they suffered from a feeling of loss or alienation or deception, but it didn't interfere with their writing novels if they had talent enough to write them. What they would reaffirm in the novels was a number of very old and simple values—in Hemingway, for example, these were courage, love, drinking, and the obligations of one's craft or métier; in Faulkner they were pride, courage again, compassion, and love of earth; in all the leading novelists of their age-group the values were intended to be fundamental, down-to-rock, and thereby fitted to survive. It was as if these writers had watched many high systems of judgment collapse around them and had afterward tried to build humbler and, so they felt, solider structures in the rubble.

Now the process of losing and finding values seems to be starting over with another postwar generation—and why shouldn't it start? The depressing feature of Aldridge's complaint, which is being echoed by many young novelists, is that this time it *is* a complaint and not even subconsciously a boast or an incantation or a program for rebuilding. The new demand for pre-existing values in the moral world seems to correspond with the new demand for security in the economic world. Just as students who plan to go into business say that they want stable employment with a big corporation and an income of ten thousand a year—not too large, but dependable—so the young novelists would like to start out with an income-bearing capital of values that would be like securities listed on a moral stock exchange. But who can discover and choose among values, who can reaffirm the best of them, if not the novelists themselves, along with the poets and dramatists and critics? Isn't that a function which writers in the past have always helped to perform? What do the new writers expect, after all? To find new thresholds, new anatomies, and at the same time retain the values they absorbed with their mothers' milk? To be great explorers of the soul, like Melville and Baudelaire, and at the same time to be respected citizens, academic dignitaries, and vestrymen of the Protestant Episcopal Church? It is true that the new novelists have a special reason for their feeling of deprivation. Just as many young Englishmen of the 1860s, and young Americans two or three decades later, lost their faith in a divine providence that watches over the human species, so these others have lost their faith in progress, whether automatic or directed by human intelligence, and along with that faith have lost the old American conviction that most people are good and that evil is merely an accident. But the loss might well be their opportunity as writers, instead of being a handicap; it might launch them into the effort to speak for the new age as other writers spoke for the past.

In simple fact there has never been a society or a new generation without values. Some of these, like food, shelter, sex, rest, are imposed on us biologically. Other values are imposed on us by the nature of human groups and—as Kenneth Burke has pointed out—by the general nature of language, which helps to determine group judgments. Of this second type are the personal values like courage and prudence in varying proportions, loyalty to the group, integrity of the person, and the ability to get along with others. The emphasis changes from age to age—for example, the prudent man is now preferred to the courageous man—but the values themselves are permanent. There is also a third type of values, impermanent by definition, that are associated with particular societies. These are values in the sociological sense—that is, ideals, customs, institutions, and social ranks or functions, toward which the people of the group have an affective or emotional regard. New values of the sort always take the place of old ones that are lost. New and old, they hold a society together; if it had no such values of its own it would cease to exist as a society.

It seems to me that the lives of ordinary Americans are rich in all three sorts of values—biological, personal or moral, and social or institutional—as well as in esthetic values that include elements of the other three. We say of a friend that he is a good guy, and that is a value judgment on the personal level. We speak of a good dinner, and that is a biological judgment, perhaps with touches of the esthetic. We speak of good luck, good manners, good stories, good reputations, and good roads. "A good car" is a more complicated value; the judgment here is partly of physical properties (the car gets us quickly and dependably from place to place), partly esthetic (it is the most beautiful object owned by many households), and partly a hint that all this power and beauty confer a higher social status on the owner. As for purely social or institutional values, we speak of good neighborhoods, good country clubs, good citizens, good government, good or favorable developments on the international scene, and usually our hearers understand exactly what we intend to say, since they share most of our notions of good and evil.

On the other hand, if we use terms like disloyal, bigoted, fascist, pinko, do-gooder, godless, intellectual, forward-looking, democracy, sound literature, renegade, Uncle Tom, or subversive, our hearers are likely to interpret them in different fashions, depending on the special language of the political or religious or racial groups to which they belong. That difference seems to me a mark of the age: not the lack of values, which exist in profusion, but the conflicting systems of value, Christian and agnostic, Catholic and Protestant, liberal and conservative, highbrow and lowbrow, labor and management, orthodox and reformed—not to mention the greater conflict of values between Russia and the United States. Another mark of the age is the desperate search for certainties. In the intellectual world this has been a time of conversions, apostasies, and reconversions. We read the life story of a man who became a free-thinker, then a Communist, then an Episcopalian, then a Quaker, embracing four different systems of value in succession, each with passionate loyalty, each with contempt or hatred for the abandoned system—we read and say of him, "In some ways he is a representative figure of the age."

All this has an application to the novels that might be written in our time. I would say that the younger writers are justified in complaining about the lack of a general audience for their work; books are now being read by a variety of special audiences. But I would also say that nobody has a right to complain about the lack of subject matter, since there are subjects everywhere in contemporary life. The conflicts among systems of value are dramas, most of which remain to be written. The search for values is itself a narrative that might be treated on an epic scale. I suspect, however, that any author who tried to write the epic or the dramas would be dismissed by some of the newer critics as a mere naturalist.

V.

NATURALISM:
NO TEACUP TRAGEDIES

1.

Several times in these chapters I have objected to the disparaging fashion in which some critics use words derived from "naturalism" and to their habit of applying the bad words to any novel with a social or general subject. One reason for objecting to the habit is that it conceals a purpose which ought to be clearly stated: the critics mean to advocate a rather narrow and specialized conception of what good novels should or shouldn't do. Any novel that does more than present a crisis in the lives of a few individuals they regard as "naturalistic," and not worth talking about. But there is another objection too: the critics are spoiling words that can be very useful when properly applied. "Naturalism" and "naturalistic" belong to a definite literary tradition, one that was originated by several French authors, but was taken over and named by Émile Zola in 1869. During the next two decades it spread over Europe, which in those easier days included Spain and Russia. It was introduced to this country in the early 1890s and still plays a fairly important part in American writing. It isn't my tradition, for I disagree with its doctrines and even more with the slipshod manner in which they are usually applied. Nevertheless, it has produced some admirable novels, not all of them by European authors, and it has contributed to our picture of the modern world.

Naturalism appeared in this country almost surreptitiously, with the private printing in 1893 of Stephen Crane's first novel, *Maggie: A Girl of the Streets*. Maggie's story was that of a tenement girl mistreated by her drunken mother, seduced by a tough, forced into prostitution, deserted and driven to suicide; like other naturalistic heroines, she was a pawn on a chessboard and the victim of forces beyond her control. In dedicating a copy of the book to a Baptist minister, Crane said, "It tries to show that environment is a tremendous thing in this world and often shapes lives regardlessly. If I could prove that theory, I would make room in heaven for all sorts of souls (notably an occasional street girl) who are not confidently expected to be there by many excellent people." He was helping to set the naturalistic pattern, both in his emphasis on environment and in his defiance of many excellent people.

Except for a brief period and indirectly, Crane was not a disciple of Zola's. He was to write a second naturalistic novel, *George's Mother*, but most of his short career was devoted to a less objective type of writing that was closer to his personal vision. Frank Norris—who was a year older than Crane, but less precocious—would be the first American novelist to become a formal convert to naturalism and, with a few infidelities, to cherish its doctrines to the end. He didn't learn them in France, where he spent two of his most impressionable years. Norris was a very young art student in Paris, not a writer, and the books he read were chiefly concerned with medieval history and romance. It was after he returned to this country and entered the University of California in 1890 that he discovered Zola. For the next four years, so his classmates reported, he was usually to be seen with one of Zola's yellow-backed novels in his hand.

What did he learn from the novels? In Zola's working notes, which Norris of course had never seen, but which one might say that he divined from the published fiction, the founder of naturalism had indicated some of his aims as a writer. He was trying to create a new type of fiction ruled by scientific laws, based on scientific observation, and written, so far as possible, by scientific methods; if successful, he would recapture for himself, and for literature, some of the prestige that had begun to surround the great scientists. "Study men as simple elements and note the reactions," he said. Notebook in hand, he studied them as if they were specimens in a biological laboratory. Many of the specimens were thieves, drunkards, or prostitutes, and Matthew Josephson's life of Zola tells how the great novelist and respectable family man—wearing a velvet-collared overcoat, a bowler hat, and pince-nez glasses—could be seen taking notes in houses of assignation. "What matters most to me," he said, "is to be purely naturalistic, purely physiological. Instead of having principles (royalism, Catholicism) I shall have laws (heredity, atavism)." And again, "Balzac says that he wishes to paint men, women, and things. I count men and women as the same, while admitting their natural differences, and *subject men and women to things*." In that last phrase, which Zola underlined, he expressed the central naturalistic doctrine, derived from the whole Darwinian movement: that men and women are part of nature, subject to natural laws, and indeed the helpless victims of natural forces.

The characteristics of naturalism in the proper sense of the word —not in the critics' loose sense—are derived from the practice of Zola and other novelists who accepted the doctrine. Naturalism is pessimistic about the fate of individuals; it holds that there is no reward on earth or in heaven for moral actions, or punishment for vice. Naturalism is rebellious, or at least defiant. With each new work it says again to respectable society, "Here is life with the veils stripped away; here are better men than you, broken and obliterated through no fault of their own; here is an end to your complacency." At the same time naturalism claims to be objective; it claims that an author can deliberately choose a subject, observe it, take notes, and present the results like a laboratory report. It approaches situations and characters from the outside; if the novelist projects himself into a character he is in danger of losing his objectivity. Naturalism is inclusive rather than selective, being an attempt to present the totality of a big subject; it is literature in breadth rather than depth. In practice it is careless about the sound or style of the words it uses, being based on the eyes (and the nose) rather than the ears. Things play an important part in it—not the novelist's impression of things, but the actual hard, angular, soiled, and smelly objects. In practice as in theory it leads to a magnification of forces, crowds, conditions, and a minification of persons.

Frank Norris, in his American adaptation of naturalism, carried this last tendency to an extreme that Zola never reached. "Men were nothings, mere animalculae, mere ephemerides that fluttered and fell and were forgotten between dawn and dusk," he said in the next-to-last chapter of *The Octopus*. "Men were naught, life was naught;

FORCE only existed—FORCE that brought men into the world, FORCE that made the wheat grow, FORCE that garnered it from the soil to give place to the succeeding crops." But Norris was also impressed by two other characteristics of naturalism. In an editorial on Zola, written at the beginning of his own literary career, he said:

Terrible things must happen to the characters of the naturalistic tale. They must be twisted from the ordinary, wrenched from the quiet, un-eventful round of everyday life and flung into the throes of a vast and terrible drama that works itself out in unleashed passions, in blood and in sudden death. The world of M. Zola is a world of big things; the enor-mous, the formidable, the terrible is what counts; no teacup tragedies here. . . . Everything is extraordinary, imaginative, grotesque even, with a vague note of terror quivering throughout like the vibration of an enormous and low-pitched diapason. . . . Naturalism is a form of romanticism, not an inner circle of realism.

Bigness and romance: these were two qualities that Norris tried to embody in all his novels. He thought he had found a perfect expression for them in 1899, when he laid the plans for his "Epic of the Wheat." It was to consist of three novels, the first dealing with California as producer of wheat, the second with Chicago as dis-tributor, and third with Europe (or India, in a later plan) as con-sumer. All three books, he said in a letter to William Dean Howells, would "keep to the idea of this huge Niagara of wheat rolling from West to East. I think a big epic trilogy *could* be made out of such a subject, that at the same time would be modern and distinctly Amer-ican. The idea is so big that it frightens me at times, but I have about made up my mind to have a try at it."

He had his try at it; he wrote the first volume bravely, *The Octo-pus,* and the second doggedly, *The Pit*; then he died before he could start the third. Although his trilogy—which would have been the second in the history of serious American writing, after Cooper's *The Littlepage Manuscripts*—was never finished, his dream of big-ness lived in the minds of many novelists who followed him. Dreiser, Upton Sinclair, David Graham Phillips, Sinclair Lewis, and many others tried to find epical, modern, distinctly American subjects— no teacup tragedies here—and most of them planned trilogies or whole interrelated series of novels that would be realistic in treat-ment but would be based on an essentially romantic emotion.

It seems to us now that the 1930s were the great age of naturalistic fiction. They were also the depression years and a time of social

bad conscience, so that most of the novels dealt with the under-
nourished third of the nation. If they ended with a hopeless strike or
a parade of the unemployed, or with the hero risking his life by
urging hungry men to unite, like Tom Joad in *The Grapes of Wrath*,
they were known as proletarian or revolutionary novels. Most of
these are remembered dimly for their political innocence and
wooden writing, but among them were two powerful works that
will continue to be read for a long time: one was of course *The
Grapes of Wrath*, and the other was James T. Farrell's *Studs Lonigan* trilogy. Erskine Caldwell was a naturalist and a good one in
his particular fashion; probably he is still good, although most of
the critics have stopped reading the books in which he keeps applying the same formula to slightly different groups of degraded characters. Not all the naturalists wrote about starving people. John
Marquand, with a more conservative cast of mind, became the most
accurate observer of almost upper-class families in the Eastern seaboard states, and John O'Hara the most accurate observer of café
society. Finally there is John Dos Passos, whose trilogy *U. S. A.* is
the most impressive and possibly the best of American works in the
naturalistic tradition. In any case, he deals with the biggest subject
of all—not an industry, like Sinclair in *The Jungle*; not a profession, like Lewis in *Arrowsmith*, or a background, like Farrell in
Studs Lonigan; but thirty years of the whole country, with many of
its industries, many professions, a diversity of backgrounds, and
hundreds of characters, all driven to failure, even the richest of
them, by forces beyond their control.

Although the naturalistic tradition is at present loosely defined
and widely condemned, it is by no means abandoned. Among the
postwar writers those who are naturalistic in the proper sense of
the word form a third group that might be set beside the combat
novelists (note that some of these, including Norman Mailer, are
naturalistic too) and the new fictionists. It is not a group in the social
sense, for its members are scattered over the country and seem to be
hardly conscious of one another's existence; yet their work retains
a family likeness, as if they had all inherited the same sharp eyes
and indifferent sense of hearing. In general they seem to be less certain of what they believe than were the naturalists of the 1930s. They
are also less ambitious in their search for material, and not one of
them has displayed anything like Dos Passos' curiosity about every-

thing that happens in American life. Retaining the objective point of view and the naturalistic interest in conditions that "often shape lives regardlessly," they prefer to write about a special community or background, usually their own. Some of their postwar subjects have been a small city with its interwoven lives (*Sironia, Texas*), a Midwestern county over the years (*Raintree County*), boys going wrong in the Chicago slums (*Knock on Any Door*), the motion-picture business (*What Makes Sammy Run*), a military school (*End as a Man*), and the younger generation on the Pacific Coast (*Corpus of Joe Bailey*).

The plot or theme of such novels, as distinguished from the subject, is usually simple. In some the protagonist—we can't often call him a hero—is warped by his environment, tempted into crime, and shot down by the police (or taken to the electric chair); the mood is always passive. In others the protagonist succeeds in business because of faults that keep him from being truly human. In still others a community is morally ruined by industrialism or commercialism. Almost all the characters in all the stories are victims of forces beyond their control, but there are some naturalistic novels—like *Corpus of Joe Bailey*—in which the protagonist resists the forces and achieves a sort of emotional maturity. Since the novelist is interested in the social background that leads to success, and more often to failure, and since he deals at length with many other characters who cross the path of the hero-victim-villain, he ends by writing a very long book. If a manuscript comes to a publisher's office in a single neat folder, it is likely to be new-fictional. If it arrives in a suitcase or a wooden packing box, it is either historical or naturalistic.

In their effort to achieve bigness and totality, the new naturalists, like their predecessors, are likely to be careless about the structure and texture of their novels. Some of the episodes will occupy a disproportionately large space in the disproportionately long manuscript—unless an editorial reader blue-pencils them—while others will be foreshortened. Frank Norris—not Crane, who cared about words—was the grandfather of these novelists, and he often expressed his contempt for careful writing. "What pleased me most in your review of *McTeague*," he said in a letter to Isaac Marcosson, "was 'disdaining all pretensions to style.' It is precisely what I try most to avoid. I detest 'fine writing,' 'rhetoric,' 'elegant English'— tommyrot. Who cares for fine style! Tell your yarn and let your style go to the devil. We don't want literature, we want life." Yet Nor-

ris's novels are full of fine writing in the bad sense and usually
end with a deep-purple passage. "Annixter dies," he says on the
last page of *The Octopus*, "but in a far distant corner of the world
a thousand lives are saved. The larger view always and through all
shams, all wickednesses, discovers the Truth that will, in the end,
prevail, and all things, surely, inevitably, resistlessly work together
for good." That is not only illogical, as a deduction from the story
he has told; it is shameless and self-hypnotizing in its use of language.

With a few exceptions the present-day naturalists have followed
Norris, both in his contempt for elegant English and in his failure
to see that he often wrote with bogus elegance. That is one reason
why—to make a confession of faith—I couldn't ever accept their
tradition as my own. I have always felt by instinct that language was
the central problem of any writer, in any creative medium. If he
lacks the sense of words he may be an admirable scholar, a moral
philosopher, a student of human behavior, or a contriver of big
dramatic scenes, but he isn't properly a writer. Yeats said that style
in literature is what corresponds to the moral element in men of
action. I think he meant that style is the result of an infinite number of choices, all determined by standards of what is linguistically
right and wrong. "Books live almost entirely because of their style,"
he said—and he was echoing a long line of creative artists who felt
that until the right words have been found for an action it does not
exist in words, in literature.

There are other objections to naturalism, and one of them is based
on the human implications of the doctrine. When the naturalists
say that men are subject to natural laws they usually mean that
human destinies are determined by the principles of mechanics, or
chemistry, or genetics, or physiology, or a rather mechanical type
of economics. Each novelist seems to have his favorite science: for
Zola it was the laws, or imagined laws, of heredity that bound together his enormous series of novels. For Jack London the explanation of human behavior lay in biology—"I mean," says his autobiographical hero, Martin Eden, "the real interpretative biology,
from the ground up, from the laboratory and the test tube and the
vitalized inorganic right on up to the widest esthetic and social gen-
eralizations." No activity was strictly human for London, not even
administering a charity or producing a work of art; they were all
applications of biology. For Dreiser the key science was chemistry,

and he explained the failure of his brother Paul by the "lack of a little iron or sodium or carbon dioxide in his chemical compost." For Dos Passos the laws were economic and governed the concentration of "power superpower." Every year, so he believed, a smaller number of always larger corporations was exercising a closer control over the lives of more and more Americans. His central purpose in *U. S. A.* was to explain how people were ruined by "the big money."

All these novelists and many others were trying to explain the personal by the impersonal and the complicated in terms of the simple: society in terms of selfishness, man in terms of his animal inheritance, and the organic in terms of the inorganic. Something was always omitted at each stage in this process of reduction. To say, as many naturalistic writers have done, that man is a beast of prey, or "a mechanism, undevised and uncreated," or a collection of chemical compounds, or a simple economic unit, is a faulty way of describing man, since it omits his special characteristics. It is a metaphor, not a scientific statement, and a metaphor that subtracts from literature the whole notion of responsible purposes, the whole possibility of tragic action.

Finally I would object that naturalism involves a false conception of the writer himself. It holds that a novelist or a dramatist should be a dispassionate observer, like a scientist in his laboratory; that he should choose an important subject, methodically gather material, arrange it into a dramatic pattern, and then submit his report. But good novels are seldom written in that fashion; they are written because the novelist has been chosen by his subject and because the material, forced upon him by everything in his past, urgently demands to be expressed. The fact is that most naturalistic writers have violated, in practice, their own ideal of objectivity. There is an autobiographical element in the best of the naturalistic novels, from *Sister Carrie* to *U. S. A.* and beyond; it helps to explain their emotional power. The element is present even in novels that seem far from the authors' lives, as we learn from reading their memoirs. Thus Upton Sinclair said of his best book, *The Jungle*:

I wrote with tears and anguish, pouring into the pages all that pain which life had meant to me. Externally, the story had to do with a family of stockyard workers, but internally it was the story of my own family. Did I wish to know how the poor suffered in Chicago? I had only to recall the previous winter in a cabin, when we had only cotton

blankets, and had put rags on top of us, shivering in our separate beds.
. . . Our little boy was down with pneumonia that winter, and nearly
died, and the grief of that went into the book.

After the success of his novel about the meat-packing industry
in Chicago, Sinclair wrote novels about other cities (Denver, Boston) and other industries (oil, coal, whisky, automobiles). He
demonstrated his capacity for research, for telling stories, and for
painting broad pictures, but the subjects were outside his personal
experience and he didn't write about them with the warmth of feeling that distinguished *The Jungle*. Other naturalistic novelists, almost all of them, have had the same failures in sympathy. They are
at their best not when they are scientific or objective, in accordance
with their own doctrines, but when they are least naturalistic, most
subjective and lyrical.

2.

Lately a change has been evident in the leading ideas of many
naturalistic writers. Their novels still follow the pattern established
by Crane, Norris, and Dreiser—that is, their heroes are still victims,
betrayed by circumstances into criminal follies that lead to disasters
—but now the follies are likely to be excused in a new fashion. They
used to be the result of either the heroes' bad heredity (*McTeague*)
or more often of their bad environment (*An American Tragedy,
Native Son*). In recent years heredity has played a rather small part
in naturalistic novels and social environment isn't so often presented
as the only reason why the heroes or heroines were victimized. Instead of being ruined by poverty or wealth or racial prejudice, they
are in many cases deformed by some traumatic experience in childhood. The heroine is seeking for a lost father image (see William
Styron's brilliant first novel, *Lie Down in Darkness*), or else she was
raped by an older man (as in John O'Hara's *Butterfield 8*), with
the result that she became a frigid nymphomaniac. The hero was
rejected by his mother—sometimes we are told that she weaned
him too soon—or else he hates his father as a sexual rival and an
image of authority (see *Prince Bart*, by Jay Richard Kennedy). All
the heroes are Oedipus; the heroines are either Electra or Messalina.

This Freudian myth in its various forms is of course not confined
to naturalistic novels. It appears still oftener in what I have called the

new fiction—as note all the stories about sensitive young men with possessive mothers—and even furnishes plots for musical comedies and motion pictures (with subplots for soap operas). Besides showing that the public is familiar with notions derived or distorted from Freudian psychology, this wide use of the myth is also connected with a general literary movement that seems to be dominant everywhere in Western literature: a movement from sociology to psychology, from political to personal problems, in a word, from the public to the private.

East of the Elbe—and, with variations, among the minority of Communist writers in France and Italy—there is a movement in the opposite direction, that is, from novels about individual lives to novels about masses of men, written with a public purpose. In France and Italy the purpose is to prove that the workers are mistreated and hence to prepare them for a Communist seizure of power; the novels are revolutionary. In Russia they are patriotic, conformist, and their purpose is to advance various programs of the Soviet state. Every Communist who appears in the novels is supposed to be heroic; the non-Communists can become heroic by accepting Communist leadership; the anti-Communists are always villains. All the characters represent political tendencies or attitudes toward the state, and so little is said about their private lives that they almost cease to be persons.

There are substantial rewards and punishments for Russian writers. Those who follow instructions earn a great deal of money—often more than they can spend—and occupy a more privileged social position than their colleagues in the West. Those who disobey the watchful critics aren't published at all, no matter how popular their past works may have been. Fantastic as the situation seems to us, it bears a resemblance to some American practices. Radio and television writers in this country are under almost as close surveillance by patriotic pressure groups. Some of the mass-circulation magazines—though by no means all of them—present subjects for treatment by fiction writers they can trust. "Why don't you do a two-fisted serial about oil prospecting in the Gulf of Mexico?" the editor says persuasively. "It's very much in the news." During World War II the imposed subject was often the result of a government directive: for example, the Air Force asked for help from the mass-circulation magazines when it had difficulty persuading men to be tail gunners on bombing planes, and the magazines obliged by ordering stories with tail gunners as heroes. Even in peacetime some of our weeklies outdo the Russians by presenting a novelist with both a subject and a ready-made plot, asking him only to provide descriptions and dialogue.

Here the parallel ends. If the American novelist refuses the subject or the plot, if he prefers to deal with more personal themes, he has other avenues of publication. Many writers earn comfortable incomes without once appearing in the mass-circulation magazines, and they are admired for preserving a sort of artistic chastity. For a real parallel with Russia we should have to imagine that the *Saturday Evening Post* and *Collier's*, with a very few others, were the only magazines to print fiction, that they were interlocked with the only publishing houses, that they were staffed by government and party functionaries, and that novelists who wouldn't follow their directives not only couldn't be published but would become politically suspect. We might also have to imagine that a novel approved and published in 1945 would have to be withdrawn from circulation in 1948, although it was still extremely popular, because the directives had changed. Exactly that happened in the case of Fadeyev's *The Young Guard*, whose author had to make a public confession of error and then had to revise his picture of the war before the novel could be reissued by the State Publishing House.

It would be a mistake, however, to judge Soviet literature in theory by its practice of the last few years. The theory, known as "socialist realism," has always taken for granted that literature exerts a direct effect on social life, and therefore has always been willing to admit that a wise society, a workers' society, would control its novelists for their own good. On the other hand, the theory did not contemplate that the control would be so rigid, so comprehensive, and so anti-esthetic as it has been in Russia since 1948. There were special reasons for that period of repression, and the cold war was only one of them. There was the Russian habit, which is also an American habit, of carrying everything to extremes; there was Stalin's attitude toward art—that of a tired businessman; and there was the single-minded Communist efficiency of Andrei A. Zhdanov, who had taken charge of cultural affairs. In 1953, after both men were dead, signs appeared that artists in all fields, including fiction, might be granted a somewhat greater degree of freedom.

Even the bureaucrats themselves were beginning to admit that "a creative problem cannot be solved by bureaucratic means," as Aram Khachaturian, one of the composers scolded by Zhdanov, was finally allowed to say in the magazine *Soviet Music*.[1]

As a theory, socialist realism should be judged by its achievements in years like those from 1932 to 1936 and from 1943 to 1947, when novels were being written and published with somewhat less interference from the Soviet bureaucrats. It might also be judged by novels of the school that were produced in France, England, and America during the 1930s and are now being produced by Communist writers in France and Italy. On this basis, that of its best periods and productions, socialist realism proves to be a theory of fiction which, like naturalism, has produced many valuable and impressive works. As a matter of fact it developed out of naturalism, at least on the technical side, and has retained many characteristics of the earlier school. Some of these are the close study of social environments, the interest in the behavior of crowds, the approach to characters from the outside—as if they were specimens for dissection—and, most of all, the emphasis on subject matter at the expense of form. In Russia "formalism" and "subjectivism" are serious charges against a writer, almost the equivalent of political crimes. The Russian doctrine resembles naturalism in holding that novelist can deliberately choose a subject for treatment, almost without respect to his past experience, but it goes a step farther by holding that the subject can also be chosen for the novelist by the workers' party or by the state.

In 1948 Russian writers were collectively scolded because they hadn't produced a sufficient number of articles about the new irrigation projects. In 1953 some of those projects were deferred, and the Central Committee of the Communist Party adopted a new program calling for a greatly increased production of foodstuffs and consumer goods. In December of that same year the writers were scolded again, this time because the new program, after three months, still hadn't been reflected in more and better novels about the collective farms. Although writers were being given a little more freedom, consumer goods and foodstuffs were the pressing

1. By the summer of 1954, Khachaturian had been reproved for his bourgeois deviation; the bureaucratic control of literature was being tightened again.

need and hence an imposed subject for novels. Said the *Literary Gazette*, in a leading article translated for the *New York Times*:

No substantial improvement in the activities of the secretariat of the Union of Soviet Writers is evident, even since the September plenary session of the Central Committee. . . . A great and difficult task lies before our writers: to produce books that help the people in their great creative activities. To depict accurately and profoundly the life of the people in all its aspects and in every sphere of activity, to express the all-pervasive grandeur of the Soviet man and to express the fundamental and typical processes of our epoch—such is the task of Soviet literature. But contemporary Soviet life will not be truly portrayed unless it is shown that the struggle for the prosperity of collective and state farms has become a matter of supreme importance for the people in general.

The *Literary Gazette* was explaining that writers' aims, even in a period of comparative freedom, must still be those of the state, and that a socially imposed subject must be executed without delay.

Earlier in this chapter I tried to explain the faults of naturalism. Socialist realism has almost all of them, and it also has a serious fault of its own, growing out of its political conformity: novelists are expected to "depict accurately and profoundly the life of the the people in all its aspects," but their picture must agree with that of the Central Committee, which is the final judge of literary truth. Old-fashioned naturalists look for and sometimes discover truths of their own. With this exception, however, socialist realism has most of the virtues of naturalism. It presents us with big, dramatic subjects, it treats them in a bold fashion, and it gives the reader a feeling that the novelist isn't running away from life but is embracing it in all its ugliness and infinite fertility. The doctrine also has one virtue in which naturalism is conspicuously lacking: it offers a system of moral values and allows its characters to choose between good and evil. Sometimes they choose to do good at the cost of their lives, and then the socialist realist is able to write in something that approaches the tragic spirit. When Malraux was a socialist realist he wrote *Man's Fate*, which is a tragic novel. *The Silent Don*, by Mikhail Sholokhov, is a collective tragedy, that of the Cossack people, and it is the novel of our time that comes closest to being another *War and Peace*. I might add that both Malraux and Sholokhov were writing from experience, or from an imaginative projection of experience, and that neither of them produced his book to order.

It has sometimes been suggested that the ideal might lie some-where between the present Western and the present Russian prac-tice. One could start with either, I have heard it said, and arrive at better novels by a mixture of qualities selected from West and East. Thus, one could start with the Soviet novel, subtract the bu-reaucratic control, add a greater psychological depth and more attention to form, and the result would be possible masterpieces. Again, one could start with the American novel, give it broader subjects, more interest in contemporary problems, more social re-sponsibility—without surrendering any of its virtues—and the re-sult would be almost the same. The one weakness of this most at-tractive program is that novels aren't compounded by a judicious mixture of ingredients. Sift together one cup of psychological depth with two cups of subject matter, knead into form, bake in a medium oven, and the result is nothing.

The Western ideal of novels based on personal experience is essentially right and the present Russian ideal of socially useful novels produced to order is wrong. The Western ideal is right be-cause novels should be true at all levels and because such truth can't be achieved without a long accumulation of feelings and observa-tions. The Russian ideal is wrong because social aims and political programs—especially new ones—are likely to be accepted only on the top level of the mind. It is always conceivable that some nov-elists might write very well about the new irrigation projects or about the new program for collective farms, but that would be chiefly by accidents of personality. That is, the novelists might be obsessed, as many persons are, by the image of running water; or they might have risen from the peasantry and might be excited by the vision of new lives for families like their own. But where one novelist would write well about the projects and programs, a dozen others would be unable to make the personal connection, and their books would be dutiful, shallow, and nonexistent as literature.

The newer American criticism has provided us with methods for understanding the weakness of novels written to order (including those whose authors agreed with the order and thought they were performing their simple duty). If we examine the language and structure of such books; if we analyze their rhythms, their images, their use of symbols, their choice of significant details, we find that all of these are out of keeping with the novelists' conscious purposes. The optimism is revealed to be forced, the convictions to be hollow, the characters to be not of a piece. Subconsciously the novelists have rebelled against the subject imposed on them and have refused to assimilate the information gathered in a pile of notebooks; it is merely information, not experience. "Man," said Marcel Proust, "is the creature who cannot get outside himself, who knows others only in himself, and when he says the contrary he lies." That is an extreme statement of the limitation under which we operate as writers and human beings, but the limitation can be transcended, as Proust showed in *Remembrance of Things Past*. Man does know others, if only in and through himself, and each life is the mirror of many others. By looking intently at our own experience, each of us can find social institutions and values, the diminished reflection of the world in which we live, so that even the purest type of personal or subjective novel has implications for its age and country. When Proust started to explain what a dinner party meant to himself, he ended by explaining a considerable area of French society.

The weakness of many American novelists today is that the books they write are based on a narrow segment of their experience and that the experience itself has been too narrow. Life on a college faculty or in a narrow circle of sophisticated people doesn't often give the novelist a sense of living in history, nor does it often lead to any broad knowledge of men and manners. I should hesitate to advise a change of life for anyone who has already made a place for himself, though I do think that apprentice novelists should pause and reflect before they decide to combine writing with teaching. For somewhat older novelists there is the possibility of making a more intensive use of what they are. "Look in your hearts and write," I heard one of them say to his students with an apologetic smile. If the novelists looked deeply enough into their own hearts and minds, they would find a broader image of American life than most of them have been presenting. I think of one example, that of William Faulkner, who lived in a Mississippi town and wrote essentially for himself, sometimes without thinking, so he said, that strangers might read what he wrote; yet when strangers did read it they found that his books contained a picture of the Deep South and an interpretation of Southern history—even a system of values and a myth of the sort that critics had been admiring in Hawthorne and Melville.

3.

Two men are spending the night in a police station on Division Street, in the Polish quarter of Chicago. They aren't sure why they have been arrested, but they work for Zero Schwiefka, who runs a gambling house, and they guess that he tried to get out of paying his weekly tribute to Police Sergeant Kvorka. One of the men is Francis Macjinek, alias Frankie Machine, who is a wizard with cards but can't do anything with people, including himself. Frankie has two great sorrows: that his wife Sophie is a psychotic invalid and that he can't stop taking morphine—"can't get the monkey off my back." His one devoted henchman is the other prisoner, Sparrow Saltskin, whose trade is steering clients into the gambling house, when he isn't stealing dogs or committing other forms of petty larceny. Sparrow is "a little offbalanced," as he likes to say, "but oney on one side. So don't try offsteerin' me, you might be tryin' my good-balanced side."

In the morning a roach falls into the slop bucket in their cell. It reminds Frankie of his own fate and he starts to rescue it, but then he changes his mind. "You ain't gettin' out till I get out," he says. Zero Schwiefka bails out his two employees. Climbing the stairs to freedom, Frankie turns back to take the roach out of the bucket, but finds that it has drowned. The roach is the familiar animal symbol that is introduced at the beginning of so many naturalistic novels; one remembers the land turtle in *The Grapes of Wrath*, crawling obstinately to no destination, just as the Joad family would crawl westward on the highway; and one remembers the cornered rat that Bigger Thomas killed in the first chapter of *Native Son*, as Bigger himself would be killed at the end of the story. This time, however, the symbol is a mixture of the grotesque and the absurd, with a hint that the author feels a wry affection for his characters and even for the roach.

I have been retelling the first episode of Nelson Algren's novel, *The Man with the Golden Arm*. The rest of the story will follow the naturalistic pattern, but with a mixture of new qualities foreshadowed by the symbol. Frankie is another hero as victim; he was an orphan and never had a chance; he had been expelled from parochial school when the coppers raided a crap game and took him off to jail; he had never been taught a trade except dealing cards; Sophie had forced him to marry her by pretending to be pregnant; in the Army he had been severely wounded and had been given morphine to deaden the pain, until he learned to steal the drug when the doctors stopped prescribing it. Back in Chicago he had smashed a second-hand car when Sophie and he were drunk, and Sophie, in her subconscious desire to retain his affection, had convinced herself that she was hopelessly crippled. Now the pattern of victimization will be traced to the end. Frankie will be badgered into killing a dope peddler; he will be hunted by the police, while Sophie is taken to the county asylum; he will be hidden for a time by a strip teaser who loves him (she is another victim); then at last he will be cornered in a cheap hotel and driven to commit suicide; all his life will be written in the passive mood. Most of the minor characters are also driven and deformed by conditions beyond their power to change, as in every naturalistic novel since Zola, but there is something different in the author's approach to the story. Instead of repeating that vast forces are grinding these people down, he takes the forces for granted. What he emphasizes is the other side of the picture, the rebellions and lies and laughter by means of which they retain, even the most repulsive of them, some remnants of human pride.

The most repulsive of all the characters is Piggy-O, the blind dope peddler who hates more fortunate people and hasn't bathed since he lost his sight, because he enjoys the idea that he is inflicting his smell on mankind. Like the others, he drinks in the Tug & Maul bar, but Anton the Owner makes him stand at the end of the bar, next to the men's toilet, so that the smell of disinfectant will deaden the smell of Piggy. Anton asks him why he hasn't pride enough to bathe, and Piggy-O answers, "I got *my* kind of pride, 'n you got yours—I'm proud of being how *I* am too." That pride in being themselves makes the characters something more than the specimens they would be in purely naturalistic novels. Instead of being a clinical study in degradation, the book comes close to being a poem about degradation, written in sometimes lyrical prose. Instead of leaving us with a feeling of defeat, it celebrates the unconquered personality and humor in the lowest of men: hustlers, junkies, stoolies, dips, stewbums, "the Republic's crummiest lushes . . . even the most maimed wreck of them all," the author says, "held, like a pennant in that drifting light, some frayed remnant of laughter from unfrayed years."

The Invisible Man, by Ralph Ellison, is another novel that starts
with social conditions and ends as a defense of the separate personality. Its unnamed hero, who tells his own story, has been expelled from a Southern Negro college for no fault of his own. Still
eager to succeed, he finds work in a white-paint factory on Long
Island and is injured through the malice of another Negro. In the
factory hospital he is given electric-shock treatments because the
doctors want a subject for experiment. The scene shifts to Harlem,
where he is recruited by the Communists and, on revealing a talent
for public speaking, is made their district leader. Soon the Communists abandon and betray him; they have changed their policy
and decided to foment a race riot by supporting a group of Negro
fanatics. In the midst of the riot he is pursued by the fanatics and
narrowly escapes being lynched. Once again the hero has been a
victim whose story can be told in the passive mood, but *The Invisible Man* is far from being a naturalistic novel. The technique is
closer to that of the expressionists: every scene is exaggerated, even
caricatured, in order to convey what the novelist thinks is the
essential truth about it. Almost every act has a symbolic value, and
many of the scenes are too patly symbolic—like the picture of black
men working in a sub-basement to make a black liquid that, when
carried upstairs into the sunlight, will turn paint dazzlingly white.

At the end of the novel even the plot ceases to be naturalistic and
becomes a sort of parable. The hero falls through a manhole into a
coal cellar and thus escapes from the black mob that is trying to
lynch him. After finding an unused basement room, he lives there
alone and meditates on his past life. He decides that everybody has
regarded him simply as a material, a natural resource to be used.
Nobody has ever seen him as a person; he has been the invisible
man. For all the resentment he feels against the white race, he
realizes that his dilemma is not merely that of a Negro; it is the
dilemma of all men in a mechanized civilization. "Who knows," he
says to the presumably white reader at the end of the novel, "but
that, on the lower frequencies, I speak for you?"

Still another novel—*The Adventures of Augie March*, by Saul
Bellow—leads by a more roundabout path to a somewhat similar
conclusion. This time the background is Chicago in the depression
years. The hero is a Jewish boy who, at the beginning of the story,
is living with his meek, half-blind mother and his two brothers. The
youngest, Georgie, is feeble-minded, and the father is a shiftless

failure who has deserted the family. At present the Marches are miserably poor, but this isn't the sort of novel that will pursue them to the point where their lives are crushed out by conditions and forces. Simon, the oldest brother, has an inner force that is capable of surmounting conditions. He is determined to get rich, he makes a brilliant marriage, and at the end of the book he is an overbearing, pot-bellied, unhappy man of affairs. Augie March is less certain of what he wants to do. He is bright, engaging, uncommitted, so that dozens of persons want to pick a career for him, enlist him in their schemes, adopt him as a son, or take him for a lover—and Augie always consents in the beginning, but there is something stubborn in him that makes him follow his own path even though he isn't certain where it goes. Always he remains uncommitted; always he breaks away and is ready to start a new adventure.

Some of the adventures are criminal: Augie is the friend of gangsters, he helps to rob a leather-goods store, and later, while attending lectures at the university, he supports himself by stealing books. Other adventures are grotesque, as when he becomes chauffeur and delivery boy for a boarding kennel that calls itself a dogs' club, or when he is employed as secretary and ghost writer by a demented millionaire. In one chapter he is a union organizer pursued by goons; in the next he is driving to Mexico with a rich woman bent on hunting iguanas with an eagle. The adventures, interesting as they are in themselves, are chiefly occasions for introducing new characters. Each of these has a separate life, and many have something more than that, a sort of demonic power. Among others there is Anna Coblin, who appears at the beginning of the book. "As she had great size and terrific energy of constitution," Augie says of her, "she produced all kinds of excesses. Even physical ones: moles, blebs, hairs, bumps on her forehead, huge concentrations on her neck; she had spiraling reddish hair springing with no negligible beauty and definiteness from her scalp." Most of Bellow's Chicago characters are like that: excessive, but with definite features of no negligible beauty.

Augie, who tells their stories, has a feeling for the integrity of each separate person; he is ready to love and admire them all, so long as each embodies a different pattern or principle of life. His own development from one episode to another is simply toward a greater awareness of his own nature. "I have always tried to become what I am," he tells a wise old rascal named Mintouchian, whom he also loves and admires. At the end of the book Augie is living in Paris and acting as Mintouchian's agent in black-market deals. He adores his wife, but she is getting ready to deceive him with a French aristocrat, and he has had to relinquish his dream of starting a foster home in which to educate many children. But he is happy enough simply observing people in their endless variety. "Why," he says at last, "I am a sort of Columbus of those near-at-hand and believe you can come to them in this immediate *terra incognita* that spreads out in every gaze."

All three of these novels have "big" subjects of the types that are usually treated in naturalistic fiction. All three are concerned with social forces, but they don't leave us with the impression that the forces were everything or that the characters were "nothings, mere animalculae," as Norris called them at the end of *The Octopus*. A few other novelists have been writing in much the same spirit; I might mention Herbert Gold (*Birth of a Hero* and *The Prospect before Us*) and Harvey Swados (*Out Went the Candle*). I suspect that these novels and others belong to a new category of postwar fiction, smaller but no less important for the future than the categories described in earlier chapters. Is there a name for this new tendency or group or school? Perhaps the name is suggested in Swados' first novel, which I read in manuscript. At one point the hero, on a visit to Pompeii, is accosted by a little boy selling filthy souvenirs. He buys them all and throws them away. "There are times," he explains, "when you have to do things you know are useless. . . . It isn't just conscience-salving. It's a way of proving to yourself that you're still a person. And that's something you have to prove over and over."

Since all the novelists end by affirming the value of separate persons in conflict with social forces, I have thought of calling them personalists. The name, of course, has been used in other connections, but it has the present advantage of applying to the different styles in which the novels are written as well as to the doctrine they all imply. Each of the novelists seems to believe that the author himself should be a personality instead of a recording instrument, and therefore he keeps trying to find a personal approach and a personal manner of writing. The effort is sometimes carried too far and in fact all the novels have faults that are easy to discern: Algren, for example, keeps falling into a burlesque of himself, Ellison sacrifices his sense of reality to his passion for symbols, and Bellow, though he writes with more authority than the others, still has trouble holding his long book together and making it more than a series of adventures. These faults, however, are the price each of them pays for taking risks that other novelists have been a little too willing to avoid.

Yet other postwar novelists have written some admirable books, whatever the category in which we place them—new fiction, combat novels, or old-fashioned naturalism. There is a weakness in the topographical or taxonomic method I have been following in these chapters—I mean the method that consists in surveying American writing as if from a distance and naming its recent types and tendencies. The method reveals the sorts of qualities, usually faults or foibles, that are common to a group, but not the more important qualities that make a novel survive as a separate work of art. Take for example *The Member of the Wedding*, by Carson McCullers. From the taxonomic standpoint it belongs to the genus New Fiction, species Southern, variety Coming to Knowledge of Pre-adolescent Girl (or *rite de passage*), and thus can be filed away with half a dozen books by other writers. What the survey does not reveal is that it is written with an intensity of feeling and a rightness of language that the others fail to achieve; it has the power over the reader of a correctly spoken incantation.

Or take a not widely read novel by Harriette Arnow, *Hunter's Horn*. This time the genus is Naturalism (with symbolic overtones), the species Hillbilly, the variety Obsessive Pursuit of a Wild Animal. Once again the survey does not reveal the special quality of the novel, which is partly the poetry of earth, partly the sense of a community, and partly a sort of in-feeling for the characters, especially the women, that hadn't appeared in any other novel about the Kentucky hill people since Elizabeth Madox Roberts's *The Time of Man*.

The postwar period has not produced any novels that the future is likely to call great—only the future is entitled to speak of greatness—but it has produced many works, famous or neglected, that are unique in their species and varieties and deserve to be read for many years. Perhaps the central fault of the period is that novelists as a class have been cautious in their choice of subjects and methods and timid about expressing their convictions. As justification for timidity they can plead the climate of the age, which has not been friendly to experiments in living or thinking. Yet the age has effected some fundamental changes in the American character, and these have not been mirrored in the novels, most of which are traditional in their form, as in their sense of life. Many of the novelists are serious, skillful, and perceptive, but one feels that most of them are without a definite direction—not stumbling, or not enough, but walking briskly, heads erect, eyes forward, within imaginary fences. A very few, including those I called personalists, have been more reckless than the rest, and perhaps they are finding directions that others can follow. The immediate future of American writing depends largely on the writers themselves. At the same time it depends on what the naturalists would describe as conditions and forces—that is, on the state of the world and whether it remains at peace, on the continuing vigor and freedom of American culture, and on the daily lives of men and women who write for the public. Since their books have to be printed before they are read, the future of literature also depends on the health of the publishing industry.

VI.

CHEAP BOOKS FOR THE MILLIONS

1.

In January 1954 I was working at the Newberry Library in Chicago and living in a small apartment maintained by the library on North State Street. The apartment lies west of the jagged, gradually changing, and sometimes indefinite line that separates the Gold Coast from the rest of the Near North Side. East of the line are luxury hotels and restaurants, big apartment buildings, old houses—some of them occupied by their owners—and an assortment of big and little shops for the carriage trade: big ones on Michigan Avenue, smaller ones on the side streets—art galleries, interior decorators, dress shops, florists, prescription pharmacies, and haberdashers with silk dressing gowns in the windows. West of the line are smaller apartment buildings, shabbier houses, lunch counters, chili parlors, saloons, Clark Street with its twenty miles of honkytonks, a Negro quarter near Division Street, and beyond it the Polish quarter that is the scene of Nelson Algren's novels. There is also Bughouse Square, devoted on summer evenings to free speech—hence its nickname—but peopled on January mornings by hundreds of pigeons and a few disreputable squirrels.

At the point nearest the Newberry Library, which faces Bughouse Square, the dividing line now lies a few doors east of Rush Street. The northwest corner of Rush and Oak is occupied by a Walgreen's drugstore, devoted to serving people chiefly from west of the line —and it serves them well, not only with drugs, candy, ice cream, tobacco, and cosmetics, but also with stationery, household appliances, rubber goods, bottled goods, and reading matter. One could live for weeks without patronizing any other shop—eating at the soda fountain, smoking the cigars, drinking the liquor, and curing one's hangovers at the drug counter. For reading matter, besides an assortment of magazines, there are two wooden display cases full of pocket books with brightly varnished paper covers.

There were four such cases on my first visit to Walgreen's, and they contained the latest volumes issued by two or three publishers. On my third visit two of the cases had disappeared to make way for an expansion of the bottled-goods department. All the remaining paperbacks had been issued by Pocket Books, Inc., the first and still the largest of a dozen publishers in the field, although I should judge that the choice was accidental. "Take out that case," the manager must have said, pointing to one that stood in a strategic position. The case went out, and with it all the Bantam Books. "Take that one too," he must have added, pointing to the case beside it, which was devoted to Signet or Dell or Avon books. The average drugstore manager regards one case of paperbacks as the equivalent of any other. Fortunately for the customers of that particular store, Pocket Books, Inc., offers a wide choice of titles. The contents of the two remaining cases, changed every month and now including an admirable series of art books at fifty cents apiece, would furnish intellectual sandwiches, sundaes, and cosmetics for a lifetime.[1]

In my rambles west of the dividing line I found many drugstores and newsstands that carried an assortment—it couldn't often be called a selection—of paperbacks. A small rack of them hung outside one of the green wooden newspaper boxes that stand on Chicago street corners. The books were covered with soot and a few flakes of gritty snow and looked as if nobody had disturbed them for a long time. The largest and most interesting assortment was in a combined drug and department store at the corner of Clark and Division. It was composed of several hundred books issued by

1. That is, if the manager let them stand there. On a later visit I found that one case of Pocket Books, capitalized, had also been removed and that a case of Bantam Books had come back again. This too contained some excellent works, if one was looking for something, or anything, to read on an idle evening.

many publishers, including Westerns, detective stories, Mickey Spillanes, historical romances, sex thrillers, a history of Western art, a poetry anthology, American classics, British moderns, and translations from the French of Jean-Paul Sartre and Jules Romains. The novel by Romains was called *The Lord God of the Flesh* and its cover showed a rather attractive young woman starting up from bed, where she had been sleeping without a nightgown. At first I couldn't place the book, then I remembered it as a half-fictional, half-philosophical study in extra-sensory perception (or sexual intercourse by telepathy) that I had yawned my way through in French more than twenty years before. The book by Sartre was a collection of short stories called *Intimacy*, with another almost naked young woman on the cover, who seemed to be saying, "Get intimate!" Although the collection includes his most famous story, "The Wall"—which has nothing to do with sex—its sale in the American trade edition must have been less than three thousand copies. Reissued as a paperback, it must have had a first printing of two hundred thousand or more.

An old man in a shabby overcoat looked at the covers of the books, opened two or three of them, but shambled off without making a purchase. A younger man came over from the cigar counter, inspected the Westerns, and chose one with two blazing guns on the cover. A broad-beamed housewife, her head wrapped in a soiled babushka, had been bustling among the kitchenware. Now, with her purchase under her arm, she passed the book racks, examined the Sartre, rejected it, and instead picked out a Mickey Spillane, *The Big Kill*. It had taken her less time to buy a book than to buy a saucepan. I looked again at the collection as a whole and decided that it was curiously appropriate to the city and the neighborhood. It was rich, random, gaudy, vital, corrupt, and at the same time innocent; it put culture at the disposal of the plain man, even the poorest, for less than the price of a bar whisky; it was impersonal, friendly, egalitarian, and it proclaimed as dogma its lack of discrimination. "Here we are," the books in the big racks seemed to be saying, "the mud and sapphires of our time, and for one or two pieces of silver you can take your pick of us. If you are fooled into reading Sartre by a naked woman on the cover, you have no right to complain. No clerk is helping you to choose and no one is holding you back; here everyone starts even. But hurry, hurry, before we are bought by others or returned to the publisher, for few of us will reappear at the corner of Clark and Division."

I was tempted to answer their plea, fill my overcoat pocket with books, buy a pint of whisky at the liquor counter, and sit reading and tippling among the pigeons in Bughouse Square. Instead I walked eastward and southward into the Gold Coast. West of the dividing line I hadn't seen any hard-cover books displayed for sale (though I might have seen them even on Clark Street if I had gone north toward Lincoln Park or south toward the Loop). East of the line there weren't many paperbacks, because there were few newsstands or drugstores, but I passed four or five bookshops, including one large and busy one, the Main Street Book Store. I entered one of the smaller shops. It carried a very small selection of new books, mostly best-sellers, a larger selection of gifts and greeting cards, and maintained a rental library. There were three or four customers in the shop, all middle-aged women, quietly dressed, unhurried, and on friendly terms with the proprietress. "I'm sorry, Mrs. Roberts," she was saying to one of them in a soft and well-articulated voice. "The book isn't in stock, but I can order it downtown and have it for you tomorrow afternoon." She saw me inspecting the books on the rental shelves. As a group they weren't much better, but merely newer, than the assortment in the drugstore; they included more nonfiction, more detective stories, and very few Westerns. "May I help you?" she asked. "Please don't bother," I said, feeling that I had re-entered a less disturbing world of politeness and personal relations.

On Michigan Avenue I passed another shop and recognized the name on the window. Although the salesroom wasn't large it was filled with new books lining the walls or piled on tables. There were also two big racks of long-playing records, and a hidden phonograph was playing Mozart as I entered (feeling again that I was a long way from Clark and Division). The books on the shelves included almost everything published during the last two or three years that I had any curiosity about reading. In two fields the collection was especially good: psychiatry and books by Chicago authors. I introduced myself to the proprietor, Stuart Brent, and found that he was passionately interested in books, in the solution of other people's personal problems, and in his native city. Many of his customers are young people just out of college. Sometimes they tell him about their problems and he says to them, "Read this book. You might find the answer there." He is mildly famous in the trade for his ability to sell hundreds of copies of a book that arouses his enthusiasm: for example, he has probably found more readers for Harry Stack Sullivan's *An Interpersonal Theory of Psychiatry* than any other dealer in the country, even the largest. Collections of stories are usually slow-moving items in bookstores, although they have proved to be more popular as paperbacks. One evening Brent amazed the publisher of Nelson Algren's stories, *The Neon Wilderness*, by selling a thousand copies of the hard-cover book at an autograph party. We talked about the days when the Near North Side was full of young authors—many of whom became famous New Yorkers—and about the possibility of another Chicago renaissance, as in the years after 1915. Brent would like to do something to encourage such a movement. He complained that most of the other booksellers didn't regard themselves as integrated parts of the community and that they didn't take enough interest in the personal needs of their customers.

I might have visited other shops, but I wasn't trying to make a survey of the book trade in Chicago, or even in one neighborhood, except in so far as it revealed a general situation. The largest Chicago bookstores—Kroch's and Marshall Field—are in or near the Loop, but most of their customers live in good residential sections. There is a smaller concentration of bookstores on the South Side, near the Midway and the university. Brent's complaint against the booksellers may well have been justified, from his point of view, but a visitor wouldn't expect to find that any large professional group was marked by his combination of interest in persons, interest in the cultural welfare of the community, and abounding energy. As a group, the booksellers I have met in many parts of the country are widely read, obliging, likable persons who regard bookselling as a profession and work hard at it, for lower incomes than they might receive from other activities. They would all like to sell more books, in quantities like those of the paperbacks in drugstores and on the newsstands, but they are dealing in more expensive articles, for which the public seems to be limited.

When O. H. Cheney made his broad survey of the book trade in 1931, he found that there were only five hundred bookstores in the country that did enough business for the publishers' salesmen to bother calling on them. Most of these stores were in the twelve largest cities, and they flourished in the same neighborhoods, he reported, as good florists, jewelers, and agencies for medium- and high-priced automobiles. He might also have said, " . . . as interior decorators, prescription pharmacies, and haberdashers with silk dressing gowns in the windows," for bookselling as he pictured it was one of the luxury trades. Twenty years later the situation hadn't greatly changed. Industrial cities as large as Youngstown, Ohio—with a population of 167,643 by the 1950 census—still had no regular bookstores, although pocket-size books were being sold there through dozens of retail outlets. People in smaller towns were buying more hard-cover books than formerly—often through book clubs, which are essentially a device for selling books by mail.[2] There was also a better market for books of all types in university towns and areas (like the Midway in Chicago) than there had been at the time of the Cheney Report. In other respects the audience for new books was almost the same as it had been in 1931. Most of it still consists of people living on the "right" side of whatever line divides their community.

There are advantages for American culture in the existence of this limited, but prosperous, alert, and well-educated body of readers. Most of them subscribe to magazines with book-review sections, many of them read the literary quarterlies, and in general they know what is happening in the world of books. They are much more willing than the general public to accept novelties and experiments. They help to perform the essential function of setting new styles in reading matter, some of which will afterward be followed by a larger public. Bookstores often serve as their meeting places —in this country without literary cafés or salons—and often keep a stock of the magazines, phonograph records, and reproduced paintings that appeal to them. In cities like Chicago many stores have developed an audience for books in one special field: psy-

2. There were very few book clubs in 1931, and Cheney wasn't inclined to believe that they would ever play a larger part in the publishing industry. By 1953 there were seventy-four clubs that recommended books for adults and eleven others that selected books for children. The membership of the two oldest clubs had declined sharply since 1946, when it had reached a peak, but new clubs continued to be founded every year. Most of the new ones specialized in some particular type of book or audience. The fear had been that the clubs would encourage a general uniformity of taste in the American public, and instead they were, to some extent, encouraging a diversity.

chiatry, drama, art, music, literature, technology, advance-guard writing, or the occult. The stores are helping in this fashion to maintain the diversity of American culture against the many forces that are working to make it uniform. By personal contacts—something entirely lacking at the newsstands—they find readers for valuable works that couldn't otherwise be published, and later they keep the works in stock. The bookstores are quiet voices pleading for permanence, variety, personality, discrimination. The pity is that the voices don't carry far enough, even in prosperous neighborhoods, and are scarcely heard on the other side of the dividing line.

2.

Meanwhile the publication of pocket-size books is a business success story that has also become an exciting development in the field of popular entertainment and education. The success story begins in 1939, although there had been some earlier efforts to distribute paper-bound books to a mass audience. After World War I the efforts had been commercial failures for several reasons, one of which was that the publishers hadn't yet found a way to manufacture really low-cost books. Another reason was that they expected to sell the books simply because they were cheap, instead of giving the public what it wanted at a price it was willing to pay. Some of them tried to give the public what they thought was good for it and found, as always, that it wasn't interested. Another reason for the failure of these earlier series of paperbacks was that bookstores, with their limited patronage, weren't equipped to sell cheap books in quantities and sometimes refused to handle them.

The situation changed in 1939, when Pocket Books, Inc., was founded by Robert F. de Graff and developed a new approach to mass-market publishing. De Graff and his associates started by finding a convenient, reasonably attractive, and highly salable format that made it possible for books to be printed on high-speed rotary presses, like magazines, and sold at a profit for twenty-five cents each—if the public would buy them in sufficient numbers. The first ten items to be issued in the new format were all items that the public could be expected to like: for example, they included *The Good Earth*, of which more than a million copies had already been sold in hard-cover editions. But finding the right books and manu-facturing them cheaply were only two of the problems that had to be solved by the new publishing house; a bigger problem was how to distribute them.

Obviously if the books were to reach an audience comparable to that of mass-circulation magazines they would have to be displayed almost everywhere that magazines were sold. That wasn't enough, however, and they would have to find other retail outlets besides the usual newsstands, drugstores, cigar stores, and hotels. By patient efforts Pocket Books, Inc., succeeded in having its publications displayed in thousands of chain groceries, dime stores like Woolworth's and Kresge's, neighborhood department stores, and supermarkets in the suburbs. Housewives bought them while marketing—a dozen eggs, a cowboy story, a pound of hamburger—and roulette players could buy them too, for they were sold in gambling clubs in Reno and Las Vegas.

Books were being distributed by what had already come to be called the saturation method of distributing novelties and magazines. Instead of being widely advertised, the product is simply placed on sale, but in the largest possible number of outlets and usually in impressive quantities, until it has been displayed to every potential customer and the market is saturated. The method proved to be highly effective. Ten million Pocket Books—capitalized—were sold in 1941, and twenty million in 1942. By 1943 they were already being distributed through more than six hundred jobbers to fifty-two thousand retailers of every type, in every sort of neighborhood, while most of the hard-cover books were still being sold by five hundred bookstores.

Rival publishers were entering the field: first came Avon Books, then Bantam Books, with a selection of standard new fiction and some nonfiction titles that might be expected to reach a wide audience. Penguin Books, an English company, founded an American branch, which developed into an independent enterprise, the New American Library of World Literature. This new firm made more experiments: most important of these was its Mentor Books, consisting of informational and scholarly works sold for thirty-five cents each through a smaller number of outlets. Signet Books, chiefly fiction, are also published by New American Library; at first they included many novels that had been passed over by other reprint houses as being too literary or eccentric. Some of the novels—notably those by William Faulkner—soon proved to be popular items on the newsstands. In spite of competition, Pocket Books,

Inc., continued to distribute more copies of more books each year; in 1952 it issued 46 million copies and 109 new titles. New American Library, then second in the field, issued 42 million copies and 80 titles; Bantam Books, 35 million copies and 94 titles. Then came Dell (26 million), Avon (22 million), Popular Library (21 million), Gold Medal (21 million), and Permabooks (10 million). In all, more than a dozen pocket-book publishers printed 252 million copies and 882 new titles in 1952.[3] The books were distributed through more than a hundred thousand retail outlets.

Although the saturation method has proved effective in distributing almost any sort of low-priced and tempting product, it involves a good deal of waste in the form of unsold stock. If the stock consists of pocket-size books they can be returned to the publishers, and the dealer receives credit for them. Year after year, as more publishers issued more paperbacks, the percentage of returns continued to rise. Newsdealers no longer had space to display all the new titles that were issued, or more than a small percentage of them, and there was no longer any single book, even the most popular, that saturated the market by appearing in almost all the retail outlets. The trade began talking about the problem of "premature returns"—that is, cartons of new books that were sent back to the publishers without being opened. In 1953, when the pocket-book business seemed to be reaching a climax, or crisis, the publishers issued 259 million copies and 1061 titles, but they had in their warehouses more than 150 million undistributed or returned copies, largely of earlier publications. These were a heavy liability for any business that operates on a small margin of profit. Observers were saying that there would have to be consolidations or bankruptcies before the business was placed on a stable foundation, but they were also taking for granted that pocket-size publishing would continue to play an important part in American life.

Any new medium of entertainment is patronized at the expense of some older medium, since everyone's leisure time is limited. Where does the time come from that is spent in reading soft-cover books? One answer is that some of them aren't read, but are merely picked up as bargains and carried home to gather dust, whereas

3. The production figures for individual publishers are taken from an article in the September 1953 issue of *Fortune*; the total for all publishers is the annual estimate made by Bantam Books, Inc.

the more expensive hard-cover books are regarded as investments that must be made to yield returns. The fact remains that hundreds of millions of man-hours each year are spent with paperbacks. What other avocations suffer? Some of the hours might otherwise have been devoted to activities, or inactivities, like listening to the radio, watching television, going to the movies, playing cards, pub-crawling, or sitting empty-handed in a train. Most of them are taken from other types of reading matter—but from what particular types?

The effect of paperbacks on the general cultural level depends largely on this last question, which isn't easy to answer. Perhaps the hard-cover reprints have suffered most; even the better ones are losing their audience, and the cheaper ones—like the novels formerly published by Grosset and Dunlap and Triangle Books—have disappeared. New hard-cover books have been less affected, and nonfiction not at all; the decline in sales is among new hard-cover novels written for a popular audience. Many book clubs, especially the larger ones, have been losing membership, although it isn't certain how much of the loss can be attributed to paperbacks. A similar doubt exists in the case of public libraries, which reported a decline in attendance during the early 1950s, but were inclined to blame it on television or prosperity; their attendance is highest in depression years. Rental libraries have also lost patronage, though not uniformly; some continue to flourish, but many have been discontinued.

Meanwhile there is one type of reading matter with which the paperbacks are directly in competition. Stand long enough in any drugstore and you will see how they compete. A customer looks at the magazine racks, then at the pocket-size books, and usually makes a choice from one or the other, but seldom from both. It is possible that for every two or three sales of a pocket-size book, one copy of a magazine fails to be sold. The big, glossy magazines can stand the competition, and most of them have been holding their circulation, but the pulp-paper fiction monthlies have clearly suffered. They have disappeared from some newsstands where they used to be prominently displayed—and so too have the unsmiling comic books, which are now as hard to find in some middle-class neighborhoods as they once were hard to avoid.

These observations give a sort of base-line for estimating the effect of pocket-size books on the general cultural level. At their very worst they are immensely better than the comics. Still at their worst, they are a little better than the pulps; often they are written by the same authors, but with somewhat more care and consecutive effort. At their best they are better than any of the mass-circulation magazines—and the statement remains true even if we set aside the pocket-book series that have achieved some literary or scholarly distinction, like Mentor Books, Anchor Books, and Penguins imported from England. Except for a few Mentors, these seldom appear at newsstands in shabby neighborhoods, but even there the assortment is likely to include some admirable works that were never before available at low prices. Pocket-size books as a class are making possible a considerable improvement in the reading habits of the American public.

It used to be thought that "serious writing" and "best-sellers" were mutually exclusive categories: the popular book never had literary merit, and the work of distinction would never be popular. The paperback experiment has destroyed that superstition and has proved that literary merit doesn't interfere with the broadest sort of popular success—unless the merit depends on subtlety, allusion, or the defiance of popular notions. If the merit has come to be widely recognized and the book is regarded as something of a classic, the public will buy it in quantities simply for that reason, as happened with the pocket editions of *A Farewell to Arms* and *The Great Gatsby*—though I doubt that it could happen with Kafka's *The Castle*. Success with a large public and literary merit are separate and incommensurable qualities, like density and color; they may exist together or exist separately. Examples are the two best-selling items in the history, to 1954, of pocket-book publishing. One is *God's Little Acre*, by Erskine Caldwell, which is written with poetic feeling about a group of characters who, when the book was published, were new to fiction. Afterward Caldwell declined into formula writing, but this early novel, for all its obvious faults, is a work of literature. The other book is *The Big Kill*, by Mickey Spillane, which is one more of the author's many stories about a detective named Mike Hammer. The detective is a folk hero who is also a homicidal maniac with a passion for ripping the clothes from women and shooting them in the abdomen. The other characters have no emotions but lust, cupidity, fear, or hatred, the writing is stereotyped, and the literary standing, or recumbence, of the novel is several stages beneath the utterly worthless. Like

God's Little Acre, also published by the New American Library, it has had a sale of more than six million copies.[4]

In 1953 Spillane was drawing abreast of Caldwell, and his novels as a group were being printed more rapidly and sold in larger quantities than any other fiction series by a single author in the history of publishing. Mr. Spillane explains their popularity by two ingredients found, he says, in all his books: fast-action plots and a walloping surprise ending. Both these ingredients should be examined at some length; perhaps they will cast light on the popular success of a series that illustrates the worst side of the paperbacks as a cultural phenomenon.

The fast-action plots consist of a linked series of episodes, with each of the episodes conforming to the same double pattern. First Mike Hammer goes to see an incredibly beautiful woman; there are five or six of these in each novel. The woman makes a shameless attempt to seduce him, usually by exposing herself; sometimes she tears open her dress from throat to waist. Mike has a wriggly feeling up and down his spine; time and again he has that feeling, but he usually manages to resist temptation. "Some other night, baby," he says between clenched teeth; then he jumps into a high-powered car and speeds off to discharge the sexual tension by killing or maiming a hoodlum.

This second part of the episode is likely to culminate in a scene of pointless and half-mad brutality. Here, for example, is a passage from *The Big Kill*, telling what happened in the toilet of a waterfront saloon when two gorillas tried giving the works to Mike Hammer:

The little guy stared too long. He should have been watching my face. I snapped the side of the rod across his jaw and laid the flesh open to the bone. He dropped the sap and staggered into the big boy with a scream starting to come up out of his throat only to get it cut off in the middle as I pounded his teeth back into his mouth with the end of the barrel. The big guy tried to shove him out of the way. He got so mad he came right at me with his head down and I took my own damn time about kicking him in the face. He smashed into the door and lay there

4. After these came two Pocket Books, capitalized: the *Pocket Book of Baby and Child Care* (five million copies by 1953) and the *Pocket Dictionary* (four and a half million). These standard works are kept on sale year after year and eventually should have a sale larger than that of any novel, even the worst or best.

bubbling. So I kicked him again and he stopped bubbling. I pulled the knucks off his hand then went over and picked up the sap. The punk was vomiting on the floor, trying to claw his way under the sink. For laughs I gave him a taste of his own sap on the back of his hand and felt the bones go into splinters.

Sometimes in the story the fierce joys of sadism—"for laughs" —give way to the subtler delights of masochism. Mike Hammer is captured by gangsters and tied to a chair, while they try to make him turn over some information. One of them wraps a wet towel around his fist and keeps working over Mike's head. "I only had to shake my head once and that fist clubbed it again. It went on and on until there was no pain at all and I could laugh when he talked to me and try to smile when the delivery boy in the corner got sick and turned his head away to puke." But Mike laughs harder at the end of the chapter when he wipes out the nest of gangsters by filling their guts with lead. Soon he is back in the high-powered car, ready to visit another incredibly seductive woman and start a new episode.

As for the second of the ingredients to which Mr. Spillane attributes the success of his novels, the surprise ending is always walloping, but it may not be completely a surprise. The reader of one Mike Hammer story can guess the villain of the next. He can guess that the perpetrator of all the cruel murders in the book—except those committed by Mike Hammer—will be one of the beautiful women who have tried to seduce the hero. He can also guess that Mike will face the woman in the last chapter and, after tearing the mask from her sins and the clothes from her body, will shoot her down with hot slugs from his Luger that "ripped through guts and intestines."

In these final walloping scenes Mike reveals something about himself that the reader may have suspected from the beginning. It has to be emphasized that I am talking about the hero, not the author. Mr. Spillane, born in Brooklyn, is a former cadet instructor and fighting pilot; in 1952 he joined the sect of Jehovah's Witnesses and said that he would put less sex into his future books (though he said nothing about sadism). I have no doubt that he is a pillar of society, but he is not the hero of his novels. The hero, Mike Hammer, is a homicidal paranoiac who exhibits all the clinical symptoms of his disease, including delusions of grandeur, of having a "mission," and the belief that police and criminals are leagued in a conspiracy against him. Like other paranoiacs he has strong homosexual tendencies and, when he tries to suppress them, they drive him into acts of violence. In each book Mike—not Mickey— projects his feelings of guilt on a bad woman who has tried to seduce him. He looks at her with hatred "dripping out of me," he says, "and scoring my face. My eyes burned holes in my head and my whole body reeled under the sickening force that pulled me toward her." The quotation is from *Vengeance Is Mine,* a novel that ends with a peculiarly nauseating wallop. As Mike's bullets go ripping through her intestines, we learn that the incredibly seductive woman is a man in disguise.

I am not used to having Jack the Ripper presented as a model for emulation and I confess that Mike Hammer frightens me. It has been argued that the stories have no relation to American life; that they put together the ingredients of the Western novel, the pursuit thriller, the comic strip, and the animated film cartoon into a cock-eyed fairy story that has no more social significance than the fun house at Coney Island. The publishers, I suppose, would like to accept this explanation: what fun! Others might say that these fairy stories are entirely too close to one side of American life at the mid-century. There is a sullen resentment against American women that we have already seen in the war novels; sometimes it leads in life to acts of aggression. We have also been hearing about more and more crimes of violence, especially those directed against women. Police statistics show that, while old-fashioned burglaries are decreasing, rapes, mutilations, and violent robberies are growing in number from year to year. I wouldn't say that Mike Hammer has anything to do with police statistics, and the fact might be that reading the stories is a means of channeling off the dangerous impulses into daydreams. But Mike Hammer—like many comic books and some of the animated cartoons—helps to show that the impulses are there, in the midst of our elaborate and internally peaceful culture. I remember reading about a sailor who was arrested in Brooklyn after a career of robbing women in lonely streets. He snatched their handbags, then knocked them down, kicked them in the abdomen—like Mike Hammer—and left them gasping and vomiting on the sidewalk to wait for the ambulance. Perhaps he wasn't a reader of the Mike Hammer stories, but he was part of the same moral configuration.

3.

Just before *The Big Kill* was issued in its first soft-cover edition of two and a half million copies, the largest in publishing history, New American Library announced that it also planned to issue a twice-yearly selection of contemporary prose and poetry, under the title of *New World Writing*. It would be using the soft-cover method of distribution for what was, in effect, a literary magazine, comparable in quality with the quarterlies, but with its emphasis on creative writing instead of criticism and with a first printing of something more than a hundred thousand copies. Since then the magazine has continued to appear every six months and has carried out the publisher's program of providing a showcase for new writers, besides paying them for their work. The writers have been chosen with a sense of literary *chic* that is a desirable quality in magazines (though I detest it in critics), and their stories and poems, besides being interesting in themselves, have been a promise of books to come. *New World Writing* has even been a commercial success on a modest scale, so that other soft-cover publishers have ventured into the field. Pocket Books, Inc., brought out *Discovery*, which was devoted to new American stories and poems; Permabooks brought out *The 7 Arts*, with new critical papers and interesting reproductions.

Since the disappearance of the *Century* and *Scribner's*, and the transformation of *Harper's* into a very useful journal of opinions and observations, we have had in this country no literary magazine that reached a wide body of readers and helped to impose general standards of taste. *New World Writing*, and possibly some of its rivals, might someday move into that empty position, if they can overcome one great weakness. The literary magazines of the 1890s weren't merely selected bodies of material presented at stated intervals; they were also a relationship existing among editors, writers, and readers. The readers were educated by the magazines, but not passively; they told the editors what they didn't like and what they wanted to learn; there was a process of exchange that ended by establishing a cultural level and a tradition that remained vital until 1910—if we must set a date for the decline of these great institutions. One's complaint against the pocket-book magazines would be that the writers are simply published. the readers simply presented with a body of writing they are likely to enjoy, but without their often feeling—as did readers of the old *Century*—that they had some participation in the choice of material and that the magazine was written and edited specifically for them.

This lack of participation is a weakness of the pocket-size books as a class: they don't arouse in authors or publishers the sense of their being read and liked or disliked that is felt in the case of hard-cover books. Readers of hard-cover books are an articulate group; they tell the bookseller what they think about a new novel, and he repeats their comments to the publisher's salesman, who carries them back to the office; later the author may hear about them, besides receiving letters, as he almost always does, from readers who think he has spoken for or against them. The case is different with the author whose book has been reprinted in soft covers. He doesn't feel that he is speaking directly to this new audience that he has reached partly by accident; he can't even picture to himself the faceless thousands who buy his book at the newsstands, perhaps read it absorbedly, or perhaps toss it aside after a few chapters. Why are they absorbed or repelled? The author will never know, and the publisher is in doubt; he isn't even sure whether this particular book was bought by young or old, women or men, rich or poor, housewives, white-collar workers, factory hands, or the unemployed. He is dealing in consumer goods for a vast market, and in general he knows less about his customers than do the manufacturers of cosmetics or detergents.

In effect, pocket-size books are launched into the void; if they stay launched they are followed by others of the same category; if they come back to the publisher he tries another type of product for the faceless multitude. A few editors—like Freeman Lewis of Pocket Books, Inc.—have studied popular tastes and can speak about them with some authority, but mostly the rules of the business are rules of thumb. Any nonfiction book of moderate length can be reprinted at thirty-five cents a copy if it is reasonably certain to have a sale of seventy-five thousand. Any short novel can be reprinted at twenty-five cents if the reasonably certain sale is at least a hundred and fifty thousand. Among nonfiction titles now being issued by trade or hard-cover publishers, not one in twenty will be judged capable of reaching the minimum soft-cover sale; among novels, not more than one in four or five.

The usual rule of thumb requires that any novel reprinted in soft covers should contain certain ingredients. There must be a story line; in other words, the novel must create enough expectancy in its readers so that they read on from beginning to end. It must have a great deal of action and preferably a great deal of sex; at least the heroine must arouse desire and the hero be capable of feeling it. The novel must have characters with whom the reader can identify himself. It must have a background in which ordinary people are likely to be interested, one not too intellectual or otherwise limited in appeal. All these ingredients can be present in a novel that also has literary distinction, but the fact remains that distinction is harder to achieve when the author is forced to comply with a series of extra-literary requirements. Perhaps he writes best about persons who are too complicated or neurotic to win the sympathy of a mass audience. Perhaps his background is one that the audience doesn't enjoy reading about —or isn't thought to enjoy by the soft-cover publishers, who assume the right to speak for the voiceless millions. After 1950 their fiction requirements began to be reflected in many bookstore novels too. That was only to be expected when we consider that publishers receive part of their income from reprint rights; they would be more likely to accept a novel that the reprint houses would bid for than one that would reach only the bookstore audience. In that respect, and not in that alone, the new mass market for books is working toward conformity rather than diversity in American fiction.

It has also created a new danger of censorship. For twenty years or more the censors had been busy with motion pictures, radio, and education; they had taken to letting the bookstores alone. Since their purpose is chiefly to control the mass mind, they have been more excited by little heresies, real or imagined, in schoolbooks than they have been by greater heresies in scholarly works or in serious novels that hadn't reached a mass audience. But when some of the serious novels reappeared on the newsstands, the censors became aroused. They seemed to object to literary distinction as much as they did to pornography, or even more. Although they said little or nothing about Mickey Spillane, in several cities they tried to forbid the sale of novels by Faulkner, Hemingway, Steinbeck, Farrell, and even of a volume of essays by Sigmund Freud.

In each of the cities a committee of parents had been formed; pious and prosperous citizens always call themselves "parents" when they want to suppress a book. Using a list of paperbacks compiled by the National Organization for Decent Literature, the committee would pay a visit to the prosecuting attorney or the chief of police. The committee members would insist that their children, or grandchildren, were being corrupted by books on the newsstands. They didn't stop to ask whether the children were reading them, or reading anything, though the question would seem to be pertinent. After some observation of newsstand customers I am inclined to believe that few pocket-size books are bought by teen-agers, but the committees didn't observe; they acted on dogma or emotion. Often they persuaded the chief of police to make a raid on the newsdealers. He would be inclined to let the bookstores alone—at least in the beginning—but the law makes no distinction between books sold for twenty-five cents and those sold for five dollars or more. Eventually the bookstores would suffer too, and some are already suffering. The publishing industry is making a vigorous and often successful defense of free speech, but it isn't disposed to offend the censors unnecessarily. One result of pocket-book publishing may be that all authors, not merely those whose work is republished in soft covers, may be limited in their freedom to treat some subjects, and that bookstores may choose to stop selling some types of books.

Publishing for the mass market is an important and exciting development in American life, but we shouldn't delude ourselves about its possibilities. It doesn't necessarily mean that the sort of books we personally admire will be reprinted for millions of new readers. Some of them will be reprinted, but others, in the future, may offend the censors or fail to meet commercial requirements and so not be published at all. I can't imagine that a publisher with his eyes on the mass market would display any interest in the manuscript of *The Sun Also Rises*—if the novel had just been written— or in those of *The Sound and the Fury* or *The Bridge*. New authors comparable to Hemingway or Faulkner or Hart Crane might benefit, at most, by having samples of their work printed in *New World Writing*. Before the mass audience read whole books of theirs, such authors would have to make themselves famous by other methods, not excluding suicide. In some ways the situation in literature is coming to resemble that which we find in other popular arts. Just as the public is getting more books reprinted at low prices, so it is getting more plays (on the movie or television screen), more

music on records or by radio, and more paintings in better reproductions. Everything that has to do with the diffusion of culture
is being handled with more and more technical efficiency. For that
we should be deeply grateful, but without forgetting that the creation
of new cultural objects, new novels, new poems, is another and more
difficult problem. The pocket-book publishers have been doing a
little, in spite of themselves, to make that problem more difficult,
as they have been doing a little more, and consciously, to make it
easier.

VII.

HARDBACKS OR PAPERBACKS?

1.

The business of publishing new hard-cover books has been suffering from a mild but prolonged crisis. Essentially the crisis results from high production costs and weakness in the system of distribution. There simply aren't enough bookstores, as we have seen, and they don't reach a wide enough segment of the American population. Of recent years their patrons have been saying that books are too expensive, although the increase in price has been less than that of other commodities, including the goods and services that publishers must buy. Many booksellers have reduced their stock and the space devoted to books, while introducing some other line of merchandise. In some of the largest department stores, including Macy's, the book department has been exiled to an upper story. There is—to use commercial jargon—a continuing strong demand for nonfiction titles. The demand is appreciably greater than it was before the war, but publishers used to make their profits out of best-selling novels and today there aren't so many of these, nor do their sales reach anything like the wartime figures.

At the same time the public has been buying more copies of many popular novels than at any time in the past. Television and other new forms of mass entertainment haven't destroyed the reading habit, at least not among adults, although they may be doing a

more thorough job with children. But instead of going to bookstores
the adults have been buying their novels at various types of newsstands and at prices from twenty-five cents for shorter ones to
seventy-five cents for a very long book like *From Here to Eternity*;
at that price two million copies of *Eternity* were sold in a few
months. It was, of course, the pocket-size reprint of a novel of
which several hundred thousand hard-cover copies had already
been sold at $4.50.

Because of the enormous sales of pocket-size books, many persons have asked why all novels—not merely those with a bookstore
success behind them—couldn't be cheaply printed from manuscript
and sold on the newsstands. Isn't this in the spirit of a new civilization bent on distributing the greatest possible number of commodities to the widest possible circle of consumers at the lowest possible
prices? Books are the chief cultural commodity. As a step toward
making new books more popular, shouldn't other publishers follow
the example of Gold Medal, Avon, Ballantine, and the other companies that have been distributing soft-cover "originals"?

Instead of answering the questions directly, I should like to make
a few points about the publication and distribution of new books.
The first is that the present system, which involves publishers, whole-
salers, bookstores, book clubs, and book-review sections—not to
mention book printers, binders, jacket designers, illustrators, advertising agencies, indexers, free-lance editorial workers, literary
agents, and all the other specialists listed in that valuable handbook
The Literary Marketplace—is dependent primarily on the sale of
hard-cover books. If the sale collapsed, the system would collapse.
Some other system would take its place, since books are a necessity
in our culture, but first there would be a period of anarchy during
which all the bookish professions would suffer.

There are reasons for doubting that the new system would be
better for serious writers—and for the culture as a whole—than the
inefficient system that now prevails. Efficiency leads to standardiza-
tion and doesn't encourage the handicrafts—of which writing is
one—or the production of original work except in standardized
laboratories. Efficiency would require that there be fewer publishers
to issue fewer books in larger quantities and hence at lower prices.
Even the soft-cover publishers are inefficient in these respects.
There are more than a dozen of them, with the number growing
from year to year, whereas it is obvious that two or three really big

firms could better exploit the market. The 1061 soft-cover titles issued in 1953 were possibly twice as many as the newsdealers could effectively display. What shall we then say of the seventy-two trade-publishing houses listed in *The Literary Marketplace*, or of the almost ten thousand new titles they issued that same year? Each house has its own editorial staff and, to some extent, its own notions of literary merit and salability. House competes with house, and book with book, in an outrageously inefficient fashion. Yet the system has the advantage for writers and for the public that good manuscripts are eventually accepted by one of the seventy-two houses—if their authors have reason to believe in themselves and have enough pertinacity. Publishers are always being advised to issue fewer books—"and better ones," the adviser is careful to add; but I have noticed that when a publisher shortens his list of forthcoming titles, some of the better manuscripts are usually found to be arty, difficult, or lacking in general appeal and are rejected with the bad ones; the shortest list isn't often the most distinguished.

Among the ten thousand new titles issued by trade-book publishers, some of the best—and a few of the worst—will be reprinted as paperbacks. Others of the best, and thousands that are useful for various reasons, will never be reprinted, but will be available in public libraries. They will also be available for years to anyone who orders them through a bookstore. Trade publishers keep their useful books in stock, list them in catalogues, and supply them on demand, so long as an effective demand continues. That too is an inefficient practice from the standpoint of good merchandising, which requires the merchant to get rid of his slow-moving inventory, but it is a useful practice for readers. Some pocket-book publishers follow it with respect to various special series: for example, Mentor Books, Anchor Books (issued by Doubleday), and Gold Medal "originals" can be ordered from catalogues. A general rule, however, is that paperbacks are distributed like magazines, in competition with magazines. Having once disappeared from the stands, most of them are as hard to find again as last month's *Ladies Home Journal*.

There is a final point to make, that trade-book publishing is a skilled profession as well as a business. It requires a great deal of training, effort, and capital invested in such activities as reading unsolicited manuscripts, finding new authors (often among contributors to little or big magazines), suggesting books they might write (and receiving counter-suggestions), helping to support the authors financially and morally until the work is finished, judging the work and often finding ways in which it might be improved, editing copy for the printer, sending advance proofs to critics who might be enthusiastic, designing attractive books (with jackets that truly suggest their contents), writing catalogue and jacket copy that will help to sell them, convincing the booksellers that they can be sold, and then persuading the public, always conservative in its preferences, to read new stories told in a new manner—if the authors have written that type of stories. Every new book presents a different series of problems. Every new author is a new system of human relationships.

Because of the problems and relationships, there is no "best" publisher, any more than there is a best lawyer. Some trade publishers are generally better than others, and there may be a best publisher for some type of book or for an individual author. Sometimes an author receives a disproportionate share of editorial attention, which his work may justify in the end. The editorial staff of Scribner's worked for years with James Jones before *From Here to Eternity* was ready for the printer; then the sales and promotion staff worked for months with the book before bound copies were placed on sale. The late Maxwell Perkins of Scribner's had worked still longer with Thomas Wolfe, as Jones had heard; the younger novelist greatly admired Wolfe, and that was one reason for his choice of publisher. If he had finished *Eternity*, which was his first book, without editorial advice it would have been a less effective novel. If it had been submitted to any publisher of soft-cover "originals"—except possibly Ballantine—it would have been rejected merely for its length, or else might have been reduced to one-third the length by omitting all but the more sensational and sexy passages. The pocket-book publishers, with their smaller margin of profit, simply cannot afford to spend much time on professional activities and human relationships. Neither can they afford to plan sales strategies for an individual author—unless he approaches the popularity of Mickey Spillane—or to make advertising appropriations for separate novels. They are engaged in the business of mass distribution, and they have to find products for which there is an actual or easily stimulated mass demand. Usually the products are books that have previously been edited and promoted by a trade publisher.

2.

A peculiarity of paper-back publishing is that the book itself—or rather the front cover of the book—serves as its principal advertising display. There are four features on the cover that help to sell a pocket-size novel (nonfiction is a different problem, approached by more conservative methods). The first feature is a sentence or phrase, called the skyline, which is usually printed above the title; it tells why the book should be read ("A tense, gripping tale of lust and larceny"). The second is the title itself, which should be simple and vigorous, or suggestive; often the title of a novel is changed for the soft-cover edition. The third feature is the author's name, which may serve as evidence of some desired quality in the book—especially if the name is Caldwell or Spillane—and the fourth is a scene from the story, illustrated in five or six glaring colors.

Almost always the scene is intended to suggest one of the universal human emotions. Sexual desire is regarded as the strongest of these, although the emotion suggested may also be horror, curiosity, or combativeness. Effective covers are thought to be those containing some recognized sexual symbol: a blazing gun (for potency), a whip, a rumpled bed, or a half-dressed woman with a visible cleavage between her very large breasts (cleavage, in the pocket-book trade, is known as "gow"). Still more effective covers might combine several symbols: for example, they might show, or have shown, a gun blazing at a woman with lots of gow as she collapsed on a rumpled bed. I am speaking here in somewhat historical terms. After 1953 the threat of police censorship had one desirable effect, among others that were ominous, and cover artists were instructed to be more discreet. Many of the newer illustrations came to depend on "situation sex," which might mean a fully dressed prostitute waiting for clients, or again might be the face and bare shoulders of an enticing woman looking out through a crack in a bedroom door. Other illustrations were "down-sexed" and depended on their appeal to necrophilia, masochism, or repressed aggression.

Questions of gow and cheesecake, of illustrations that are up-sexed, down-sexed, or situation-sexed, are carefully explored by paper-back publishers, who sometimes regard the cover as being more important than the text. "Give me the right cover," said a newcomer in the field, who was fresh from directing pulp-paper magazines, "and I could sell two hundred blank pages. I could sell *Finnegans Wake* on Skid Road as a book of Irish jokes." It is possible that he could sell a first soft-cover printing of *Finnegans Wake* in the shabbiest neighborhoods,[1] but he couldn't sell a second. The generalized public can always be fooled, but individual members of the public don't like to be fooled a second time. They won't complain to the publisher, and probably not to anyone, but they mightn't buy another pocket-size book. I'm not at all certain that displaying Jean-Paul Sartre's short stories, for example, with a half-naked woman on the cover isn't one way of fooling the public. Misbranded merchandise is still misbranded, even if it is better than the article described on the wrapper—and even if it isn't merchandise at all, but a seriously intended work of literature. The misbranding might interfere with the sale of other merchandise that is accurately labeled, and I think this happened for a time in the pocket-book field. Many of the less educated buyers must have been afraid of getting another collection of difficult avant-garde stories disguised with a suggestive title and a sexy illustration.

The items of merchandise that have actually been popular on the newsstands, except in special neighborhoods—the books that have justified their wide distribution by going into second and third large printings—were usually novels with strong story lines, lots of action, and the other ingredients I mentioned as being those of soft-cover fiction. Not enough of the novels were being issued by trade publishers to supply the demand for new titles. The result was that any novel with the right ingredients became the subject of competitive bidding, sometimes while it was still in manuscript. "I'll make a payment of fifteen thousand dollars against future royalties," one of the soft-cover publishers would say. "I'll guarantee twenty thousand," another would answer. In several cases the advance guarantee has risen to a higher figure: forty thousand for *The Naked and the Dead*, a hundred thousand for *Eternity*. Half of the sum, by the terms of most contracts, has gone to the trade-publishing house and half to the author.

1. The audience for Anchor Books, Penguins, and Mentor Books would buy *Finnegans Wake* and know what they were getting. Actually there isn't one audience for paperbacks; there are many audiences, reached—except in the case of these named series—by a generally random method of distribution, as if the publishers were using fine birdshot to fire at a mixed covey.

Any novel that received an advance guarantee of fifteen thousand dollars or more was known as a "premium" book. By its gratifying sale, *Eternity* earned enough in soft-cover royalties to cover the guarantee, as *The Naked and the Dead* may also have done, but the earnings of most of the premium books have been less than the advance payment. That has been one complaint of the pocket-book houses; another has been that, even after making what seemed to them unreasonably high bids, they still didn't get the novels they wanted. The next step was obvious: some of them explored the possibility of publishing new fiction for themselves. The fiction might be easy to find, if they merely relaxed a few of the requirements that had been imposed by trade publishers—for example, if they were a little less exacting in matters of originality, credibility of plot, consistency of motivation, and good writing. All these were less important for newsstand sales than telling a headlong story with lots of sex, empathetic characters, and a picturesque background. Scores of novelists trained by the pulp-paper magazines were able to tell such stories: why not choose the most experienced, give them kitchen-tested subjects, and set them to work? In 1950, Gold Medal Books announced the first series of pocket-size new novels. It was a sensation in the publishing world, and other companies entered the same field.[2] In 1953 they brought out two hundred and twenty-five "originals," or more than one-fifth of all the new titles issued as pocket-size books.

One publisher of new soft-cover fiction has followed a different policy from the others. Ballantine Books, founded in 1952, has tried to find and publish new novels of some literary merit (while avoiding what the company describes as "authors whose style and subject matter are extremely specialized"). Ballantine covers part of the editorial or professional costs by working, wherever possible, in cooperation with a trade publisher. Many of its novels have appeared simultaneously in two editions, one sold in bookstores for a dollar-fifty or more per copy, the other at newsstands for thirty-five cents (or ten cents more than ordinary pocket-size novels). The plan is attractive to authors, whose royalties are paid at more than

2. Some of the companies were Dell and Avon (the two most active), Popular Library, Pyramid Books, and Lion Books. The three largest soft-cover publishers—Pocket Books, Bantam Books, and New American Library—stayed out of the new-fiction field, although they issued some non-fiction "originals," which were thought to offer less competition to trade publishers.

the usual soft-cover rate; also they needn't be divided with a trade-book publisher. But royalties depend on total sales, as well as on rate per copy, and in 1954 Ballantine hadn't solved the distribution problem; for example, in the Near North Side of Chicago I saw only a few Ballantine novels on sale, at only one of the drugstores and newsstands I visited. The experiment also hadn't proved that newsstand customers prefer "originals" to reprinted novels.

The customers, however, will buy "originals" if they have an unoriginal look—in other words, if they fall into some popular and easily recognized category of writing. That is the chief lesson to be drawn from the commercial success of Gold Medal Originals, Dell First Editions, and two or three other series of soft-cover novels that are written to order, on subjects approved or even imposed by the editor (who sometimes furnishes the ready-made outline of a plot), and then published from manuscript. There is no misbranding of merchandise, unless the high-breasted female on the cover promises a little more titillation than has been provided by the author. Dubious customers need only read the skyline of the novel, which, besides telling why it should be read, also places it in some definite and familiar category of fiction. If they like the novel after reading it, they can find others in the same series described in excerpts from the publisher's catalogue that are often printed at the end of the book. Here, in the case of Gold Medal Originals, are some of the excerpts:

178.   CABIN ROAD   *John Faulkner*

A slice in the lusty passionate back country life that made Tobacco Road a classic. John Faulkner's best book.

222.   SPRING FIRE   *Vin Packer*

A novel of love between two beautiful women. Honest, provocative, it deals with a theme too important to keep from the light.

256.   STREET OF THE LOST   *David Goodis*

Here is the story of Ruxton Street, in the city's lowest slums. A street of prostitutes, workers and dope pushers. But a street where people live and love as they do on any back street in your home town.

No. 178, by William Faulkner's younger brother, clearly belongs to the Tobacco Road category, as well as to the older one of stories about the farmer's lusty passionate daughter. No. 222 is Deviant or Off-Beat Sex (or well-of-loneliness). No. 256 is

Proletarian Sex, a category that has proved to be much more popular on the newsstands than in bookstores. People who live—as many newsstand customers do—in respectable working-class neighborhoods like to read about other neighborhoods that have escaped from respectability.

People in slums also buy pocket-size books; they like to read Gangster and Waterfront stories, always with lots of sex in them and often with a tough detective for hero. They like even more to read Cowboy stories (now usually with sex), and in fact this category is the one that chiefly nourishes the American daydreams of the less-educated classes, including real cowboys. The prosperous classes find their dreams of escape in Mysteries, with less sex and a series of clean murders solved by a gentle and cultured detective. One notes that rental libraries, usually situated in prosperous neighborhoods, have little call for Cowboy stories but keep a large stock of Mysteries. A middle position, economically speaking, is occupied by Science Fiction (with or without sex), whose readers—according to a survey by University of Chicago sociologists—have incomes a little but not much above the national average. These are the familiar categories that have furnished most of the fast-moving items among "originals" on the newsstands: Tobacco Road, Off-Beat Sex (now declining in popularity), Proletarian Sex, Gangster and Waterfront, Cowboy (now rising again), Mystery (still the largest category, but declining), Science Fiction (steady), and always, one might add, Historical Sex, with bitchy heroines. There has been a continuing strong market for novels about pros, or prossies, and nymphos, but those about psychos, dipsos, and junkies are said to be in weakening demand.

Books of all the categories are produced, honestly packaged, and distributed as merchandise. There is always the possibility, of course, that some of them might turn out to be "originals" in another sense of the word than that used by their publishers. Category fiction isn't necessarily bad fiction, and authors like Dashiell Hammett and Raymond Chandler—not to mention dozens of others—have written it in a personal style and with some freshness of treatment. Not a few relatively serious and talented authors have been tempted by high advances, and sometimes by the closing of other outlets, into writing novels for the newsstand audience. One thinks of John Faulkner, W. R. Burnett, MacKinlay Kantor, Jerome Weidman,

Richard Wright, George Milburn, and Benjamin Appel (to whom I am indebted for some of my facts); in 1954 all these, and many others, were under contract to soft-cover publishers.

The larger houses in the field were able to offer guarantees of three thousand dollars for each novel, based on a first printing of about two hundred and fifty thousand copies; some novels go into second or even third printings and earn additional royalties. Some manuscripts prove to be better from a literary standpoint than the publishers had bargained for. The publishers have no objection to literary merit—in fact they welcome it in any novel that also contains the required newsstand ingredients—but neither do they object to lack of merit, if the ingredients are present. Most of their authors will give them what they require and nothing more. Most of the "originals," now and in the future, will be interesting chiefly as sociological documents that cast light on the dreams of escape and the sexual fantasies of the broader American public. If we hope to find new novels that are not categorized, not written to specifications, not expected to reach a wide audience because novels just like them have reached it already, we must continue to look first to the trade-book publishers.

CODA: THE LITERARY STOCK EXCHANGE

But trade-book publishers, for all their greater independence of choice, are affected in their own way by literary fashions. Critics are affected by them too, probably more than they realize; they keep trying to express their personal judgments, but in any given season they all seem to be praising the same group of authors for about the same reasons; soon it will be the turn of another group. For a long time I have been following the rise and fall of reputations on what might be called the literary stock exchange. There are market quotations on the work of every prominent author, living or dead, and the quotations change from year to year, sometimes from week to week. With a mixture of curiosity and skepticism I have watched the common stock of some authors climb steeply from a few dollars per share to the equivalent of five hundred or more. Other stocks come crashing down from five hundred to zero, until trading is halted and the authors' names are removed from the Big Board—and all this without any change in the authors themselves.

The literary stock exchange might be defined as the process of bargaining among critics and would-be critics that determines the standing of prominent authors in any given month or year. There are bulls and bears in the market; there are pools, tipsters, speculators, long-term investors, and specialized traders; there are even planned campaigns in various literary stocks. Finally a balance is reached between short selling and buying for the rise, and that balance serves as a market quotation on the author's work.

The quotation doesn't answer the question of how many copies the author's next book will sell, because most readers don't listen attentively to critical opinions. On the other hand, it helps to determine which authors will be discussed in literary journals—and in how much space—which authors will be required or recommended reading in courses in modern literature, and which authors will be studied and imitated by their successors in the new generation.[3] Publishers look at the market quotations too. Sometimes when a manuscript is being considered for publication, a senior editor will say, "We're sure to lose money on it," and a junior editor will answer, "Perhaps a little, but we ought to regard it as a prestige item." What the junior editor means is that the author of the manuscript, although lacking in sales appeal, has a high value on the literary stock exchange. He has mana, as the anthropologists would say, or what political sociologists would call charisma—that is, he has a supernatural power or virtue in which the publisher can participate by the act of accepting the manuscript.

Sometimes—by no means always—today's stock-market quotations have a prophetic value and help to determine which authors will be best-sellers in five or ten years. Theodore Dreiser was admired by the younger critics and novelists as early as 1910, but it wasn't until 1925, when he published *An American Tragedy*, that his standing was recognized by the reading public at large. By then his critical or stock-market quotation had already begun to decline. T. S. Eliot had enjoyed a high critical reputation for thirty years and had won the Nobel Prize before he published a book—*The Cocktail Party*—that appeared on a best-seller list. A general rule

3. Dr. Stanley Pargellis of the Newberry Library tells me that when first editions of an author's work appear in auction rooms, the bidding by dealers also reflects the quotations, or opinions, prevailing on the critical stock exchange. As instances he notes the steep decline in Galsworthy and Stevenson first editions after 1930. There are signs of partial recovery in Stevensons, but Galsworthys are still inactive, at a depressed level.

is that, if we are looking for indications of an author's permanent value, his present standing on the stock exchange is hardly more to be trusted than are his sales reports. On the Big Board his quotations go up and down, sometimes in a most erratic fashion, while his works are no better or worse than they were on the day of publication.

One example is the flurry in Scott Fitzgerald stock that occurred in 1950 and 1951. A whole series of events affected the literary standing of an author who had been dead for ten years and had been nearly forgotten before he died. First came a revival of interest in the 1920s as a historical period; people remembered faintly that Fitzgerald had been one of its principal spokesmen. Then came the gift of his papers to the Princeton University Library, where they were accessible to scholars and proved to be a rich field for research. Then came the popular success of a novel—*The Disenchanted*, by Budd Schulberg—with a hero suggested by Fitzgerald; every reviewer mentioned him. In the following season Arthur Mizener published a well-documented biography of Fitzgerald, *The Far Side of Paradise*; it had an appealing story to tell and, like the novel, climbed nearly to the top of the best-seller lists. Four of Fitzgerald's own novels reappeared, one after another, in pocket-size editions. His stories were collected and published with a long introduction, and many of them were dramatized for television and radio. Professors of contemporary literature and fiction writing discovered that his work was extremely teachable because of the notes he left behind him, and that students could profit even from his mistakes. By that time students were indeed profiting, in more ways than the professors intended. At several American universities—Princeton less than others—they were trying to relive the 1920s, acting with the romantic desperation of Fitzgerald heroes, and wearing their fathers' coonskin coats to football games. As for Fitzgerald stock on the Big Board, it attracted speculators, had a dizzy rise, and in the summer of 1951 it was being bought and sold at what I should judge to be two or three times its par value.

But it does have a par value, even a high one, and that is among the lessons to be drawn from the Fitzgerald story. Every author who rises above mediocrity and manages to speak for himself, instead of speaking as he likes to think that other people would like to think of him speaking—every author, that is, who really exists for us has a value in himself that operates as a kind of norm. If his reputation rises above the norm, that is, if his stock goes much above par on the literary exchange, it is certain to fall again. If its fall brings it much below par, it is almost certain to rise. There is even a law of compensation in such matters: the steeper has been the rise, the dizzier will be the fall. The longer and more completely an author has been neglected, the greater his eventual fame is likely to be—granted that he belongs to the small band of genuine authors. For Herman Melville the period of complete neglect lasted in this country for sixty years, though some of his books were still being read in England, where literary reputations are somewhat more stable. American critics rediscovered Melville in 1921, and since that year they have been making exaggerated amends to his ghost. Not only do they discuss *Moby-Dick* as the greatest American novel—as it well may be—but they try to persuade us by their explications that even his feeblest works, like *The Confidence Man*, are superior to the best of Thoreau (whom they have stopped reading) and Emerson (whom they disparage).

It is characteristic of operations on the literary exchange that critics usually praise an author by disparaging others. They know, but keep forgetting, that true authors can seldom be compared in any real sense, each being unique. Though every author has a justified reputation that he deserves to keep for a long time, it depends in each case on a different system of measurement—as if the par of one author had to be reckoned in inches of growth, that of another in closeness of texture, that of another in mass, and that of still another in his ability always to surprise us with a word. No stock market would be able to record such varied computations. On the literary exchange, however, all authors are measured by the same simplified standards and all keep rising and falling in reputation as if they had prices that could be quoted in dollars and eighths of dollars, like those of common stocks.

When the price of an author goes too high, there is likely to be a market crash, as in the case of James Branch Cabell. The boom in his stock was largely a result of the excitement over *Jurgen*, when that novel was first published in 1919, then suppressed, and finally reissued. Its reappearance was such a victory over the censors that many critics began talking about the author as if Shakespeare or Melville had appeared on Publishers' Row. In 1921 Vernon Louis

Parrington, who was often a better judge of literary values, wrote a long essay on "The Incomparable Mr. Cabell." He ended it by saying, "Mr. Cabell is creating great literature. A self-reliant intellectual, rich in the spoils of all literatures, one of the great masters of English prose, the supreme comic spirit thus far granted us, he stands apart from the throng of lesser American novelists, as Mark Twain stood apart, individual and incomparable." Thirty years later Mr. Cabell was still writing books, but hardly anyone was reading them, or going back to his earlier work—except in Italy, where he still had a limited public. In this country he wasn't being praised or attacked; he was lucky to be mentioned. Although his reputation had suffered from changing fashion, it had suffered still more from his intemperate admirers and from the law of compensation. His real but rather slender and provincial talent couldn't stand the strain of his being called a great master of English prose and the supreme comic spirit thus far granted us.

When these notes on the literary stock exchange appeared some years ago in the *New Republic*, I ended them with a sort of market letter, such as a broker or investment counselor might write for his clients. Although the letter dealt with the course of values in November 1951, it may have some value as a historical record. It read as follows:

"The market has been active this month, with many stocks selling off, but with the public coming in to buy selected issues, some of which registered advances ranging from fractions to eight or ten points.

"There was brisk trading in the Lost Generation group of novelists. Faulkner common showed mixed tendencies, on account of conflicting reports as to the value of the firm's new product, but the issue gained strength in the last hour of trading on Saturday and closed at 309⅜, an advance of seven points since the first of the month.

"Scott Fitzgerald was firm, at twenty-two points below the high that was reached in the bull market last spring and summer. Hemingway suffered a loss of six points, said to be the result of short selling, but showed more strength at the close. With an extra dividend promised for next year, investors should take note of this standard issue, now thought to be seriously undervalued. Thornton Wilder was low but steady and there were signs of quiet accumulation by insiders. Thomas Wolfe Industries continued a creeping recession.

"Among issues that used to be market leaders back in Coolidge days, Willa Cather was in limited demand and Edith Wharton moved up four points and a fraction. Buyers proved apathetic to Theodore Dreiser offerings. Sherwood Anderson has been inactive at bargain prices since what has become known as the Trilling Killing, when bears of the Lionel Trilling syndicate made their famous raid against this formerly gilt-edged stock and forced it down more than fifty points in a single trading session.

"Prospects in the international field continued to be blurred, with the result that most buyers refrained from active participation. Rumors that the franc was about to be devalued led to a weakening of French equities, though Gide and Proust held firm. Sartre, a newcomer in the field, was flabby at the close and seems to be suffering from the effects of overproduction.

"There was brisk trading in Moravia, Pratolini, Snia Viscosa, and other Italian issues. Among those from Central Europe, Kafka had a drop of twenty-one points for the period, when specialists tried to realize their paper profits. The public showed no interest in offerings by Kafka's American subsidiaries.

"Apparently the Conservative victory in the recent elections had little effect on the price of British equities, although Winston Churchill was up five points and there was a lively demand for brandy and cigars. Older firms such as Joseph Conrad Navigation and Matthew Arnold Lecture Bureau continued to show strength. After a long period of inactivity, Stevenson reappeared on the ticker and made fractional gains, owing, it is said, to the rediscovery of buried treasure.

"Bernard Shaw reached a new high for the postwar years when the death of the president and founder of the company called attention to its essentially sound position. There was a flow of venture capital into some promising new issues, including Joyce Cary, Henry Green, and Ivy Compton-Burnett.

"Because of uncertainties about the immediate future, some investment trusts were transferring their funds into long-term, low-yield bonds of established market leaders. Shakespeare (up two points), Sophocles, and Dante all showed strength in mildly active trading. Milton rose fractionally, on reports that the powerful T. S. Eliot interests, which for years had taken a short position in this stock, had shifted to the other side of the market. Operations of the Great Books syndicate caused a fluttering demand for Plato and Aristotle.

"Among the American classics Melville continued to be the most active and once again ended the period with a net gain, but for the first time there was indication of short selling. Market insiders were saying that Melville backers had become overextended and that a reaction was certain to follow. Although there was little trading in Longfellow, rumors spread that the company might start an active sales campaign. Whittier was snowbound. Henry James was down three points and a fraction after the recent flurry. Emerson was firm at a depressed level with not much activity. We are inclined to believe that the issue is undervalued and offers a sterling opportunity to investors.

"The new poetry remains obscure, with not much public participation. An underlying tendency in the fiction market is the continuing slow decline of all novelists specializing in social protest and in optimistic pictures of the future. Symbolism is popular, psychoanalysis is riding high, and there is a brisk demand for original sin."

After this market letter was written, most of the tendencies it reported were carried farther. Faulkner common continued its rise and thereby strengthened the whole group of associated Southern novelists, particularly Katherine Anne Porter and Eudora Welty. Fitzgerald weakened in generally quiet trading, while remaining at levels consistently above those which prevailed before the 1950–51 flurry. The Hemingway extra dividend was announced in the summer of 1952 and led to a frenzied recovery, as our analyst had prophesied. Among the newer British equities, Joyce Cary proved attractive to more investors than competing firms, but many showed a preference for Graham Greene or George Orwell. There was less activity in American blue-chip stocks, and notably in Melville, but the limited trading was still at high prices. Overproduction led to a steep decline in Melville Critical Products. The expected rally in Emerson failed to materialize and may be delayed for years; long-term investors are advised to have patience. . . .

So I might summarize three recent years of trading on the exchange, still using the jargon of a market analyst—and may I never be forced to use it again after this chapter! But the summary is accurate enough in its rough fashion, and it shows that changes in the American reputations of famous authors—even of recognized classics—have been as intemperate as the Chicago winter climate. For living authors, especially the younger ones, whose livelihood partly depends on whether reviewers like their work, the changes may be tragic, even fatal to their careers. After a chorus of unfavorable reviews, perhaps undeserved, their next books mightn't be published. That, as we shall see, is only one hazard of the literary profession.

VIII.

A NATURAL HISTORY
OF THE AMERICAN WRITER

I hope the title of this chapter isn't too pretentious. Natural history is defined in the *New Century Dictionary* as "the science or study dealing with all objects in nature, now esp. animals and sometimes plants; also the aggregate of knowledge connected with such objects; also, a work dealing with such objects." I should like to discuss present-day American writers as objects in nature. Though more informally, I should like to write in the spirit of Margaret Mead when she described various tribes of New Guinea, including the Arapesh, the Mundugumor, and the Tchambuli, or in the not dissimilar spirit of Robert S. and Helen Merrell Lynd on their two expeditions to Middletown U.S.A.

I have none of the equipment these others carried with them, no doctorate in anthropology or sociology, or learning that would justify a doctorate, and I haven't even buttons or plug tobacco to bribe the natives. On the other hand, writers are my own tribe, and I can claim some such knowledge of them as was shown by Sir Peter Buck when he described the customs of his own Maoris. I have been living among them—writers, not Maoris—since I underwent the initiation rites of young manhood. During all those years I have been making random notes on subjects like "Where Writers Come From," "How They Get Started," "How They Earn Their Livings," "Their Domestic Habits," "Their Public Status," and "The Writer's Psychology." It was after reading a book on this last topic that I decided to make further notes and reduce them to some sort of order. The book was *The Writer and Psychoanalysis*, by Dr. Edmund Bergler, and I recommend it for its value as an irritant; it should be introduced into every writer's private library like a grain of sand into a pearl-bearing oyster.

Dr. Bergler is a Viennese psychoanalyst, now practicing and writing in New York, whose specialty is treating the occupational disease known as "writer's block." The disease, or group of symptoms, is almost as common among writers as morning sickness among pregnant women. Sometimes it cures itself in a day or a week, and the writer works steadily until his book is finished. Sometimes the book refuses to be born and the symptoms develop into a serious mental illness. "Many and varied," Dr. Bergler says, "are the maneuvers of the truly blocked writer in his attempts to get started again: the poor man"—and I have often found myself in his plight—"sharpens his pencil to take notes, then finds the point still not sharp enough; the typewriter stares up at him like a reproachful face; he is simply not in the mood, but will be tomorrow (except that tomorrow never comes); he feels a slight nausea and must first cure his upset stomach; he would like a drink, but one drink calls for more, and more drinks make him sleepy; he indulges in fantasies of grandeur, cashes in on achievements never reached, and at the end of all his twisting and turning feels only deep depression."

Perhaps the nausea and thirst and depression are accurate physical comments on the story he is trying to write. Perhaps in many cases—the possibility must be considered—writer's block is a mechanism designed to limit the production of bad literature, and perhaps Dr. Bergler's blocked patients, when they asked to be cured, were defying a law of providence and nature. There had been thirty-six of these patients, or analysands, when he wrote his book in 1950. Some of them, he says, were talented, but the statement isn't borne out by the plots of their stories, as the doctor repeats them, or by the samples he gives of their poems. The plots are commonplace, the poems are awkward and uninspired, and the reader can't help wondering whether Dr. Bergler wasn't performing a disservice to the public at large by encouraging these unhappy men and women to produce more stories and uninspired poems without the pangs of conscience they had spontaneously felt before they carried their troubles to the tribal medicine man.

Dr. Bergler rightly believed, like most physicians, that his duty to his patients came before his duty to the public. He subjected all thirty-six to deep analysis and reports that almost all were freed from their symptoms. Most of them went back to writing, although a few decided wisely that they hadn't enough talent and found other occupations. After meditating on all the case histories, Dr. Bergler wrote this book to put forward a general theory that is also a pretty sweeping condemnation of writers as a group. I have discussed the theory with several of his professional colleagues without finding any who accepted it. Dr. Bergler speaks for himself, and, if his notions are in any way representative, they represent only one type of analyst. Unfortunately the type is numerous, or at least vociferous; it consists of those who rush into print with dogmatic and simplified explanations of complicated patterns of behavior. The explanations are always put forward as scientific truths, but they usually conflict with one another except at a single point: almost all these print-hungry analysts want us to believe that the characters of men and women in society are determined at every step by the experiences of infants in the womb, or a few days out of it. But before trying to criticize Dr. Bergler and his fellow dogmatists, let me summarize his theory briefly and as fairly as I can.

Writing is a neurosis, the doctor says, like alcoholism and homosexuality. It is the symptom of an illness that goes back to the earliest stage of postnatal life, when the infant regards himself as an omnipotent monarch. But soon his omnipotence is threatened: the infant feels hungry, and the mother keeps him waiting for her breast. Reduced to helpless rage, the tiny monarch fancies—according to Dr. Bergler and some of his colleagues—that the mother "intends to *starve, devour, poison, choke, chop to pieces, drain, castrate* the child. . . . That 'septet of baby fears' becomes deeply embedded in the child's unconscious." He tries to revenge himself on the mother by acts of aggression, but finds that they lead to punishment. Thereupon the normal child diverts his aggressive impulses into games and make-believe. The future neurotic persists in the aggressive acts, is punished time and again, and finally learns to enjoy punishment—even to provoke it, so that he can luxuriate in a sense of guilt. He becomes an "orally regressed psychic masochist."

Such is the mechanism that—according to Dr. Bergler—underlies writing, alcoholism, and homosexuality. Since all these are types of oral regression, "there is nothing remarkable in the fact that they are frequently found in combination, or that the combination of writing and alcoholism is even more frequently observed. It must be stressed, however," the doctor adds judiciously, "that the triad is *not* typical of all writers." What is typical of them all—besides their masochistic attachment to the mother as "that giant ogre of the nursery"—is the depth of their regression and inner guilt. As an adult, every writer is "a perpetual defendant indicted before the tribunal of unconscious conscience. To counteract that indictment," Dr. Bergler says, "an alibi is instituted—the artistic creation. The inner alibi goes like this: 'I am not masochistically attached to Mother; Mother does not even exist.' Thus, in the process of productivity, the writer acts *both* roles: that of the 'giving' mother and [that of] the 'recipient' child: he gives himself, out of himself, beautiful ideas and words, thereby establishing autarchy."

Having described this mechanism, which, he says, is followed by writers "with amazing monotony," Dr. Bergler is able to explain in a few words the meaning of terms that critics have argued about for centuries. Aristotle tried to define the work of art, but the doctor has no patience with his attempt; the work of art, he says, "is nothing but an unconscious *secondary alibi defense.* . . . One sees the lawyer and hears his plea for the defendant; the resulting *plaidoyer,* when applied to the unconscious, is called, in creative people, a work of art." Here, as elsewhere, the italicized phrases in quotations are italicized by the doctor himself, who likes to be emphatic. Words, he says emphatically, are equivalent to milk for the writer. "This identification of *words* with *milk* is of great significance." His definition of poetry is quoted approvingly from the late Dr. A. A. Brill: "Poetry is a sensuous or mystic outlet through words, or, as it were, through a chewing and sucking of nice words and phrases." For the definitions that follow, Dr. Bergler himself is solely responsible:

Publishing one's work "is a form of exhibitionism."

The critic is usually "an inhibited writer filled unconsciously with undigested anger against the less inhibited of his confreres in the writing profession. . . . His unproductivity as a writer also results in a predilection for mediocrity, because mediocrity is, unconsciously, more easily forgiven by the sterile than is genuine talent."

"The basic drive which underlies imagination is voyeurism; imagination is the 'purified' successor to infantile peeping."

Talent "reduces itself to a palpable biopsychological entity. The difference in talent in writers can also be formulated: *it corresponds to the amount of compromise the unconscious Ego can wrest from the inner conscience*," or Superego. "That amount can be analytically increased"—in other words, Dr. Bergler can make authors more talented, "at least in some cases."

The writer is "just a neurotic operating his defense mechanism, without knowing it. . . . The idea that the writer is objective, and the highest representative of the time or of the culture in which he lives is, politely speaking, ridiculous." Elsewhere Dr. Bergler, speaking less politely, accuses every writer without exception of being a masochist, a sadist, a peeping Tom, an exhibitionist, a narcissist, an "injustice collector," and "a *depressed* person . . . *constantly haunted by fears of unproductivity*." The masochistic impulse lies deepest in his character, but it is concealed by sadistic acts that serve as "a pseudo-aggressive alibi—hence the chronic rebellion of the writer and his chronic attack on institutions, mores, prejudices." And so with another pair of symptoms: "The writer is an exquisite voyeur (imagination), who transposes the voyeuristic tendency into exhibitionism as a defense: by writing, he exhibits before the reader." "Being himself a neurotic, [he] is as competent to describe love as a blind man is to describe colors." "Writers concern themselves in their work exclusively with abnormal human reactions. Normality is not a subject dealt with in poetry of any kind."

"How about normal writers?" Dr. Bergler asks, and then dismisses the question. "The *epitheton ornans* 'normal' does not suit the writer; it corresponds to a *contradictio in adjecto*. It is as if one were to say: Hot snow, humanitarian Nazi, fragrant putrefaction. I have never encountered a normal writer, either in my office, or in private life, or in studying the life history of writers. I doubt if anyone has met such a phenomenon as a 'normal' writer. Normal people just don't feel impelled to write."

Dr. Bergler feels impelled to write, and has published ten books, in some of which he plays the part of a literary critic. By his own principles he would stand convicted of various abnormalities, including masochism, sadism, voyeurism, exhibitionism, narcissism, and a predilection for mediocrity. He wants us to understand, however, that his principles don't apply to the exceptional race of psychoanalysts, whose knowledge exempts them from human faults. "In twenty years of psychoanalytic practice," the doctor says, "I have seen a great deal of neurotics, *intra* and *extra muros*. The most depressed, pitiful, and sordid lot has been that of writers. True, a few writers achieve fame and wealth; but these make up at best 0.001 per cent of all writers. The majority are poor, never achieve material success, are habitually misunderstood, struggle along, either scornfully making a poor living in some tangential profession (journalism, copywriting in advertising concerns, teaching, clerking, et cetera) or being lifelong parasites. . . . And still the true writer takes all this in his stride, not knowing, of course"—but Dr. Bergler knows—"that he chooses masochistically, because of his inner wish to suffer, a poverty-stricken profession, in which he will achieve neither fame nor money, nor acknowledgment and esteem. A writer sacrifices unconsciously everything else to his defense mechanism—this is his *modus vivendi*."

I have lived among working writers ever since I left college, and I simply can't recognize my friends and acquaintances in Dr. Bergler's picture. The writers I know are sometimes more depressed than "normal" persons—whoever those may be—but at other times they are more than normally elated. They laugh more than the business people I know. They like to have parties at which they eat very well, with lots of wine at dinner, talk excitedly about persons and places, flirt and flatter, play word games, and late in the evening they like to dance—if they are under fifty; sometimes the older ones dance too, but often they merely talk. Young and old, they are usually good talkers, which means they are also good listeners; they get attention because they give attention.

Dr. Bergler makes us feel, I hope mistakenly, that his thirty-six patients would have been unpopular in any group composed of working writers and their families. The patients were too depressed and pitiful, as he says, they were too self-centered, and most of them lacked the professional qualifications that would entitle them to join any such group. A few had written successful plays or novels, but had found themselves unable to continue their careers. Most of the patients—to judge from the doctor's account—would seem to have been advertising or publicity men, schoolteachers, and women living on alimony. Each of them had written some poems or stories in adolescence, and that is one reason why Dr. Bergler feels justified in calling them writers. The other and stronger reason is that they all showed symptoms of what he calls "the writer's neurosis." Why

shouldn't it be called the non-writer's neurosis? "Here is a clinical
example," the doctor says. "A writer who had published six books
(one of them a good one) entered analysis when the lack of success
of his last book became apparent." In other words, he came to Dr.
Bergler because the public told him clearly that he had ceased to be
a writer.

Whatever the doctor says about knowing some writers *extra
muros* and studying the biographies of others, his conclusions are
based primarily on his thirty-six analysands. Perhaps that explains
why the conclusions are different from mine: we are talking about
two separate groups of persons. My subject is writers, and particularly working writers; Dr. Bergler's subject is persons who suffer
from the malady that has come to be known as the literary temperament. A great number of failed or frustrated writers show signs of
being afflicted with that temperament. They are described by some
of the doctor's colleagues—for example, Daniel E. Schneider, author of *The Psychoanalyst and the Artist*—as symptomatic artists, on
the ground that they have the symptoms but not the art. Many working writers start out with the symptoms but lose them as a result of
their professional experiences. Eventually the literary temperament
—if they ever possessed it—is so disguised in them and overlaid with
other traits that working writers appear to be persons of another
type, or of many other types. Dr. Bergler's patients, so he says,
repeat the same pattern "with amazing monotony." Writers in my
sense of the word follow many patterns of conduct and may be as
different in personality as, let us say, Henry Miller and Sir Winston
Churchill, or Truman Capote and Robert Frost, or Faith Baldwin,
Dylan Thomas, and Virginia Woolf.

WHAT WRITERS ARE, AND WHY

For me a writer is a man or woman who writes. Simple and all-
embracing as the definition seems to be, it starts by excluding most
of Dr. Bergler's patients and ends by having implications in several
fields—vocational, social, functional, and psychological—that it
might be useful to explore.

In vocational terms, the writer is a person for whom writing is the
central activity—though it isn't always the activity that takes most
of his time. Until each of them was in his sixties, T. S. Eliot probably
devoted more time to being a banker, an editor, and a publisher,

Wallace Stevens more time to being an insurance executive, and William Carlos Williams more to being a physician with a general practice, but writing was central with all of them. Of course, all three are poets, and that, in our present society, explains the division of time. Prose writers earn more by writing; hence they can—and should—make it their profession as well as their central interest.

In social terms the writer is a person *with readers*. His consciousness of having readers, now or in the future, and thus leading the most important part of his life in public, helps to determine his social character. He must assume a role, or a whole series of roles. When he talks to himself he wants his words to be overheard; note that writers' private notebooks are almost always written to be read. He wants to communicate; even the most abstract and difficult poets have some clear message for the reader, if the message is only "See how difficult my poems can be!" All writers are nourished by the sense of having an audience—or, in exceptional cases, like that of William Blake, by faith that the audience will someday be found. If they lose that feeling it is as if they had been deprived of some essential food; often they suffer from psychosomatic complaints that sometimes prove fatal, and almost always they stop writing. There is the familiar example of the German novelists under Hitler. Some of them wrote books that could be published because they flattered or at least didn't offend the ruling powers. Others weren't allowed to publish anything, but their exiled colleagues said, "Wait till Hitler is overthrown and we'll find that they've all written novels and put them away in their desk drawers." When Hitler was overthrown, all the desk drawers proved to be empty.

In functional terms, the writer is a craftsman whose medium is the written language; he works with words as a painter works with shapes and colors, a composer with tones, and a cabinetmaker with wood, glass, and metal. Like every good craftsman, he wants to make objects, or artifacts, that will have an independent existence and will play a part in the lives of people he has never seen.[1] Like

---

1. "To write something of enduring beauty, this was the ambition of every writer: as it was the ambition of the joiner and architect and the constructor of any kind. It was not the beauty but the endurance, for endurance was beautiful. It was also all that we could do. It was a consolation, even a high and positive joy, to make something true: some table which, sat on, when it was meant only to be eaten off, would not splinter or shatter. It was not for the constructor that the beauty was made, but for the thing itself. He would triumph to know that some contribution had been made: some sort

every good craftsman, he has reasons for believing in the high importance of his own medium; and the writer, so it seems to me, has the best reasons of all. Language is the specifically human gift and the cohesive force that holds each tribe and nation together. One might call it a fifth dimension of human life, for the human community exists in language almost as it does in space and time. From another point of view it is our greatest cooperative undertaking, with millions of persons each year inventing new words or turns of speech, most of which will soon be forgotten. One function of writers is to choose among these innumerable possibilities, fashion a literary medium, and invent new expressions of their own, which in turn may be used by millions of others.

Writers, of course, have other functions too: notably they tell stories that become the myths of the tribe, as well as presenting characters that can serve as tribal heroes and villains. At this point, however, I should like to emphasize their linguistic function, because it is being overlooked by so many theorists. Dr. Bergler—to mention only one—has written a whole book about writers without stopping to think that their words are intended to have a meaning for readers. Words for Dr. Bergler are simply "milk" that the writer produces out of himself; their value is purely subjective. He forgets the most important feature of the "milk." It must be transformed into products with an objective value for others, or else it will be refused and the writer may stop producing it.[2] The words of great writers may set the linguistic patterns of whole nations. Dante—not alone, but vastly more than others—set the pattern that would be followed in Italy. If Dante had been born in Venice or Rome or

---

of consoling contribution quite timeless and without relation to his own profit. Sometimes we knew, half tipsy or listening to music, that at the heart of some world there lay a chord to which vibrating gave reality. With its reality there was music and truth and the permanence of good workmanship. To give birth to this, with whatever male travail, was not only all that man could do: it was the human contribution to the universe. . . . This was it, as the poets realized, to be a mother of immortal song: to say Yes when it was, and No when it was: to make enduringly true that perhaps quite small occasional table off which subsequent generations could eat, without breaking it down: to help the timeless benevolence which should be that of this lonely and little race. . . ."—Quoted from *The Goshawk* by T. H. White.

2. Dr. Bergler, who speaks of "the alibi sickness called writing," is comparatively free from the disease. He has absolutely no feeling for the accepted value of words and makes them mean what he wants them to mean, like Humpty Dumpty; for example, he thinks that an alibi, or plea of having been elsewhere, is the same as a denial, an excuse, or a self-justification.

Palermo instead of Tuscany, modern Italian would have been a different language—and one might add that modern Italians, who think mostly in words, like people everywhere, would have had slightly different thoughts.

What happened in France is a more complicated story, but once again writers played a central part in it. Sixteenth-century French was a rich and disorderly language that in many ways resembled Elizabethan English. Classical French, as written and spoken a hundred years later, was a new medium fashioned for the needs of polite society, which was also new at the time. Among those who worked to create the new medium were some opinionated poets, led by Malherbe, all the members of the new French Academy, and many fashionable ladies who invited men of letters to their salons, where ladies and guests argued politely about the words that could or couldn't be used in polite literature.[3] One result of their discussions and refinements was that classical French became an extremely supple language with a limited vocabulary, easily learned by foreigners, in which every word had a definite meaning. It was and deserved to be the second language of cultivated people in all the other European countries. Essentially it was a prose language, but Racine proved that it could also be a medium for poetry so flawless and moving that it not only survived as part of the living theater but also preserved a whole group of social and literary conventions. In the 1920s I used to attend performances of *Phèdre* in the French provinces. I came to feel that Racine, besides writing the play, had also formed the actors and had, in some measure, created and trained the audience.

These are great names I have mentioned, but the same sort of work is being done on a smaller scale by authors of our own time and country. One of their achievements in the last fifty years was the creation of a rich and flexible prose style based on Midwestern rather than New England speech. As a literary medium, the Midwestern style derives from Mark Twain, who is still the master of

3. Words that shouldn't be used, because they were thought to be vulgar, included almost all the names of household objects and domestic animals. After 1650 the word *souris*, or mouse, probably seemed more shocking in polite conversation than the word *merde* would seem three centuries later. In 1950 Parisians were telling the story of the taxi driver who found that he had a flat tire and uttered some picturesque obscenities. His passenger, an old lady in a feather boa, leaned out of the window and asked him, "Why can't you say just *merde* like everybody else?"

American prose, but it also owes a great deal to Gertrude Stein and Sherwood Anderson. Perhaps it owes more to Hemingway, whose novels made it so popular that it promised to become the accepted vehicle of American fiction. Soon the Midwestern style was affecting the popular speech from which it had developed, so that a whole generation of young Americans learned to talk like Hemingway's heroes. Writers are always changing the language in this fashion. As craftsmen in words, bent on improving their medium and giving it force and purity, they earn a respect from others that often they don't deserve as individuals. W. H. Auden, in his elegy for Yeats, expressed what I am trying to say in three short stanzas:

> Time that is intolerant
> Of the brave and innocent,
> And indifferent in a week
> To a beautiful physique,
>
> Worships language and forgives
> Everyone by whom it lives;
> Pardons cowardice, conceit,
> Lays its honors at their feet.
>
> Time that with this strange excuse
> Pardoned Kipling and his views,
> And will pardon Paul Claudel,
> Pardons him for writing well.

In psychological terms, the writer is a person who keeps trying to find the exact and meaningful words for any situation, because he believes that such words have a magic power. It is this word-mindedness that distinguishes writers from scholars, who deal with various orders of facts, and from intellectuals or speculative thinkers, who deal primarily with ideas. Many writers are also scholars or also speculative thinkers: for example, Thomas Huxley was all three. But facts retain their value whether or not they are expressed in words that cast a spell; often they are best conveyed in pictures or in columns of figures. Many ideas are capable of being expressed in mathematical symbols, and at other times they can be badly expressed, in the wrong words—as John Dewey often expressed them—without losing their value. Dewey wasn't a writer, properly speaking, and neither was his great precursor, C. S. Peirce. William James and Santayana were writers, but that hasn't any bearing on the question whether they were greater thinkers than Dewey or

Peirce. For the writer properly speaking, language is not only the medium in which he works but also the medium in which he lives and breathes. His private universe consists of words, and no experience seems quite real for him until the revealing and magical words have been found for it. Sometimes he regards himself as a soldier fighting against the unknown and unexpressed; he is like a Roman legionary always serving on the frontier. Sometimes he is an explorer trying to broaden that civilized homeland which is the area of consciousness, by finding the proper words for new experiences.

The writer—still in psychological terms—is a person who talks to himself, or better, who talks *in* himself. Usually when alone, but sometimes also in company, he conducts a silent conversation that is often described as a solitary monologue; in most cases it is really a dialogue. Often the subject of conversation is a domestic incident or an item in the newspaper—especially one that makes him angry—but in other cases it may be the story or essay or poem that the writer is working on. One of the speakers is the writer himself, and the other is his inner audience. The writer does most of the talking; perhaps he starts by presenting a situation in what he thinks are the right words to impress the audience, which seems to consist of a single person. The audience—or I had better say the auditor—is extremely critical; perhaps he doesn't say anything, but his silence implies, "What you say isn't effective; try it again and make it clearer and more exact."

Dr. Bergler believes that the solitary monologue is simply "the unconscious plea and *plaidoyer* of the inner lawyer," presenting his client's case to the unconscious conscience. But the plea is consciously expressed and the auditor is consciously present. Sometimes his judgment is expressed in words that are clearly heard by the inner ear. "You've got yourself into a fine pickle, Mr. Snively," he says. "Better throw the whole thing away and start over from the beginning." Often the judgment is severe—so much so that the writer gets discouraged and spends the whole day polishing two or three sentences in hope of winning the auditor's qualified approval. At other times the auditor is enthusiastic. "It's good, it's wonderful," he almost shouts. "Hurry and get it down on paper before you forget the words, because they're right." Often—perhaps in most cases—the finished story is a transcription and revision of what the writer has already told his inner audience.[4]

4. Revel Denney, the only American poet I know who is also a sociologist,

CHILDHOOD AND EARLY ADOLESCENCE

Not being a psychoanalyst, and not being persuaded by the explanations of those psychoanalysts who have tried to simplify the subject, I don't know how the writer comes to develop this word-mindedness or this habit of talking in himself. Perhaps Dr. Bergler is right, and it is really some event in earliest infancy that sets him on the path he will follow through life. The question is hard to discuss in practical terms, because not one of us remembers back to the time when he did or didn't regard his mother as the giant ogre of the nursery. I can remember being punished, and pretty often, but it doesn't seem to me that I derived any conscious or unconscious pleasure from the punishment. On the contrary, I tried very hard to avoid it, sometimes by telling lies—if I didn't think they'd be found out—and sometimes even by being a good boy. There are three remembered circumstances or stages in my boyhood and early adolescence that made me think of becoming a writer when I grew up. Since the same stages can be found in the life of almost every other writer who has tried to set down his memories, they might— it is always possible—have more to do with his choice of profession than any trauma in early infancy.

First, I started reading when I was six and kept it up for the next ten years. My mother used to say that she might as well have lost her son, because he never talked to her any more and she hardly ever saw his face, it was always in a book. I don't think I got much out of my early reading, except a miscellaneous lot of historical and geographical items that somehow stuck in my head. I read in a daze and sometimes didn't remember the story of a book I had just set down. But the reading furnished subjects and scenes and characters and words, thousands of new words, for the inner conversation that had already begun when I was six and that still continues after fifty years. Later I came to believe that all writers were great readers before they started to write. The boy or girl whose nose is always in a book is likely to think about writing books of his own.

Second, I wasn't adjusted to any group and had no playmates most of the time. When I wasn't reading I often told stories to my-

___

told me that his boyhood audience was often the last author he had been reading. For a long time he conducted imaginary conversations with Horatio G. Alger: "My hero's in trouble, Mr. Alger. Tell me, what would a brave boy do?" A later auditor of his was Samuel Johnson.

self, as lonely boys are accustomed to do. The stories, though told in Pittsburgh, were usually concerned with three young Scottish Highlanders, Donald, Dugald, and Duncan, whose names I had found in a book of fairy tales. Donald, the leader, was an honest, brave, resourceful lad, but when I was ten years old I began to get bored with him and introduced another character named Allison, who was brilliant, reckless, and always getting into trouble. I didn't know at the time that Alison, written with one "l," was usually a girl's name. My fictional character was named for my best and almost my only friend, Allison Crawford, whom I had met outside the East Liberty branch of the Carnegie Library. He was two years older than I, a sandy-haired boy with a high, thin bridge to his nose that gave him a look of quizzical contempt. I thought, and still think, that I had never met anyone so brilliant or so far beyond his years. At fifteen he wrote some stories that are still remembered by his high-school classmates. He also began to visit the red-light district that flourished on Second Avenue, chiefly because he thought it was the reckless thing to do. At sixteen he contracted gonorrhea, which was never cured. At seventeen he got into a street fight with an amateur boxing champion. He was kicked in the bladder, complications set in, and he died a few months later. At twelve and thirteen, when I knew him best, he already seemed to carry with him an intimation, almost a halo, of early death. The stories I told myself about Allison usually ended with his being killed by trait'rous Southrons, after he had recklessly saved the lives of Donald, Dugald, and Duncan, who would never forget their friend. After I had followed the real Allison to high school, I wrote a story about the fictional Allison that was admired by my English teacher and was read aloud to the class—but that marked the beginning of a third stage in the future writer's career.

Before discussing it, I should say that loneliness at some period in childhood or adolescence is an experience of all the writers whom, as Dr. Bergler would say, I have met *intra et extra muros*. Their isolation hasn't always been physical. Sometimes the future writer is part of an affectionate family group, but still he has a feeling—whether or not it is justified—that he is neglected by his brothers and sisters, disregarded by his schoolmates, left standing pitifully alone. There may be any one of a hundred or a thousand different reasons for the feeling. One boy is persecuted for looking effeminate—"Yah, sissy!"—and another for being poor and not dressing like other boys. Still another is an alien, the only Jew in his class, a Negro in a white neighborhood, or a Yankee in the South. Often the future writer has a physical defect that may be ugliness, short-sightedness, a disfiguring birthmark, or a club foot like Philip's in Somerset Maugham's *Of Human Bondage*. The novelist explained later that he had given Philip a club foot because it seemed to be the psychological equivalent of his own boyhood stutter. Sometimes the isolation is the fault of the child's parents, who are richer or better educated than their neighbors and won't let their son or daughter make friends. Sometimes it starts from an accident of residence, as it did in my own case: we lived in a flat next to my father's office in a business district, and there were no other boys in the block. Like many other lonely children, I didn't wear the right clothes or use the same words as my schoolmates.[5]

The isolation might also be caused by a domestic tragedy. When a famous poet was eleven years old and living happily in Savannah, his father went mad, killed the mother, and committed suicide. The children were separated, and the future poet was sent north to live with his aunts in New Bedford, where, having no playmates at first, he read and dreamed. A still more famous author, Nathaniel Hawthorne, suffered an injury to his foot that kept him confined to the house for two of his boyhood years; they were the years in which he acquired his taste for solitude. At Harvard I knew a young man who was handsome, tall, came of a good family, belonged to several clubs, and wrote poems. I told him that he reminded me of the riddle: What animal has soft fur, sharp claws, catches mice, and barks? Of course the animal was a cat. When you asked why it barked, you

5. Reuel Denney tells me that American physicists, of whose lives he has made a study, were also lonely as children. But they thought or daydreamed about *things* and how to make them work, where the future writers told stories about imaginary people. In "Why I Write," an essay reprinted in *Such, Such Were the Joys,* George Orwell describes a writer's typical boyhood. He says in part:

"From a very early age, perhaps the age of five or six, I knew that when I grew up I should be a writer. . . . I was the middle child of three, but there was a gap of five years on either side, and I barely saw my father before I was eight. For this and other reasons I was somewhat lonely, and I soon developed disagreeable mannerisms which made me unpopular throughout my schooldays. I had the lonely child's habit of making up stories and holding conversations with imaginary persons, and I think from the very start my literary ambitions were mixed up with the feeling of being isolated and undervalued. I knew that I had a facility with words and a power of facing unpleasant facts, and I felt that this created a sort of private world in which I could get my own back for my failure in everyday life."

were told that no riddle should be too easy. My friend's poems were like the cat's bark—or so it seemed until he explained that he had injured his heart as a boy. Kept alone in his room, he had read a great deal and had begun writing poems to keep himself company.

All these are examples of wounded people, although the wounds are of various orders, physical and emotional. What they suggest is something a little different from Edmund Wilson's theory of the wound and the bow. Wilson presented his theory by retelling the myth of Philoctetes as it appears in Sophocles' drama of the same name. The hero had been deserted by the other Greeks because of a foul-smelling wound in his foot and because of his agonized cries. But he owned a magic bow that never missed its mark, and the Greeks begged him to come back after they had learned from an oracle that his bow was the only weapon capable of defeating the Trojans. In Wilson's interpretation, "The victim of a malodorous disease which renders him abhorrent to society and periodically degrades him and makes him helpless is also the master of a superhuman art which everybody has to respect and which the normal man finds he needs." Moreover, ". . . the bow would be useless without Philoctetes himself. It is in the nature of things . . . that they cannot have the irresistible weapon without its loathsome owner, who upsets the processes of normal life by his curses and his cries."

That statement of the myth would apply to some great men of letters, and also to men who were great in other fields, but it wouldn't apply to the typical and not always highly talented young writers whose early careers I have been trying to describe. Sometimes they recovered from their wounds and became well-adjusted and popular with their classmates without losing the desire to write. Always the wound itself was less important than the isolation to which it led. The isolation gave them time to read and tempted them to conduct imaginary conversations with imaginary playmates. It heightened their feeling of identity, or separateness—sometimes to a dangerous degree—and helped to furnish the sense of perspective that writers have to possess. Forced to live somewhat apart from their classmates—and later from their business associates—they could look at them as if from a distance and might even learn to move about almost invisibly—"in the fourth dimension," as Kipling said that he did in his Indian days. Finally—since they fancied that other boys and girls looked down on them—they tried to assert their personal worth by the best available means: by telling others, or by writing down and trying to publish, stories like those they had already told themselves.

That begins a third stage in the future writer's career, the stage at which his work is received with a measure of social approval. Usually this public appearance is overlooked in theoretical discussions of the writer's life, though it is often described in autobiographical novels. Dr. Bergler doesn't even mention it—but then he doesn't mention the first two stages either, since his theory is based on the pre-verbal behavior of infants in the nursery. The third stage belongs to adolescence, and I think it is crucial. People sometimes ask why all the boys and girls who are passionate readers, who spend much time alone and fall into the habit of telling themselves stories, don't try to become writers. One answer is, of course, that not all of them have enough talent—or a chance to be treated by Dr. Bergler, who says he can increase talent analytically, "at least in some cases." But how do they learn, in terms of practical experience, whether the talent is there to be expressed or increased?

Quite simply, they show something they have written to a teacher or to their classmates and find whether it is approved. Perhaps their compositions are read aloud in class and the class listens, or even laughs at the jokes. Perhaps the adolescent writer is seized by the itch for publication and hand-letters or typewrites or mimeographs a school newspaper that is passed from one student to another; if there are favorable comments the future writer hears them. Perhaps the school paper already exists, and he contributes jingles or stories. He is told that a girl he has always admired, but has been afraid to approach, was impressed by one of the stories and said it was "positively brilliant." That is strong wine for a high-school boy, especially for one who has always fancied that he was disregarded or even despised by his classmates. A football or basketball player might take the praise for granted, but it intoxicates the boy who has been a lonely reader. Dreaming of victories, he determines to go on writing—or, if there are no victories and nobody likes his work, he wonders whether he mightn't win success and social approval in some other profession.

I am simplifying a process that continues through high school and college, and sometimes for years after graduation. In the end one might say that the writer has been nominated by his teachers and classmates and elected by a body of readers; his choice of a profession has been socially confirmed. I have never met a young writer of promise who wasn't eager to have his work printed and praised. "Exhibitionism!" Dr. Bergler has told us, but his remark is an example of a bad habit to which many psychoanalysts are addicted, I mean the habit of explaining all types of social behavior in terms of sexual aberrations. An exhibitionist, in the primary meaning of the word, is a man or a woman—but usually a man— who gets a sexual thrill from indecently exposing himself. A young writer exposes his mind, sometimes indecently, but his desire to be read and praised is completely normal in this world where all of us are hungry for social approval.

All of us, artists and salesmen, executives, mechanics, and day laborers, are engaged in a competition for social status, and the competition is perhaps fiercer in high school than it is in later life. The status of future writers isn't exalted. In a big-city high school there are always the athletic crowd and the social crowd. Usually there is also the literary crowd, which ranks below the other two and is somewhat distrusted for being eccentric—but still, it does have a status, and that gives a little security to its members and sets them somewhat above the undifferentiated mass of students.[6] There are times when the skills of the future writers are needed by the others, as Philoctetes and his bow were needed. School news must be gathered and written, a class oration must be delivered, and graduation exercises don't seem complete without a class song or a class poem. Very early the future writers acquire the habit of being read, and soon the reader has become an essential part of their writing. Some of them will afterward create the image of an ideal audience; they will write for the approval of Goethe and Tolstoi, or of Yeats and Rilke; but they will also count on having readers among the living. If they lose the sense of having those readers, of being socially useful and approved, they will often suffer from writer's block, and some of them might go to Dr. Bergler to have their professional status reaffirmed.

Dr. Bergler would tell them, of course, that they "want to be masochistically refused"—if he wrote English he would say that they wanted to enjoy the masochistic pleasure of being refused— "by the pre-oedipal mother, that giant ogre of the nursery." In offer-

6. At Harvard in 1954, the social crowd, the athletic crowd, and the literary crowd were known respectively as the clubbies, the jockstraps, and the arty party.

ing this explanation he would be illustrating still another weakness
of many psychoanalytical theorists. Most of the Freudian analysts
don't share the weakness, since they are quick to acknowledge that
we live in a world of complicated social relations. Many others, however, are obsessed with a desire for simplification that takes a metaphysical and even a theological turn.[7] Like Dr. Bergler they want
to find a pre-social pattern for every form of social behavior, and
they try to trace the pattern back from the crib to the bassinette
and thence to the womb. One pictures them dripping with amniotic
fluid as they tell us, scientifically, just how it feels to be a happy
foetus. Often they describe the birth trauma as if they had just under-
gone that shattering experience; they tell us, scientifically, that it
is the cause of all our psychological ills. Dr. Bergler is a little less
radical than some of his colleagues. He is willing to grant the infant
a few weeks of life in the outer world—say eight or ten—before it
begins to exhibit that primal pattern of neurosis for which the doctor
has been seeking. Once found, however, the pattern proves to be
so broadly inclusive that it explains, scientifically, both alcoholism
and homosexuality, as well as the behavior of every writer from
Shakespeare to Mickey Spillane. It even explains the difference in
talent between the two writers, for Dr. Bergler would tell us that
Shakespeare's unconscious ego was able to wrest a greater degree
of compromise from his inner conscience, or Superego: the compromise was *Hamlet*.

In addition to the unscientific dogmatism of such a theory, and its
complete lack of literary feeling, it also reveals a serious logical weakness. Logically the first form assumed by any psychological condition
isn't the same as its cause and isn't the same as the condition existing today. We might take, for example, the baby's reaction to its
mother. Although we don't know how the baby feels, we might reasonably assume that the mother (or the nurse at the hospital, who is
never mentioned in psychoanalytic theories) is its first experience of

7. The picture of human life presented by many analysts can easily be
translated into terms of Christian theology. First comes the Garden of Eden,
or the womb, and then the Fall of Man, which is variously interpreted by
different analysts: sometimes it is the birth trauma, sometimes (as in Bergler)
it is masochistic dependence on the mother, and sometimes it is the Oedipus
complex. Afterward man lives in a state of Total Depravity (or neurosis),
unless he achieves Salvation (or "sublimation," or "adjustment") by an act
of Charity (which is called "transference"), or else is snatched from the jaws
of hell by Divine Grace. This last takes the shape of intervention by the
analyst, whose insight is another word for the Divine.

what might be called "otherness." That is, the mother appears as something outside the baby, immensely more powerful than the baby, capable of granting or withholding benefits, and essential to the baby's nourishment. Later this conception of otherness would be extended to the father, by a process of analogy that is deeper than logic. Still later it would be extended to many other persons and institutions, or natural conditions, so that it would seem quite reasonable for us to speak of mother earth, mother nature, alma mater, the mother tongue, and the mother country. At last it would be society at large that occupied the mother's place and assumed her functions; here again was something outside the adult, immensely more powerful than the adult, and capable of granting or withholding benefits. The nourishing milk of society would take the form of personal income, or simply of money.

Many psychoanalytic formulations make better sense if we change two simple words in them: if we read "money" when the analyst says "milk," and "society" when he says "mother." "You suffer from a feeling of insecurity," the analyst may tell his patient (or subtly lead the patient to conclude for himself), "because your mother took her breast away; she weaned you too soon." Psychoanalysts almost always talk about breasts, even though most of their patients were bottle babies. Perhaps, if the patient is a writer, he suffers from insecurity because his last book didn't sell, and a manuscript was returned by the *Saturday Evening Post*, and he doesn't know where the money's coming from. Writers have other worries too, like everyone else in this imperfect world, but they are engaged in a financially hazardous profession—as we shall see—that makes them think a little more about money than most Americans are forced to do. I know a distinguished writer named, it doesn't matter, but let's call him George Ollendorf, who had suffered a quite serious breakdown when he was forty. At that time he was already a pretty famous man; he had a family to maintain, a position to support, and very little income. "I worried all the time and couldn't work," George said. "My friends found me some very good doctors and therapists, but I don't think that any of them helped me in the least. Then Betty inherited a good deal of money, enough to keep us going for a long time. I felt better right away, and I've been working ever since."

IX.

A NATURAL HISTORY, CONTINUED

Where Writers Come From

The republic of letters is in some ways desperately snobbish, but nobody is excluded from it because of his family background; in that respect it is a true democracy. By the middle of the twentieth century American writers might come from any economic level and any section of the country, if they weren't born abroad. They might come from any college or university, or none, and from almost any of the racial stocks and cultural groups that compose this nation of peoples. They were, however, more likely to come from certain backgrounds; as sociologists would say, the incidence of authorship was higher in some groups than it was in others. It was very high among the children of professional families, of many racial origins, living in the Northeastern states, especially if the children were educated in Eastern preparatory schools and at any of the Ivy League colleges. The lowest rate for the native-born was among Indians and Spanish-Americans living in the Mountain states; it came close to being no rate at all. On the other hand, there was a high incidence of authorship among Mormons born in the same region.

I don't know that sociologists have ever studied what they would call the racial provenience of American writers, although it would make an interesting subject for a doctoral dissertation. Our nineteenth-century authors were mostly of English stock, with an admixture of Dutch blood in New York; Melville and Whitman were both half Dutch. Elsewhere there were some Pennsylvania Germans, French Huguenots, and Scotch-Irish (though not many of these), with a thin sprinkling of O'Briens and O'Reillys. Bret Harte was our first famous author of Jewish descent. After 1890 the newer racial stocks began to come forward one at a time, as if to mark, in each case, the integration of a new group into American culture. First the still foreign-sounding names had appeared as those of boxers, then as those of politicians in the working-class wards down by the river; then came the businessmen, the college football players (in the second generation), and finally one of the names would be signed to a best-selling novel. There had been another pattern in literature. First we read about members of the new group as apparently stupid but really shrewd and lovable persons who made funny remarks in broken English (like Hashimura Togo, the Japanese Schoolboy). Other members of the group would then be presented in angry books, as tragic or pathetic spokesmen for their people. Still later their children would be presented simply as human beings to be valued for themselves.

The literary pattern is clearest in the case of the Irish, because of their group consciousness and their long experience as an oppressed minority. The first Irish-American author who won, and deserved to win, a national reputation was Finley Peter Dunne, in the 1890s. His Mr. Dooley was a saloon keeper who discussed national politics with a mixture of innocence and wisdom and whose eyes filled with tears—though we don't read the sadder dialogues today—when he discussed the sorrows of Irish immigrants. If we except Donn Byrne, that romantic Orangeman, Scott Fitzgerald was the next really famous Irish-American author. Like Dunne he had been accepted into the ruling Protestant group, and unlike Dunne he wrote about that group, so that his Irishness was a little disguised, but it remained an undertone in all his stories; it gave him a sense of standing apart that sharpened his observation of social differences. He liked to give his heroes Irish names or, at the very least, an Irish lilt to their voices. James T. Farrell, beginning in the 1930s, wrote about the Irish on the South Side of Chicago, not far from the saloon where Mr. Dooley used to hold forth, but there wasn't much humor in Farrell's stories, nor was there any attempt to please the ruling group. Most of his characters were pathetic creatures, oppressed by conditions, and his underlying mood was indignation at their being denied a chance for a better life.

By the 1950s there were distinguished Irish writers in all branches of American literature, including the criticism of abstract art (James Johnson Sweeney) and the translation of Greek tragedies (Robert Fitzgerald). *The Trouble of One House*, by Brendan Gill, is good enough in itself to stand for much of the newer Irish-American fiction. Gill tells the story of a cultivated and prosperous family that happens to be Catholic and of Irish descent, but whose troubles are those of human beings everywhere in modern life. Although his novel is more skillfully written than anything by Farrell, or even by Scott Fitzgerald, it lacks the emotional power of those earlier books conceived at a time when the American Irish were still in some ways an oppressed group. That loss of power belongs to the pattern too, for the sorrows of a novelist—including his racial sorrows—are part of his emotional stock in trade.

The Irish were literary pioneers and were followed by dozens of other racial and cultural groups. After 1900 there appeared in succession—though not in quite this order—the South German Catholics (Dreiser), the North German Protestants (H. L. Mencken, Ruth Suckow), the prosperous and highly cultivated German Jews (Gertrude Stein, Paul Rosenfeld), and the Scandinavians (among them O. E. Rolvaag, who lived in Minnesota, wrote in Norwegian, and translated his own novels into English). Soon there were also scores of writers among the newly arrived Polish and Russian Jews, perhaps beginning with Mary Antin and Abraham Cahan. Negro writers had been published for many years, but after 1930 they spoke with more authority and appeared in greater number. Richard Wright was the most distinguished, and Frank Yerby the most cynical and successful; he published romantic novels about white Southern planters and was the first American Negro to earn a million dollars by his writing. The Armenians appeared in 1934, with William Saroyan, and the Italians in 1939, with Pietro Di Donato's *Christ in Concrete*. I am thinking of writers who learned their trade in this country, not of adult immigrants or refugees who had learned it in Europe. Had I included those others, I might have mentioned precursors in several groups, going back as far as Lorenzo da Ponte, who died more than a hundred years ago, after teaching New Yorkers to like Italian opera.

By 1950 there were professional writers who represented many newer and sometimes rather localized groups, including the Greeks (A. I. Bezzerides and Kimon Friar), the Croatians (with the late Louis Adamic), the Sicilians (Jerre Mangione), the Dutch in Michigan (David Cornel DeJong), the Icelanders of the Dakotas (Holger Cahill), the Frisian Islanders (Feike Feikema), the Nisei (S. I. Hayakawa), and even the Koreans (Younghill Kang). A few of the larger racial groups were still seriously underrepresented in American literature; they included the Poles (Marya Zaturenska), the French Canadians (John Kerouac), and the Hungarians (represented chiefly by refugees). These groups were still at the stage of producing businessmen and football heroes. Others, like the Mexicans and the Puerto Ricans, were such recent arrivals and were so handicapped educationally that they had no writers to speak for them in English; their admired representatives were still boxers or baseball players. Their time in literature will come. Every group has something of its own to contribute, a special experience or sense of life, and all of them will someday do their part to enrich American writing.

Economically the provenience of American writers—or one might better say their background and class loyalty—has changed more than once during the last sixty years. In the 1890s writing was regarded as a leisure-class occupation. Few of the writers themselves had leisure-class incomes; more of them than today were starving in garrets, but they wrote for a privileged audience, and their fictional heroes regarded themselves as gentlemen born. Successful writers were entertained by Andrew Carnegie and might even be supported by William C. Whitney, who gave more than a million dollars, in the course of years, to his friend Finley Peter Dunne. It was a time when Lorenzo de' Medici was a pattern for millionaires. The National Institute of Arts and Letters, founded at the turn of the century, was subsidized by Archer M. Huntington, as the National Arts Club was subsidized by Spencer Trask. Later Trask's widow endowed their mansion, Yaddo, near Saratoga Springs, as a summer retreat for writers and artists. She hoped that they would regard themselves as well-bred guests of the family.

All this munificence encouraged writers to accept the leisure-class standards, and the standards were also enforced by the truly great magazines of the 1890s: *Harper's*, the *Century*, and *Scribner's*.

When Edith Wharton, then a young society matron, first ventured into literature by writing three poems she thought might be published, she sent one poem to each of the magazines, with her calling card. All three were accepted, and possibly would have been accepted if they had come from Kokomo, being fairly distinguished poems, but the calling cards helped the editors to make up their minds. Theodore Dreiser, the poor German boy from Indiana, felt that the magazines and their contributors existed on a happier planet. "These writers," he said in *Newspaper Days*, "seemed far above the world of which I was a part. Indeed I began to picture them as creatures of the greatest luxury and culture, gentlemen and ladies all, comfortably housed, masters of servants, possessing estates, or at least bachelor quarters, having horses and carriages, and received here, there and everywhere with nods of recognition and smiles of approval."

Dreiser would write about his own class of small-town boys and girls making their way, or failing to make it, in Chicago and New York. His early work, which had fervent admirers in literary circles, may have had something to do with the change in economic loyalties after 1910, though I suspect that the change would have taken place if Dreiser had never written. Many of the younger writers were professing radical sentiments and joining the Socialist party. Millionaires were withdrawing their support from literature, and, on the other hand, a broader, well-educated middle-class public was being formed that was willing to buy sophisticated novels. After 1910 writing came to be regarded as one of the middle-class professions, open to young men and women who were highly trained for the work. Writers talked less about being gentlemen or ladies and took to presenting middle-class heroes, but they tried not to follow a middle-class pattern in their personal lives. Even if they earned comfortable incomes, as many of them did after 1920, they spent the incomes for travel and services and entertainment, rather than houses or motor cars, and lived in the style of prosperous gipsies.

Once again I am offering a few general remarks on what might well be a subject for sociological researches. I can picture the postgraduate students setting out with questionnaires and coming back with charts. "Where were you living in 1930?" they would ask a number of writers in succession. "Did you own your house? How did you support yourself during the depression? What was your income in 1930 and what was it ten years later?" Putting together the answers to questions like these, our students would find that there was, after 1930, still another change in literary loyalties. Instead of being leisure-class or bohemian, the younger writers of the time began to picture themselves as genuine proletarians. More of them than before came from working-class families. For others the role of oppressed worker was easy to assume, since they were living on very small stipends from the Federal Writers' Project, but their behavior was not without an element of inverted snobbery. Young men from good Eastern universities disguised themselves in dirty cotton-flannel shirts while they tried to write proletarian novels like those admired in Russia. Most of the novels were merely stylish, for the time, and were based on second-hand feeling, but some of them revealed a serious effort to broaden the horizons of American fiction. We began to read stories about coal miners, turret-lathe operators, filling-station attendants, production-line workers, oil drillers, lumber-mill hands in the Northwest, Southern sharecroppers, and fruit pickers in California—employed, unemployed, or on strike. All sorts of backgrounds and occupations, or the lack of them, appeared in literature for the first time, as if to remind us that earlier novelists had failed to present many broad levels of American society.

The horizons of fiction narrowed again after World War II, except in stories about fighting men overseas; most of the new stateside novels had college-bred heroes and heroines. The novelists themselves, with a few exceptions, had stopped acting like bohemians or proletarians, and it was getting hard to tell a writer from anybody else. Many of the younger ones lived on residential streets, owned their homes—or were trying to buy them—and were active members of the Parent-Teacher Association. Unlike most writers of the 1920s, they worried about public opinion outside their own group and were letting themselves be absorbed into the new white-collar classes. In some respects, however, there was a curious reversion to the leisure-class standards of the 1890s. The institution of literary patronage had been revived and extended, although it had ceased to involve many personal contacts between writers and millionaires; now the money was given to foundations, which disbursed it in the form of fellowships. The genteel tradition of the 1890s had also been revived in fiction, and many of the new novels had an air of decorum that would have pleased William Dean Howells in his later years. It is never genteel to talk about money, and the novelists didn't talk about it much, but one could see that their characters hadn't many financial worries. My friend George Ollendorf, who reads the novels attentively, has been impressed by the financial progress of characters in American fiction since the days when novelists wrote about the unemployed. "To make a rough estimate," he says, "the annual incomes of heroes and heroines have increased in the last twenty years by at least five hundred per cent."

I mentioned the question of college background. At the beginning of this century young writers went to Harvard if their parents could afford to send them; any other university was a second choice. "I went to Harvard," says Van Wyck Brooks in his memoirs, "just as students in the twelfth century went to Paris, because, for me also, Abelard was there; for I knew I was a writer born—I seemed always to have known this—and I supposed that Harvard was the college for writers." Harvard retained that reputation for many years after Brooks was graduated in 1907, and partly retains it today. The most famous literary class was 1910, with T. S. Eliot, Jack Reed, Walter Lippmann, Heywood Broun, and others who then seemed of equal promise. After 1915, however, active literary groups appeared at other universities: first at Princeton, with Edmund Wilson, John Peale Bishop, and Scott Fitzgerald; then almost simultaneously at Yale, Columbia, Pennsylvania, Ohio State, and Chicago; then came the young poets at Vanderbilt who published the *Fugitive*. In those days it seemed that writers usually came forward by college groups, but Hemingway, Hart Crane, and a few others had never been to college. Faulkner had briefly attended the University of Mississippi.

The situation is a little more complicated today, though Harvard still has a higher incidence of authorship than any other American university. In the last few years it has been producing novelists and poets, and more than its share of future publishers. Princeton, which probably ranks second, has been producing novelists, poets, and new critics, most of whom have studied under Richard Blackmur. Yale is more public-minded and seems to specialize in reporters, including many of those who have made reporting a twentieth-century art form, but it also trains a good many critics and maintains a famous school of the drama. Kenyon College, in Ohio, has attracted young poets and critics, largely because John Crowe Ransom teaches there. On the Pacific Coast the universities popular with young writers are Stanford and California; in the South they might be Alabama and Tulane. Often the attraction of a university has been a single famous teacher, like Hudson Strode at Alabama. Iowa has a school of creative writing with a group of able teachers, and enrolls postgraduate students when they appear—as they do today— from colleges anywhere in the country. It would seem unlikely that any university will ever again establish the sort of undisputed literary prestige that Harvard enjoyed at the beginning of the century.

The sectional background of American writers becomes an interesting topic, not when we ask where they were born (the answer being almost anywhere), but when we ask what the sections were to which they have felt an emotional loyalty. For half a century after 1830 the section was likely to be New England. It was so much the center of the literary life that several authors born west of the Alleghenies became New Englanders by adoption, like William Dean Howells of Ohio and George Washington Cable of Louisiana. Even Mark Twain, who didn't get along with the Bostonians, spent much of his life in Connecticut. At the end of the 1880s, however, the center shifted to New York City, which was a section in itself and exercised a magnetic force, stronger than that of New England had been, on authors born in other sections. The most fashionable New York writers of the years after 1900 were Richard Harding Davis, of Philadelphia, and the playwright Clyde Fitch, who had grown up in Schenectady. The most loyal New Yorker was O. Henry, who was born in North Carolina and trained as a newspaperman in Texas. Except for Henry James and Edith Wharton, who lived in Europe, hardly any of the prominent authors had been born in New York, but nevertheless it was the seat and shire of the writing clan. Although its central position was threatened twice by Chicago—in the middle 1890s and after 1915—and once by Paris, in the 1920s, New York always retained the publishing houses, the magazines, the theatrical producers, the literary agents, and so the writers couldn't stay away.

It was in the depression years that one first began to notice a geographical diffusion. Young writers were still coming to New York, but there were not so many as before, because the city had ceased to glitter with opportunities. The glitter was in Hollywood, if the young men wanted to earn a great deal of money. If they simply wanted to keep alive while writing, they tried to join the

Federal Writers' Project, and it was always easier to be certified to the Project if they stayed at home in Missouri or Idaho than if they moved to New York. There was no Writers' Project after World War II, but by then the magnetic attraction of the big city had weakened. Young writers were studying or teaching in universities all over the country. Many established writers had moved to Connecticut, just beyond the New York suburbs, but others had continued to live in California or Mississippi; perhaps they felt that air mail and the long-distance telephone brought them close enough to the publishing industry. As always, that industry was centered in New York—it was now almost confined to New York—but in some branches of serious writing, especially fiction, the prestige of leadership had passed to the South.

I have often wondered about the reasons for this dominant position of Southern novelists at the mid-century. Like everything else in literature, it can partly be explained in terms of personality: one novelist—in this case, William Faulkner—had found a path that many others could follow. But Faulkner had several distinguished and quite independent contemporaries; one might mention Katherine Anne Porter, Caroline Gordon, Robert Penn Warren, and Eudora Welty in what is now the older group of novelists, as well as poets-and-critics (the term should be hyphenated) like Ransom and Allen Tate. Faulkner has also had many able successors—so many, in fact, that the new position of Southern writing seems to call for additional explanations in social terms.

One explanation among others is that Southern writers belong to what is really a national minority with its own tradition, which they feel to be endangered and which they are bent on reaffirming in literature. Another explanation is that the rural South hasn't many commercial amusements, with the result that its people have been forced to amuse one another, largely by telling stories about local characters. Southerners have a good deal of practice in story-telling even before they begin to write. Still another explanation applies to Southern fiction, though not to criticism or poetry. It depends on the definition of novels as *long stories that deal with changing relationships*; these relationships are easiest to study when they exist among members of the same family. Many novels, of course, deal with relationships of other types, from narrow ones like those between lover and mistress to the broad relationships among members of any social group (for example, an army platoon, a business office, or a college faculty). The family, however, makes an ideal subject for a novel and thereby simplifies the task of Southern writers—for the family is more important in the South than anywhere else in modern America (except among some cultural minorities, notably the Jews and the Italians, who have also been producing many young novelists). The South alone has preserved what sociologists call the extended family, or clan—that is, a group which includes aunts, uncles, and even distant cousins, as well as parents and children. The Southern family, at least in the smaller towns, is also likely to include persons of many different callings and levels of income; often there are rich and poor farmers, storekeepers, filling-station attendants, a doctor, a banker, and even a novelist in the same family group. From earliest childhood the novelist has been acquainted with a great diversity of characters, and he finds it easy to present them in action. Northerners travel more, but know fewer persons intimately. Most of their friends are likely to be on their own economic level, even in their own profession, with the result that their novels may be lacking in variety and color.

The South, of course, is not the only section with interesting writers. Today they are appearing in many regions, and often their work bears a sort of regional imprint. Publishers' readers learn what to expect; sometimes they look at the return address on a manuscript and wager what kind of story it will be. "It comes from Maine," I heard a reader say. "I'll give you odds that it's a historical novel about the great days of the shipbuilders." Novels from the Pacific Northwest and from Utah are also likely to be historical; in one case they might deal with covered wagons and in the other with Mormon pioneers and their plural wives. Novels from Hollywood are often slick jobs about a topic of current interest. Novels from Chicago are usually naturalistic; Chicago is the homeland of American naturalism. About novels from Connecticut one can never be sure; the writers who live there come from many states, and most of them haven't yet acquired the regional color of their new home.

How They Get Started

In the early 1950s there were more apprentice novelists than ever before, and fewer of them were breaking into print; only about half as many new novels were being published each year as in the early 1900s. "How can I become a professional writer?" was a question young men and women kept asking in a hundred different fashions, and one never knew what to answer them—except to say, "Keep writing, if that's what you want to do, and get published as soon as you can." In the new age there were many byways that might lead to literary recognition as if by accident. There was, however, only one marked pathway open to most young writers, and it might take them to the wrong destination.

A hundred years ago there were several types of apprenticeship. One of them was the Harvard Divinity School, and it is interesting to note how many American authors started in life as clergymen; they never really stopped preaching, and—except for Emerson, who isn't read enough—we don't read most of them today. More of the good authors started in the printing shop of a daily or weekly newspaper, after leaving school at the age of fourteen or fifteen. The apprentice was taught to read proof and set type, and that was sounder training than any professor of creative writing (English 209, meeting at three o'clock MWF) could offer him today. At the very least he learned to spell and punctuate, a simple form of knowledge that many college students never acquire. His work with a type-metal alphabet might also give him a tactile sense of words; each of them had weight and body, the shorter ones were easier to handle, and any useless word wasted his time, as it would waste the reader's. Whitman, Howells, Bret Harte, Mark Twain, and Lafcadio Hearn all set type at some stage in their early careers, and each of them learned to write fluent and accurate English. After setting type for a newspaper, they each wrote stories for it. The best of these were reprinted so widely that magazine editors, then book publishers, began asking for their work. They were launched into the literary life, sometimes without really knowing how.

After 1890 most of the newspaper printing shops were unionized and no longer offered casual employment to young men serving their literary apprenticeships; the new path to recognition led through the city room of a big-town newspaper. There the pay was likely to be miserable—ten dollars a week to beginners (as late as 1915); eighteen or at best twenty-four dollars a week for those with two or three years of experience; thirty dollars to star reporters. Underpaid and overworked, the reporters drank too much and changed their jobs after every big spree,[1] so that there was always

---

1. Those who kept drifting from one paper to another were called "boomers." Among the last of the species was big, curly-haired, broken-

a place for promising young men. If these survived the first few years of newspaper life—as not all of them did—they learned to get their facts straight and in proper sequence, though most of them never acquired the same feeling for words as the older authors who had worked in printing shops. Dreiser, Mencken, James Gibbons Huneker, Stephen Crane, and David Graham Phillips—in fact, most of the new writers who appeared between 1890 and 1915—got their start as cub reporters. But that path began to be closed too, after the First World War, by the disappearance of many dailies and the fiercer competition for jobs on those that remained. Later, with the founding of the Newspaper Guild, reporting ceased to be a poorly paid apprenticeship and became a career in itself.

The 1920s were the bohemian period in American literature. Young writers went to Greenwich Village or Montparnasse and lived partly on the bounty of their relatives but chiefly by their wits. They found odd and impermanent jobs, mixed their own gin, rolled their cigarettes at home, and talked their way out of paying bills, but they also worked hard to get ahead. Besides writing book reviews, which were often assigned to beginners in those days, they started their first novels and sometimes finished them, with the help

---

nosed Lionel Moise, a brilliant reporter who was also a poet, a cop-slugger, a heartbreaker, a singer of barroom ballads, and a great teller of barroom stories. He liked to start a story by saying, "Did I ever tell you about the time I was in jail in Pocatello [or Fresno or Savannah]? I was but a lad. . . ." The story would explain that he was in jail because of a three days' drunk, and it would end with his being released and, very often, getting another newspaper job. Besides telling stories, he liked to stand with his foot on a brass rail and discuss the art of writing fiction.

I knew him first and best in 1919, when he was working briefly for the New York *American*. It was Lionel as much as anyone who saved my life when I was delirious with influenza; he cradled me in his arms as if I were a rag doll and carried me into the hospital. Much as I liked and admired him, I thought that he was one of the many brilliant reporters of the time who had half-baked themselves by reading Nietzsche. "Goest thou to women?" he liked to quote. "Forget not thy whip." He could be cruel to women, and one year in Chicago there were two attempted suicides because of him. Both girls sold their stories to the Hearst papers, and Lionel lost his job on the *News,* but he was soon hired by a Milwaukee paper; by that time he was a pretty famous character. He had talent enough to have become a famous writer too, if he had ever acquired the discipline of the trade. As it was, he exerted a real influence on American writing, through the cub reporters who learned their jobs under him. Reading Charles A. Fenton's book, *The Apprenticeship of Ernest Hemingway*, I learned that Moise had worked for the Kansas City *Star* in 1917, when Hemingway was a cub there and listened to his lectures. "Pure objective writing," Moise would say time and again, "is the only true form of story-telling."

of advances from hopeful publishers. Advances were easier to
obtain than in later years, and they went farther too, considering
that young writers and their wives could live in the country for a
hundred dollars a month, and in France for even less. If the novels
were published they had a good chance of being successful. Literary
fashions were changing and new authors were likely to be praised
and overpraised by new reviewers, who were also making their
way. Some of the authors were able to support themselves by writing almost from the day they left college, though none of the others
lived on the scale of Scott Fitzgerald, who earned eighteen thousand dollars in his twenty-fourth year.

The new writers of the 1930s couldn't afford to be so happy-go-
lucky. If they came to New York, as not all of them did, it was at a
time when some of the most hopeful publishers had gone bank-
rupt—among them the lordly Horace Liveright—and when there
wasn't as much hack work as before. Jobs were hard to find, except
on the expanding Luce publications, which offered a few positions
at high salaries, but gave the editors no time to write for themselves. Some writers married New York schoolteachers, who were
regarded as affluent persons in the depression years, and others
scraped along on home relief. After 1936, however, there was the
Federal Writers' Project, which kept hundreds of young people alive
while they were struggling with their first novels; and there was
Hollywood, where, in the early days of sound pictures, the studios
were willing to hire almost anyone who had published a book; Hollywood was a writers' project retailored in mink.

After World War II there were no more projects of the sort. Although jobs were plentiful, there were few openings for apprentice
writers, and in fact for apprentices in most professions. Instead of
learning to write by writing for publication, while they were paid
just enough to keep them alive, like other apprentices, young men
and women now stayed in college and studied to become professional authors, just as others studied there to become personnel
managers or public-health nurses. The popularity of courses in creative writing is a fairly recent development. These used to be called
by the less flamboyant name of "Composition," and they didn't
attract much attention except at a few universities—notably Harvard, where they were entrusted to famous teachers like Lewis E.
Gates and later C. T. Copeland and Dean Briggs. The English 47
Workshop, in which George Pierce Baker taught playwriting to

thirteen selected students—"Baker's dozen"—started at Harvard and later moved to Yale, where a school of the drama was built around it. Yale also offered—and still does—an excellent course called Daily Themes, and there were popular teachers of composition at a few other universities, but they were rather the exception. In the 1950s, however, even the smaller colleges had courses in Creating the Novel (or the short story, or the drama, or sometimes all three). State universities had all these courses, which were often assigned—this was something new—to writers who had made a name in their profession. Many state universities (and even country high schools in the State of Washington) also taught Scenario Writing and Writing for Television—usually after arguments about whether these subjects belonged in the English department or in the school of journalism.

At Harvard in 1953 there were fourteen half-courses, open to qualified undergraduates, that centered on the writing of fiction, with others on the writing of plays, poetry, and nonfiction. Several universities taught the writing of criticism, usually as a subject for postgraduate seminars, and Indiana each year appointed a Critic in Residence. Other universities had a Poet or a Novelist in Residence, or a Visiting (and salaried) Writer. Still others held writers' conferences each summer, attended by the amateurs of the region, whose work at the conference was sometimes counted toward a college degree. The postgraduate school of creative writing at the University of Iowa regularly conferred a master's degree, with the student submitting a novel or a book of poems as his magisterial thesis. When I taught for one term at another state university, my assistant had just finished a novel, which he asked me to read. I told him that it was a creditable piece of writing, as indeed it was, but that it had a rather shopworn plot and probably wouldn't be accepted by a publisher.

"I guessed as much," the assistant said, for he wasn't in the least conceited. "But you haven't answered the sixty-four, I mean the important question. Does it show that I have enough creative talent so that I should try to live by writing?"—he was married and already had two children. "Or should I play safe and take a teaching job?"

I hesitated, thinking that the answer to the first question is always no, because the born writer doesn't ask it. "What would you teach?" I said.

"A college workshop in creative writing. I've been offered the job."

Since World War II many young men have gone straight from studying creative writing into teaching it, without any interlude for writing creatively, or even commercially. Some of them, including my former assistant, have proved to be capable teachers. Others whose work I have seen were awkward in expressing themselves, unable to construct a simple story, and I wonder what sort of knowledge or ignorance they have been passing on to their students. Most of the students, incidentally, should be taught grammar and rhetoric—two subjects that have fallen into neglect—instead of being permitted, even encouraged, to start by trying to create stories full of myth, symbols, and "meanings on different levels." It is as if they were being launched into the stratosphere in turbo-jet planes before they had learned to ride bicycles.[2] Perhaps the least qualified of their instructors were giving them critical analyses that were too advanced for most of them; that is a habit of bad teachers. As for the best teachers, they were highly talented men and women who, in another age, would have lived far from a campus and would have supported themselves by writing for publication.

College teaching, whether in creative writing or in English literature, or occasionally in some other department, had become the one clearly marked path to recognition that was open to most young writers. That didn't mean, of course, that other paths were completely closed. Young men who had distinguished themselves in college, as not all writers do, might win a Rhodes Scholarship to Oxford, or a Fulbright Fellowship that would let them study in France or Italy (and the Fulbrights were also open to women). They might try to do a book abroad, while neglecting their courses. At home there were still openings in the magazine world, though most of

2. Once at a writers' conference I was asked to give a "workshop period" in poetry to a class of sixty students. After talking for five minutes about some common problem of verse structure, I noticed that many students had begun to look as if they didn't want me to see that they didn't understand what I was saying. I stopped and asked, "How many of you know what an iamb is?"

Nobody answered.

"An iambic foot in poetry," I amplified. To make the term clear I wrote it on the blackboard. "Now do you know what it is?"

This time a half-dozen hands went up, but waveringly, as if even the best-informed students weren't quite sure of the difference between an iamb and a spondee or a dactyl. I spent the rest of the workshop period giving an elementary talk on English metrics, to which the class listened with attention.

these went to graduates of the older Eastern universities. Other young men and women might follow the bohemian pattern of the 1920s and move to New York, where they planned to get along on odd jobs while somehow writing a book. Although most young writers of the 1950s—say, ninety per cent of them—are less bohemian than their predecessors, the others are more desperately bohemian—"hipsters," they sometimes call themselves—and live in cold-water flats, or "pads," on the edge of a world peopled with car thieves, dips, and junkies. Their meeting places are in Greenwich Village, but sometimes they hitch-hike across the country to spend a season in the half-literary underworlds of Denver and San Francisco; it is a life that has been described in three or four published novels. The fact remains that this bohemian path to recognition no longer seems attractive or even possible to most young writers. They have wives and children to support; early marriage has become a mark of the new generation. Needing an assured income, no matter how small, hundreds of them have been finding it in the universities, where, after taking their degrees—often with the help of monthly checks from the Veterans' Bureau—they have been appointed to junior posts on the English faculty.

Most of them soon find that teaching and writing are two separate professions, and hard to reconcile. Some few have combined them successfully: the first example that comes to mind is Robert Penn Warren, who is an admired novelist, an influential critic, a poet of distinction, and also has made a brilliant academic record. Warren says that teaching helps him with his literary work, although I note that he now teaches, at Yale, for only half of the academic year. Kenneth Burke, at Bennington, has a still less exacting schedule: "every other year, for every other week." Some of his books started as informal talks to his students. John Crowe Ransom, at Kenyon, is a poet-and-critic who, to judge by the success of his former students, has had a wider influence than any other teacher of English in the country. But already with Ransom, who writes very well—unlike some of the critics who studied under him—there is a question that keeps rising in one's mind: wouldn't his literary work have been still more impressive if he had given all his time to it? If there is a doubt in Ransom's case, there is none in that of other writers on college faculties; either they have been erratic and slipshod teachers, or else more frequently—for they are men of conscience—their writing has been neglected or has fallen into the academic mold.

College teaching is an engrossing career in itself, and it encourages the writer to spend his time amassing and imparting knowledge of an objective type, instead of expressing his personal truths. What he writes for publication is likely to take the form of long critical articles in the quarterlies, for the simple reason that such articles grow naturally out of his academic work and help to improve his academic position. Sometimes they do most to improve it when they are written in that impressive jargon known as the academic style.[3] In lecture halls the professor speaks from above, to a captive audience of students who have to understand what he is saying or flunk the course. Some professors don't bother to interest their classes, but merely try to be concise and informative. Others are actors and hold the students' attention by a dramatic projection of their personalities. In both cases they lose the habit of addressing readers outside the classroom, who can't hear the dry methodical voice, or the dramatic one either, and simply close a book if they are bored.

Besides these literary temptations, the academic life in itself has disadvantages for the young writer. The work, if done well, is absorbing and even exhausting. The salaries for beginners are generally below the wages of unskilled labor, and the long vacations are an illusion, considering that most instructors—and all the married ones with children—have to spend part of the summer working to pay their bills; many of them teach for six or twelve weeks in summer schools. It is several years before they are granted job security, or academic tenure, and the instructor who does brilliant work, or is popular with the students, isn't always the one to be given a permanent appointment. "It's his own fault," I have heard it said of an instructor whose contract wasn't renewed. "He offended the older

3. When I first worked for the *New Republic* we used to receive many contributions from professors of sociology or government, and many others from reporters on small-city newspapers. An old office argument was which of the two classes wrote worse. As a copy editor, I preferred the reporters. After you had unmixed their metaphors, unwised their wisecracks, corrected a few obvious errors in grammar, and run the short paragraphs together, their contributions made pretty readable English. The professors' style was grammatically correct, but it was harder to unscramble, owing to their habit of constructing sentences around two abstract nouns, each guarded by an adjective (or by another noun used as an adjective). The two nouns would be connected by some form of the verb "be," or else by a causal verb like "result in" or "effectuate." Instead of writing, "The crowd felt bewildered and stood still for a moment," the professors were likely to write, "Mass bewilderment resulted in [or effectuated] a momentary stasis."

men in his department by having too many ideas. He knows his subject, but he doesn't know the folkways of academic life." The young professor works for an institution, forms part of an academic community, and has to observe the rules of both if he wants to get ahead. As a teacher he can't afford to do what writers do—that is, risk his career with every new task he undertakes and every book he publishes. He has superiors to placate, and the superiors have to worry about the board of regents and the state legislature. A rash book by a young professor might result in a diversion of funds from the college of liberal arts to the medical school, or it might mean a smaller legislative appropriation for the whole university.

If the young professor writes his book in spite of everything; if it is published and talked about and even has a sensational sale for a first novel, what then? Perhaps he resigns his academic post, buys or rents a farmhouse in Connecticut, and sets to work on another book; but he finds that it is harder to finish than he had expected, and soon he learns that its sales prospects aren't too bright. The second novel has been the stopping point for many writers, either because it marked a backward step—often the author has used his best material in the first novel—or else because the improvement wasn't as great as reviewers had hoped to see. They are almost always harder on the second book than on the first. It isn't until the third book appears that an author can regard himself as really launched on his career—and even then he is likely to find that in America today very few people can earn a living merely by writing books.[4]

4. Several of the observations on "How They Get Started" were first made in an essay I contributed to Bruce Bliven's symposium, *Twentieth Century Unlimited*, copyright, 1950, by Bruce Bliven. Later there are quotations and revisions from the essay—called "How Writers Live"—on pages 171, 175, 177–79, 218–19, and 226–28 of this volume. I am grateful to Mr. Bliven and to J. B. Lippincott Company, publishers of the symposium, for permission to use this material.

X.

A NATURAL HISTORY,
STILL CONTINUED

How They Earn Their Livings

According to the 1950 census there were some fifteen thousand professional authors in the United States, or about two thousand more than there had been in 1940. These men and women—with other thousands of part-time writers—played an essential part in several American industries. Book and magazine publishing in all its branches couldn't have existed without them. Compositors and pressmen by the scores of thousands were employed in reproducing what they wrote. Booksellers and newsdealers distributed it to the public. Librarians preserved it. Actors performed it in theaters, in motion-picture studios, and for transmission by radio and television. The advertising industry depended on their work, as printed or performed, to obtain an audience that would buy the products of manufacturers who advertised. Yet authors as a class were replaceable persons who received only a minute portion of the wealth they helped to create. Those who wrote books for publication were somewhat more respected than other types of authors, but they created less wealth of a tangible sort and hence received an even smaller reward financially. Aside from the hard-working authors of textbooks, standard juveniles, mysteries, and Westerns, I doubt that two hundred Americans earned the major portion of their incomes, year after year, by writing hard-cover books.

There had been a brief period at the end of World War II when writing books was a profession that supported hundreds in comfort or luxury. In those days a romantic novel that was chosen by one of the major book clubs and sold to the movies might yield its author as much as half a million dollars. There weren't many of these bonanzas, but most books were selling well, many publishers were making excess profits, and even the authors of unsuccessful novels could find well-paid writing jobs in Hollywood or on the staffs of big-circulation magazines. A large share of their literary earnings went to the Bureau of Internal Revenue, for the income-tax laws have never been kind to writers, actors, glamour girls, professional athletes, national heroes, and others with brief periods of prosperity. On the other hand, many writers were helped financially by the excess-profits tax of wartime years. Magazines and motion-picture studios didn't mind paying very large sums for stories when the sums could be deducted from taxes and the real cost of the stories was only a few cents on the dollar. Many publishers tried to reduce their excess profits by making advance payments for books that wouldn't appear until the tax had been repealed.

"I remember the Christmas season of 1945," George Ollendorf told me. "That was the end of the year when everybody was trying to force money on you, if he thought the payment was tax-deductible. I couldn't go into the office of a big publisher without being asked to write a book, always with a generous advance—'and we'll have a check in the mail tomorrow,' the publisher was sure to say. I had tax troubles of my own that year and turned down most of the offers, but two of them were so good they couldn't be refused. Then I got home on Christmas Eve and found two other checks that weren't due till February. Both publishers said that they thought I could use the money to pay my Christmas bills. 'Yes,' I said to myself, 'and your accountants can use it to defer your taxes.' "

"What about the two books you signed contracts for?"

"I wrote one of them, but it wasn't finished till 1948, and then the public wouldn't read it."

"And the other book?"

There was an unhappy look on George's square Pennsylvania-German face. "I never really got started on it, and last year I had to pay back the advance. Look at that old heap." He pointed out the window at his station wagon. "It's going to be a long time before I have money enough to buy another car."

Even in the 1940s authors had reason to complain of their economic position. David Cohn, in an article for the *Saturday Review*, compared his situation with that of a tenant farmer always in debt to the plantation store. Said Mr. Cohn:

He is a cotton sharecropper, I am a literary sharecropper. Each of us, by virtue of the system, has a certain amount of economic security even if it is at a low level. His employer, the planter, and my employer, the publisher, must keep us alive so that we may create cotton and books by the sales of which they earn their livelihood. If he gets an advance of fifteen dollars a month so that he can eat and clothe himself while he is making a crop, I get a lump sum advance so that I can eat and clothe myself while I am writing a book. In both cases, whether by calculation or coincidence, the advance always seems to be just enough to keep body and soul within hailing distance of each other.[1]

Some authors, like many tenant farmers, never got out of debt and never received a check for earned royalties, but still they managed to keep alive. In the 1950s, however, publishers had to be a great deal more selective in making advances. There were fewer small advances, offered on the chance that something publishable might come of them, and fewer big ones too. Because of higher living costs, the medium advance—of one or two thousand dollars —no longer fed and clothed an author while he was writing a book. "You'll have to finance yourself or find outside help," the publisher was saying in effect. Sometimes the book might be scholarly enough to interest one of the big foundations, and then—much oftener than in the past—the author might receive Carnegie or Rockefeller money with which to finish it. But these were special cases, and in general the sharecropping system was breaking down for writers, as it had already broken down for cotton tenants.

The book when published was less likely to hit the jackpot than in the wartime years; at least the jackpots were smaller. There were still authors with hundred-thousand-dollar kitchens in their country houses—according to Louis Kronenberger, who gets around—and authors who spent more money in night clubs than did the quiet children of Texas millionaires, but they weren't so common as they had been ten years before. Novels chosen by the major book clubs were yielding about one-third as much to their authors as they had

1. Quoted by Elmer Davis in his Bowker Memorial Lecture for 1940, "Some Aspects of the Economics of Authorship." The lecture, reprinted by the New York Public Library, is recommended reading.

yielded in 1945. Hollywood was buying fewer stories and paying much less for those it bought. Soft-cover reprints were a new and important source of income for many writers, but, except in a few cases, they didn't pay enough to balance the loss of income from other sources. Bookstore sales are hard to compare for any two decades. It is safe to say, however, that the sales of nonfiction books were higher than they had been before World War II, and those of hard-cover fiction much lower. In 1953 bookstores sold about three times as many copies of the ten leading nonfiction titles as of the ten leading novels.

Authors' royalties on bookstore sales were a little lower in percentages than in 1940 and a great deal lower than in 1910. Before the First World War twenty per cent of the retail price was a common royalty for popular novels; Kipling was paid thirty per cent. After 1925, fifteen per cent became the maximum, and it was reached at the end of a sliding scale; many contracts called for a ten-per-cent royalty on the first twenty-five hundred copies sold, twelve and one-half per cent on the next twenty-five hundred, and fifteen per cent after five thousand. In the 1950s the maximum was still fifteen per cent, but it wasn't offered in all cases, and the sliding scale had lengthened out, with royalties rising after five and ten thousand copies sold, instead of after twenty-five hundred and five thousand. Often the royalties were now based on the wholesale price of the book, at a higher percentage figure that yielded a little less money to the author—though not much less—than the lower percentage of the retail price. A novel priced at $3.50 would earn about $1750 for its author for the first five thousand copies sold, a little less than $4000 for the first ten thousand, and, depending on the method of computing royalties, a little more or less than $9000 for twenty thousand copies. If the sale went to twenty thousand, however, the novel would be entering a new field of commercial possibilities and might earn a great deal more in subsidiary rights (magazine, book-club, digest, movie, soft-cover-reprint) than it did in royalties.

In the 1950s not many novels each year had a bookstore sale of twenty thousand copies. Twelve thousand was the figure that had acquired a magical value for publishers. When a book reached that sales figure it had safely passed the break-even point—whatever that might be—and was making an assured profit. Publishers are naturally and professionally courteous to authors, except to the obviously incompetent, but the author of a serious novel that had sold more than twelve thousand copies could count on being received by them with special consideration. The word would be passed from desk to desk, "Jack Ribblesdale is here." The youngest file clerk would find an errand that carried her past the open door of the office where Ribblesdale was sitting in conference with the senior editor. "He's handsomer than in the photographs," she would report to her friends on the eighth floor. Junior editors would be called in for introductions. The promotion manager would lead Ribblesdale downstairs, present him to the sales force, and break out a new bottle of Scotch. Later the author would be taken to lunch at an expensive restaurant, given free copies of books by other writers, and perhaps there would be a coming-out party for his new novel at a Park Avenue hotel (though there weren't half so many of those parties as there had been in the 1940s).

The author whose sales hadn't reached the magical number of twelve thousand was still received with consideration, but he caused less commotion in the office and wasn't asked out to lunch at such expensive restaurants. If his sales were under five thousand he was likely to hear a great deal about business conditions and about the publisher's getting-out figure or break-even point. Each new book is a separate venture and requires a new investment in design, jacket, composition, and electrotype plates. This investment can't be figured on a per-copy basis, since it is just as large for a sale of five thousand copies as it would be for fifty thousand. A certain number of copies must be sold before the investment has been recovered and the publisher starts to make a profit; that number, different for each book, is its break-even point. For all books the point has been rising for many years, as a result of higher wages in the printing trades. Back in the 1930s the late W. W. Norton, an extremely able publisher, used to make a small profit on scholarly books after they had reached a sale of fifteen hundred copies. In the 1950s the getting-out figure for a novel of medium length and price was often said to be ten thousand—but that was the story told by publishers, and they may have been displaying a human weakness for exaggeration. Any novelist whose last book had reached a sale of five thousand copies and whose next manuscript was as good as its predecessor could be pretty sure that it too would be accepted for publication.

The fact remains that most novels didn't reach a sale of five thousand; they were losing ventures for the publisher and for the author as well. The average income from writing books was below the average earnings of Southern mill hands, and not much above those of cotton sharecroppers. An author might work a year or more on a book, have it published and favorably reviewed, and still not earn enough in royalties to cover the thousand dollars that he might have received as an advance.[2] His next book might take another year and not be published at all.

Although the publication of his first book is likely to be a very small financial transaction, it may have important consequences for the author. If the book is widely reviewed, his name will acquire some value in the literary world. He has a chance of obtaining a literary prize or a fellowship, and there are many more of these than there were before World War II. Magazines will show more interest in his articles or stories.

For more than a century writing for magazines has been the principal source of income for many authors. Changes in this field, however, have been much more sweeping than among the book publishers, who, compared with the owners of big-circulation magazines, are a group of conservative small businessmen. It was the general or family magazines that used to offer the best market for free-lance writing, but long before 1950 most of these had vanished. The *Saturday Evening Post*, *Collier's* (which had become a fortnightly), and *Cosmopolitan* were exceptions; they still printed stories and articles for all the family. Most of the other weeklies and monthlies that flourished in the new age made their appeal to a particular audience or to a particular interest of the wider audience: they were picture magazines, news magazines, women's magazines—men's magazines too, though they weren't so successful—home-and-garden magazines, fashion magazines, age-group magazines (like *Seventeen*, for adolescent girls, and *Red Book*, redesigned for young marrieds), weeklies "not for the old lady from Dubuque," farm journals, hunting-and-fishing magazines, business magazines, and magazine digests. Many of them were partly or wholly staff-written by salaried authors. All except the digests printed many pictures, thus cutting down the space for text.

2. That was by no means a new situation for authors. In 1929 I published a first book of poems, *Blue Juniata*. It was quite well received and earned a little more than the advance of $125. Poetry didn't sell in the 1920s, or in the 1950s, but prose didn't always do much better. The first edition of *Exile's Return*, in 1934, barely earned the advance of $350.

In the 1920s the text had consisted—according to commonly quoted figures—seventy per cent of fiction and thirty per cent of nonfiction; in the 1950s the proportions had been reversed. Since there was more demand for articles, their authors were being paid, on the average, much more than they would have received thirty years before; some of the new men lived so well and traveled so widely gathering material that they couldn't afford to write books. The payment for fiction hadn't greatly changed; generally the minimum was higher, but the maximum was lower except in the very competitive field of the women's magazines. No fiction writer was being paid four thousand dollars for each accepted story, as Scott Fitzgerald had regularly been paid in 1930 by the *Saturday Evening Post*. I doubt that anyone was earning as much per year by writing magazine fiction as Jack London had earned in 1910, when dollars were bigger and there was no income tax. Still, it seemed to authors in other fields that successful story writers, even in the 1950s, were making their livings the easy way.

Lecturing to forums and women's clubs was, for many writers, a more laborious means of increasing their incomes; usually it involved long journeys and low fees. The lecturers in greatest demand were the authors of inspirational books, adventurous travelers, political analysts, flower arrangers, and handsome novelists whose names were in the news. A rather new development was the increasing number of requests from colleges for lectures by serious or symbolic novelists (who mightn't be so newsworthy or handsome), new critics, and new poets. Some of these traveled from college to college in little bands and were entertained like medieval troubadours.

Many writers were employed by institutions of various types, often on a permanent basis. The salaried writer was a new figure in American society, and he wasn't always easy to recognize. Sometimes he might be disguised as a businessman, hired by a corporation to act as its spokesman or to edit and contribute articles to its house organ. Sometimes his disguise might be a military or naval uniform. The Army, the Navy, and the Air Force all had their historians and also their authors of manuals and reports, some of which were distributed by the millions, while others were designed to be read by a highly restricted audience of staff officers. The writer might also be employed by other branches of the federal government, which, in addition to its many other functions, was the largest American publishing house; most of its bulletins and handbooks were written by salaried officials. In Hollywood the writer might be employed by a motion-picture studio to write scenarios, or merely dialogue for scenarios; in New York he might be hired on a yearly basis by a national magazine, or it might give him a drawing account. Several encyclopedias maintained salaried writing staffs. Northwestern University had a bureau that accepted contracts to write business histories.

The free-lance writer—that vanishing type—might be engaged in an even greater variety of projects. Language is the medium in which our culture exists and in which its knowledge is diffused and preserved. The independent professional writer is, among other things, an engineer of language, and he never knows what institution or individual may next demand his services. An advertising agency may need his help in planning a television program for one of its clients. A charitable foundation, after making a social survey, may call upon the writer to make a readable story out of its findings. A manufacturer needs a handbook for his agents and customers. A statesman, a general, or a famous actor has been asked to write his memoirs, but lacks a gift for self-expression in words. Nevertheless a workmanlike book appears; it is the story of the public figure "as told to John Hartley Weber," who of course did the writing. Or the children of a dead industrialist decide that he should have a published memorial and engage a professional author to write his biography.

Some of these projects offered no more than a living wage or less, but others were fairly profitable: for example, an established author might be paid fifty thousand dollars for writing a businessman's biography, on which he had worked for two or three years. All the projects had one feature in common: they were undertaken chiefly because the writer needed money. If he could support himself, even modestly, by what he regarded as his own work, he was likely to keep his independence by refusing the most tempting offers from outside sources. His own work, however, might also have involved him in a variety of money-earning ventures. Even though his income was in the lower brackets, his yearly tax return might be more complicated than that of many middle-sized corporations. He might have worked part of the time for a salary, like a clerk, and part of the time for fees, like a consulting engineer, but he might also have lived part of the time like a capitalist on his Rents and Royalties. His work had involved business expenses that were hard to estimate: how much should he charge off for that month of research at the Huntington Library in Pasadena? And that party to which he invited two editors and some people they wanted to meet: would he be justified in deducting the cost of it—what cost?—as business entertainment? At last he is likely to decide that the expenses are beyond his powers of computation; he will simply pot-shot at them, hoping that his guess won't be implausible. As for the sources of his income, they have changed from year to year, but a fairly typical list might run something like this:

1. From various magazines he has received fees for writing articles or stories, and much smaller fees for writing book reviews.

2. Publishers have paid him for reporting on the literary quality of several manuscripts, usually at $25 a report, and they might also have called him into consultation about the revision of other manuscripts.

3. Another publisher asked him to edit and write an introduction to a book that was on its way to becoming a classic. (The introduction might also have been published as a magazine article and might have been used as the basis of a lecture, since the writer has tried to make each separate project yield a double or triple income.)

4. One of the minor book clubs has paid him a small monthly retainer for serving as a member of its editorial board.

5. Three or four universities invited him to lecture, usually for $100 a night and traveling expenses.

6. For a week or two in the summer he was on the staff of a writers' conference, at $250 a week and expenses, and with more free time he might have taught at other conferences, on a sort of Chautauqua circuit.

7. Twice a year he received a report from his own publisher about the sale of books he had written in the past. There wouldn't be many dollars in his actual royalty account, but sums might be owed him for subsidiary rights—say for a soft-cover reprint or for a translation into Spanish or Swedish.

By a combination of all these means—the author reflects, as he stuffs his tax return into an oversize envelope—he has managed to scrape through the year. He hadn't lost much time through illness, fortunately. Someday he would get a windfall, a sudden check from a book club or an award from a foundation, and it would enable him to write the big book he had been planning for as long as he could remember, without ever having time or money enough to get to work on it.

I have been describing the situation of a fairly fortunate writer, any one of the scores or hundreds whose names were familiar to publishers and editors and college deans, but whose works had never been widely popular. There were other writers, younger or less known, who found it much harder simply to keep going. They worked in a chaotic industry where there were no real labor unions. The Authors' League, which tried to serve in that capacity, had seven thousand members in 1954, and not all of them were in good standing. It was then divided into five professional guilds, and one of these—the Dramatists' Guild, with eighteen hundred members—had organized its special field to such an extent that it was able to negotiate on equal terms with theatrical producers. The Screen Writers' Guild, though less unified, had obtained concessions from the Hollywood studios. The Authors' Guild of the League, with twenty-seven hundred members, including about half of the professionals in the book and magazine field, had done a great deal to improve the terms of publishers' contracts; in 1954 it was fighting for higher royalties on soft-cover reprints, with a larger share of the royalties paid to the author. But the Guild had to argue and plead; it wasn't strong enough to present demands and enforce them by going on strike, as labor unions do.

Its activities hadn't contributed much to the welfare of book reviewers, translators, ghost writers, or manuscript editors and revisers, and those were the trades by which many free-lance writers had to earn their precarious livings. Fees for such work had to be set by negotiations between a small craftsman and a not very big businessman, and the craftsman couldn't often be a hard bargainer. He knew that he was replaceable and that the supply of book reviewers, translators, ghost writers, and manuscript editors and revisers was always greater than the demand for their work. The result was that he usually accepted too small a fee and worked at top speed, carelessly, in the effort to earn it before his living expenses had outrun his income. Many fields of literature had suffered from low pay and hasty work, which usually go together, but translation had suffered most of all. Translation should be something more than a trade for hopeful novices and embittered veterans who can't support themselves in any other fashion. Translation is an art that involves the re-creation of a work in another language, for readers with a different background of experience who still must be made to understand what the author means and implies. The art can't be mastered in a year or two; ideally it would be the study of a lifetime. In this country after World War II there were few professional translators, since most writers got out of the field after finding that they couldn't earn a living there by doing good work. That was one reason for the failure of many foreign books in the United States. Ineptly translated, they hadn't really crossed the Atlantic, but had been left sailing from port to port like stateless refugees.

Poetry also suffered from being miserably paid work, but the publishers were less to blame for that condition than was the bookstore audience. Many publishers liked poetry and would have issued more of it if they could have counted on an average sale of fifteen hundred copies per volume; they would have been losing a little money, but would have felt that they were performing a useful service. In the 1950s eight hundred copies was about the average for books of verse not issued at the poet's expense, and that meant a greater loss than publishers could often afford. Books for which the poet paid the cost of publication seldom had any sale, except to relatives. As for the absent readers of poetry, most of them claimed that it had become "too difficult," but it wasn't always so, and nobody argued that the less difficult poets had a wider audience than the others. The fact seemed to be that the more difficult poets were a little more likely to be praised and hence to find readers in a limited circle consisting chiefly of other poets, students of poetry, and book reviewers, who often regarded obscurity as a challenge. In effect, poets were being encouraged to write for that limited circle. Instead of saying that modern poetry lacked readers because it was difficult, one might have come closer to the truth by saying that many modern poets were difficult because they lacked general readers.

If poets earned their livings—and not all of them did, some of them having been supported by their wives or relatives, or by private or public charity—it was chiefly by other means than writing poems. A published book of verse might bring them royalties of two hundred dollars and as much again in reprint rights—or possibly more, in the course of years. For some reason anthologies of poetry had a better sale than volumes by one author and hence earned more for their editors, as well as paying fees to the poets whose work was reprinted. A few universities offered appointments to poets in residence, one at each university, but these posts weren't filled every year. There was nothing in this country like the Third Program of the British Broadcasting Corporation, which helps to support most of the good English poets. On the other hand, American poets were eligible for a good many prizes and fellowships. I should estimate that a little more than ten thousand dollars a year was distributed to poets in prize money, and a larger but variable sum in fellowships. Poets also earned a little by contributing verse to magazines, although the market was limited; only one American weekly, the *New Yorker*, printed a fair amount of serious poetry during the year and paid a good price for it. A better source of income, for those who had a platform manner, was lecturing about poetry and reading their poems to college students and women's clubs. But all these activities together wouldn't have supported twenty poets during the year, if all the income produced by all the literary efforts of all the poets had gone to those twenty. There were hundreds of poets in the country and, in the early 1950s, only two of them earned a livelihood by writing poetry: one was Robert Frost (who also lectured), and one was Ogden Nash. Many, perhaps most, of the recognized poets taught in universities, and the others supported themselves in a variety of fashions; among the better known were two businessmen, a retired doctor, a lawyer, several housewives, some men and women with small private incomes, a publisher, an editor, an ex-janitor, and a professional barfly. The barfly was Maxwell Bodenheim, who had never worked—except for the Federal Writers' Project—and who was murdered in a cheap lodging house early in 1954.

I haven't considered the situation of the many writers who, after a promising start and even after publishing several books, are forced to realize that they have lost their public. Sometimes they have lost their talent as well; their new books are badly fabricated instead of being imagined, and readers aren't held or persuaded by them. But sometimes the authors may write as well as before, or better, and find that fashions have changed. Their new books don't even impress the first audience of publishers' editors. "That man Burnside," the publishers say, "is still a pretty good novelist, but he's jinxed. We'd better not take him on." The magazine editors who used to accept Burnside's work have retired or taken other jobs;

perhaps the magazines have ceased publication. He tries writing juveniles or mysteries, but finds that both those fields require special training which he hasn't bothered to acquire. The entry about him disappears from *Who's Who*, although his name is still printed there with a sign indicating that information about him can be found in an earlier volume. Burnside looks at the name and feels as if he had been exiled, living, to the land of spooks; he can still talk, but nobody hears him, nobody knows that he exists.

There were many Burnsides in the 1950s, and some of them were my friends of long standing. I received a letter from one of them after years of silence. "This is my situation," it started:

Since the war I have written three novels and about fifteen short stories. I have placed three stories. I was struck the other day by reading that Auden said that nothing much is important, but to be published is important. As long as one is published there is a connection, there is a link, there is a functioning, there is the opposite of vacuum. The terrible thing is to feel that you're in a vacuum, that what you have done with so much effort will never, never reach anybody; that the moment will come after you're dead when the papers you have left will, unread by anyone, and discarded, start yellowing and burning. To have left no trace in the continuum is terrible. Then you are really unremarked dust. If you are published, however obscurely, there is a chance that somewhere on a dusty shelf, in some attic, lining some closet, as part of the binding of a book, there are words of yours left. Then you are still somehow alive.

I have another letter from this friend, who used to be a fairly well-known writer before his four years of military service. The second letter is undated, and fifty years ago it would have been a scrawl, but now authors go to the typewriter when they want to say something very fast and truly from the bottom of their minds. Here it is in full:

I sing the failures of the world, those who wanted-to-be but never-became. The Hemingways and Faulkners do not need my song because the glory of the world is theirs. Neither do the Kafkas and Stendhals need it any longer; the songs of others rose over their graves. I sing of the forever obscure, the failures in perpetuum, through the eventual doom. I sing of girls with thick ankles who wanted to be ballet dancers, of potentially great singers who had a permanent frog in the throat. I do not sing of evaders like Casanova who after all did escape from the Leads, but of the countless others who never got away, of those who found a pin in the corner of their cell, and who, after thirty years of digging with the pin, broke out into the open to see a guard waiting for them. I do not sing of the man who put up the main rose window in the center nave at Chartres, but of the other man who competed for the job with him, who drew cartoons and went to the bishop and was encouraged, and who was certain he would get the commission, but who did not after all get it. I don't know if there was such a man, but I imagine him and I sing of him.

I am trying to think of the most obscure person who ever lived, let's say a Chinese child who stood on the hot afternoon of July 9, 1546, and watched a lizard crawling over the very same spot where four centuries later a Chinese soldier was killed with a bullet from a rifle made in Bridgeport USA. I imagine this child at that moment of his, and during this moment of mine I sing of him. I think of all the jobs never gotten, letters never received, books never published, paintings never sold, telephone rings never heard, hopes never fulfilled, dreams never realized; I have a song for all of them, while I breathe the air that doesn't surround them and see the earth that doesn't cover them. I think of muscles unflexed, conceptions unconceived, high resolves unresolved; I not only think of them, I feel them, I experience them, and being past the mood of frustration I sublimate them into a song. But even that is a failure, a flop; it deserves the bird, a tomato in the face. I have no voice. I don't sing very well.

But my friend was unjust to himself, or boastful in an inverted fashion, as writers sometimes are. Very often he sings well, and never better than when he celebrates his failure to sing. Also he is tougher than most people I know and has a better family situation; his wife is employed, he earns money by odd jobs, and he will keep on writing until someday his work may be estimated at its true value—or at more than its value, by the law of compensation. Others in his predicament, the tender souls, are in danger of dying before their time, because discouragement makes them prone to accidents and less resistant to disease. I don't know whether insurance companies have tried to estimate the life expectancy of writers. Such figures, if compiled, might show that writing was one of the riskier occupations, comparable in its mortality rates with deep-sea diving, structural-steel working, and piloting experimental planes. A writer is always experimenting with new methods of soaring to heights or plunging into depths. He always has to struggle with the invisible opponent that is his own subconscious, and sometimes the fruits of the struggle are only exhaustion and discouragement. The mortality rate is highest among unsuccessful writers, and someday insurance agents will be cautioned against issuing policies on their lives. Successful writers—I don't mean the financially successful, but those who carry on their work from year to year with a feeling of accomplishment—are likely to live a long time. One thinks of all the white-maned nineteenth-century poets, the grandfathers; in the middle 1950s they had their successors in Walter de la Mare, Somerset Maugham, Robert Frost, and Thomas Mann. But other recognized and talented writers had succumbed at an early age, and sometimes at the moment of success, to what were in many cases occupational diseases: alcoholism, overwork, melancholia, and suicide. I have written, or have been asked to write, too many obituaries and memoirs of writers my own age or younger, my acquaintances or friends, whose work I admired: Hart Crane, Thomas Wolfe, Scott Fitzgerald, Nathanael West, John Peale Bishop, Genevieve Taggard, F. O. Matthiessen, Edna St. Vincent Millay, Dylan Thomas —not to mention others of perhaps equal talent but not so wide an audience, and sometimes none at all: Allison Crawford, Harry Crosby, Jack Wheelwright, Otis Ferguson, Phelps Putnam. There isn't one of them who shouldn't be doing his best work today.

THE WORKING DAY

It may be as short as fifteen minutes and as long as fifteen hours or more. The fifteen-minute day was that of Francis Parkman when he was writing *The Conspiracy of Pontiac*; he suffered from a nervous affliction that kept him from working longer. In fifteen minutes he could write six lines, on the average, but the lines were *written* and didn't have to be changed. The working day of fifteen hours or more is that of magazine writers meeting a deadline or novelists making corrections just before a manuscript goes to the printer. Hemingway worked on the printer's draft of *For Whom the Bell Tolls* from Miami to New York, sweating over the pages in a Pullman drawing-room where the air conditioning was out of order. Later, in New York, he rewrote the galley proofs in ninety-six consecutive hours, during which he didn't leave his room at the Hotel Barclay. But the first draft of the novel had been written on an easier daily schedule; he started after an early breakfast and stopped before lunch—though sometimes, if a chapter was going well, the lunch might be delayed until the middle of the afternoon.

As a general rule the more disciplined writers—Hemingway is one of them—have the shorter working days; they spend from two to four hours at their desks, then try to forget the book until next morning, trusting that their subconscious minds will carry it ahead while the writers are busy with other activities. Undisciplined writers often spend long days in and out of their studies. They hardly ever stop thinking about their work and never get much of it done, except in bursts.

The working day is often the working night. That schedule has the great advantage of providing freedom from interruptions: there aren't any more visitors or door-to-door salesmen, the children have been put to bed, the telephone doesn't ring. Night is favorable to certain types of writing, to flights of fancy and also to miserable hack work that is hard to do by day, when the writer's critical sense is livelier. Young writers who have to support themselves by other occupations have no choice but to work at night. I know a young novelist who runs a second-hand bookstore that opens at noon and closes at nine in the evening. He goes home, eats a late dinner, and writes until five. His schedule doesn't leave enough time for sleep, and I doubt that he will be able to continue it after he is forty.

Middle-aged writers usually work in the morning, although there are many exceptions to the rule. One exception was Amy Lowell, who rose at three in the afternoon and started working after midnight. She liked to have guests for dinner, distinguished foreign men of letters or bright innocent Harvard students, but she sent them away from her big house in Brookline at five minutes after twelve, just in time to catch the last streetcar that rumbled down Boylston Street. Then she sat in a deep leather armchair before the fireplace, with her feet on a stool, a blotting pad in her lap, and a collection of finely sharpened pencils on a narrow table, and worked until dawn. The interlined manuscripts were left in the hall to be copied by her two secretaries, who weren't allowed to use erasers and had to destroy every typewritten page on which there was a mistake. It was a schedule that required, among other things, a great deal of mental vigor and a household of trained servants. Most writers after the age of forty find that they haven't any longer enough energy to work effectively at night. They have their best ideas early in the morning, when they are also best able to criticize the ideas, and the older the writers are, the earlier most of them go to work. I know two distinguished men in their sixties who regularly start writing at six in the morning.

Let us picture the working day of a somewhat younger and more typical writer; he might be forty years old and he lives in the country with his wife. The day is one of those when he is starting work on a "piece"—which is anything short intended for magazine publication—or on a new chapter of a longer work. After sitting for half an hour over a second cup of breakfast coffee he goes upstairs to his study. There he takes the typewriter out of its case, puts in a sheet of paper, and writes a first sentence that he has been thinking about all week. But the next sentence isn't clear in his mind and he starts pacing from window to window like a caged animal. He is tempted to escape into the garden, which is getting weedy; perhaps he could think more clearly with a hoe in his hand. Resisting the temptation, he suddenly thinks of another sentence. He is at the typewriter when he hears the telephone ring and hopes the call is for his wife, who answers it—but no, New York is calling person-to-person for the writer. New York turns out to be a buzz of confused conversation, a wait, and then a clear voice saying, "I'm sorry, Miss Maybank has stepped out of the office. We'll have to call you back."

His wife drives off to the village to do the shopping. Watching her go, but not really seeing her, the writer thinks of another sentence and rushes upstairs to set it down. He reads over what he has written, tears the sheet out of the typewriter, and does a revised version of the three sentences; then he goes back to pacing from window to window. He wonders who Miss Maybank is and what she wants him to do. The telephone rings and he goes downstairs, calling out to the empty house, "I'll take it, dear." It is somebody from the school board with a question for his wife. He says, "Just a minute, I'll call her," then remembers that she is in the village. He goes to the kitchen, finds that there is some cold coffee in a pot, and puts it on a burner. The telephone rings again and this time, after another wait, Miss Maybank introduces herself. She is a fact-checker for a magazine and wants to know the source of a quotation that he has used in a forthcoming article. He runs upstairs, goes through his papers, and finds the quotation. Miss Maybank starts to thank him at length, but there is an acrid smell from the kitchen and he has to hang up; the coffee has boiled over. While he is cleaning the stove his wife appears with an armful of groceries, and they get into an argument about the mess he always makes. He goes upstairs, still muttering, and finds that he can write another sentence, but it will be the last that morning.

The mail has come, and he reads it after lunch. It includes a manuscript by an unknown author who begs him to recommend it to a publisher and thanks him profusely in advance, but doesn't enclose postage. There are galley proofs of two novels that their publishers hope he will like and say a few kind words about, to print on the jacket. An almost total stranger wants to be sponsored for a Guggenheim fellowship. The writer has saved one envelope for the last, because it looks as if there might be a check in it, but what he finds is an appeal for funds. He reflects that every established writer is regarded as a sort of unpaid service bureau for the literature industry. Why not incorporate himself and ask for tax exemption as a charitable organization? Unfortunately he has no organization, not even a secretary to take care of his correspondence. He remembers Oscar Wilde and his remark that he had known scores of young men who came up to London and ruined themselves by answering letters. Nevertheless he composes a rather testy letter to the author of the manuscript, asking him please to send return postage. Then, feeling too drowsy to stay indoors, he goes out to work in the garden. Late in the afternoon, while he is hoeing a row of beans, another sentence occurs to him. He goes back to the typewriter and works fast for twenty minutes, with the words coming easily, but then his wife calls upstairs to remind him that George and Betty are coming for dinner and he'd better get dressed and be ready to mix the cocktails, of which he will drink too many.

Next morning he starts by reading over what he has written. "This won't do at all," he says aloud as he drops the two sheets into the wastebasket; then he plucks them out again and lays them aside for reference. This day, and the two or three that follow, there are fewer interruptions, but now the writer would almost welcome them; his new obstacle is a torpid and recalcitrant mind. He tries to provoke it into activity by lying on the couch in his study and looking fixedly at a point on the ceiling. Thoughts occur to him, but they all seem unpersuasive or unusable. He paces the floor while the typewriter stares at him with its forty-two round keys like so many accusing eyes. "You damn father symbol," he says to it. He escapes the typewriter by working in the garden until he lapses into a state of brute exhaustion. Next day he takes a long walk on a dull road, hoping to hear the right words repeated by an inner voice, in time to his footsteps, but the words aren't right or writable. His appetite is poor, his sleep broken, his temper so bad that his wife keeps out of his way. He begins to worry about paying the bills, with no money coming in, and wonders whether he shouldn't consult a psychoanalyst. But we are talking about a professional writer, not one of the symptomatic artists who might be Dr. Bergler's patients. The professional has obligations to fulfill or a deadline to meet, and he usually ends by meeting it.

Gradually and in part subconsciously the story has been taking shape in his mind as he walked and worried. One afternoon he is surprised to find himself typing away at it. He eats dinner with an abstracted air, replying briefly to his wife's remarks, then goes back to his study. If he is working on a magazine piece he is likely to finish a first draft of it that night, while the conception is fresh in his mind. He seldom retains a clear picture of the hours when he is actually writing; all he remembers afterward is that the typewriter kept up a nervous clatter, with intervals of silence when he walked the floor between paragraphs, and that he filled a big wastebasket with discarded pages. Once when he came back to the room after getting a drink of water he found it foul-smelling and hazy with smoke. Most writers smoke too much when they are working, not so much for the taste of tobacco as for the need to have something in their mouths; those who stop smoking are likely to chew gum or pencils or kitchen matches.[3] This particular writer has filled a big bowl with pipe ashes, and when he finishes the piece at three o'clock his mouth feels as if he had tried to swallow a boiling infusion of bitterweed. Words and phrases keep echoing in his mind; some he decides to change tomorrow, but others are so completely right that they give him a sense of elation. There is a gray light in the window before he falls asleep.

Tomorrow—or rather this afternoon—he will revise what he has written, an easier operation that he usually enjoys; then he will send it to the magazine just in time for the issue that is going to press. The next day he will go fishing, with a good conscience, and the morning after he will start his struggle to write another piece. Magazine writers are like sprinters, always in severe training to run short races; they live in brief cycles of depression and elation. Book

3. A friend of mine signed a contract for a second book, but hasn't written it. "Every time I start to work on it," he says, "I think of all the cigarettes I'll have to smoke before it's finished."

writers are like cross-country runners, jogging along at a steady gait. After the first struggle to get started they can work on their projects for a few hours each day, week after week, always knowing that they will start each morning where they left off the night before —unless, or until, they are stopped midway in the book by some new problem that demands another period of silent wrestling with their minds; then they are off again at the steady trot that may continue to the end—though often they find themselves sprinting in the last desperate half-mile.

There is a never-ending argument about the best places for writers to work: in or out of cities, north or south, facing the sea or the mountains, in America or Europe, and at what sort of desk, in what sort of room or office or study. Hemingway once stopped the argument for a time: "——," he said, "the best place for a writer to work is in his head." The essential part of a writer's work is done there, often without any external sign that he is working, except for a vacant look in his eyes and a habit of not hearing remarks until they are repeated. Essentially his work consists in having ideas, or rather conceptions, and putting them into words. These may occur to him at curious times and places: on a train in the early morning, or lingering over a second cup of breakfast coffee, or sitting motionless in an overstuffed chair, or taking a long afternoon ramble, or waking from an uneasy sleep—perhaps the words were dreamed [4] —or in a crowded room when everyone is talking excitedly and the writer is talking too, but thinking of something else than what he says. Some writers have fixed occasions for thinking, and that may prove to be a dangerous practice: if the routine is changed by accident they may find that ideas no longer occur to them. I know one writer who, like many others, had fallen into the habit of thinking while he walked. After a siege of arthritis he couldn't take long walks any longer, and it was four years before he was able to finish his next book. The luckier writers are those who have learned to think at their desks.

The desk, which is often a table, may be large or small and may be placed in any sort of room. One of my friends works at a little

4. James Thurber said in a letter, "I get a lot of help, when I am stuck, by dreams every now and then. In one recently I was in a coupé with an artist I know and two men I didn't know, and the artist said, 'This car won't go until we get rid of these characters.' We stopped the car and put them out, and the next day I cut the characters they represented out of my book."

pine-topped kitchen table in a hall bedroom that is hardly wider than a door. "A small room is best for thinking," he explained. "It's more like a womb." He didn't tell me why he had his best thoughts in a womb. Most writers prefer a big desk or table in a room that is long enough for them to pace up and down between sentences. They like to face a wall rather than a window, which would be distracting, and they like to have a bookcase and a couch. They are lucky if the room is at a distance from their homes and hence from household interruptions and the double-damned telephone.

Usually a writer likes to be alone when he is actually writing, but he can sometimes work equally well in a roomful of strangers. Many books have been written from beginning to end in the typewriter room of the New York Public Library, where there is space for twenty persons at a long table; some of them will be reading, some typing, some looking abstractedly at the wall. Other books, but not so many, are written at the Library of Congress, which provides separate almost soundproof cubicles for research students. A greater quantity of verse and prose, including some distinguished works, has been produced at writers' colonies—notably at the MacDowell Colony in New Hampshire, at Yaddo in upstate New York, and at the newer Huntington Hartford Foundation in California. These endowed colonies invite a number of guests for specified periods, usually for two months at Yaddo, which is open all year, and for the summer season at MacDowell. Guests are furnished with board, lodging, and a place to work—all free, except that MacDowell makes a small charge for board. Each of the colonies is doing more for the arts in America, in a modest and practical fashion, than foundations that disburse much larger sums of money.

The actual writing of an essay or a story is a task that largely consists, as I said, of transcribing an inner monologue (or one voice of an inner dialogue). Sometimes the whole story exists in the author's mind—it has been silently told over, once or many times—before the first word of it is set on paper. Sometimes the writer has only the beginning of a story and a picture of how it will end; then the monologue continues while he is sitting at his desk or pacing the floor. Sometimes his transcription of the monologue will be as faithful as a stenographer's report. "I listen to the voices," Faulkner explained, "and when I've put down what the voices say, it's right. I don't always like what they say, but I don't change it." Other writers treat the monologue, or dialogue, as if they were on the copy desk of a big newspaper and as if the story had been handed in by a cub reporter; they keep changing the lead, changing the sequence, changing the words, to conform with an imaginary stylebook of their own.

The monologue can be written down and corrected by several methods and combinations of methods. Most writers now use a typewriter; some are skilled touch typists, some hunt and peck. Others, including many of those who reach a wide audience, dictate to their secretaries or—more often now—to different types of recording machines. Thomas Wolfe wrote everything with pen or pencil, then had his manuscripts copied. Fitzgerald used the same method, but not for the reason Wolfe gave, that his hands were too big for the keyboard of a typewriter. Hemingway types his short stories, but does the first drafts of his novels in pencil, counting the words at the end of each writing day. "If you write with a pencil," he says, "you get three different sights at it to see if the reader is getting what you want him to. First when you read it over; then when it is typed you get another chance to improve it, and again in proof." Thornton Wilder writes with a pen and revises with a pen; he is almost the only recognized American author who submits a holograph manuscript to his publishers. John Steinbeck has a complicated method: first he thinks about a novel for months or even a year until it is clear in his head, then early one morning he starts the first chapter in longhand. At the end of the day's work he dictates from the manuscript into a machine, changing as he goes; dictation is an essential part of the process, because what he writes is a spoken prose. His secretary transcribes the record and Steinbeck revises her transcript. At the end of the novel, the whole manuscript is copied and revised once more; sometimes it has to be copied twice before it is ready for the printer.

The difference in speed of transcription by the different methods is sometimes an illusion. A touch typist's fingers are likely to move faster than his mind, with the result that he makes several drafts of a page before it seems right to him. A pen or a pencil is slower than the mind, but that gives time for mental corrections and the handwritten words are more likely to be a final expression, like Parkman's six lines per day; many touch typists give more hours, and sometimes more days, to a book than Parkman did. Dictated prose is often easy to read, but loose and wordy, since the speaker hadn't time to be concise. Again, he may pause so often and make so many corrections that he doesn't produce more words per hour than he might have written with a pen. A wise author tries every method of putting his words on paper. By changing methods he keeps reminding himself that the words come out of his head and can always be transcribed in some fashion, even if they have to be scratched on plaster or traced in the sand with his big toe. Otherwise he is in danger of becoming so attached to a particular method that when something interferes with it—for example, an injury to his hand—he will have to stop writing. Eugene O'Neill always wrote his plays in a ledger, with a fine pen, in a script so small that his secretary had to use a magnifying glass. After he contracted Parkinson's disease, which makes the hand shake, he couldn't write any more of the plays he had already planned.

Whatever the method of transcription, there are fast writers and slow writers, and they seem to be different breeds of men. James Thurber is one of the slow ones, though he isn't a "bleeder," which is the technical word for writers who produce one phrase at a time, as if it were a drop of their heart's blood. Instead he belongs to the other type of slow writers, who like to put everything down in a burst of energy, then go back over it time and again. He said in a letter written in 1954:

> I have been trying to finish a book I started, or a long piece rather, just a year ago in Williamsburg. I have spent a thousand hours on it, although it won't exceed fifteen thousand words when it's finished, and I've done about thirty complete rewrites, but have run into the well-known blank wall. . . . This business about slaving over a piece to get every word right reminds me of arguments I've had with Elliot Paul, who almost believes you have no moral right to change what flows out of you onto the paper, and with others. Simenon, who can write four hundred times as fast as we can, happened to drop in yesterday with my English publisher, Hamish Hamilton. Fastest writers I know are Sally Benson and John O'Hara. O'Hara, like me, is no good at plotting in advance, but his only revising, even of novels, is what he calls "pencil work," a minor change here and there in final rereading. When you consider that *Appointment in Samarra* was done like that, it makes you think that the boy is a genius. One thing is sure, a genius, by definition, doesn't have to go over and over his stuff.

As a slow writer, but not the slowest, I envy and a little resent the "geniuses"—though I shouldn't have yielded to the temptation to put the word in quotation marks. I should like to believe that all those hours of labor gave my breed of writer a superior status, but that isn't always the case. Simenon writes his short novels in eight days, after thinking about them for a month, and nobody could write them better. There are some types of writing, Faulkner says, that are like riding a bicycle on a tight wire; you have to go fast or you fall off. Some of Faulkner's most involved and longest sentences were written most rapidly. The slow writers are often the deceptively smooth writers; the best of their stories, like Thurber's, appear to be very simple until you read them a second time. Other writers can learn a great deal from Thurber, where they can't learn much from Simenon, whose fecundity is no more catching than his power of invention.

In spite of typewriters and recording machines, the average speed of composition has probably decreased in the last hundred years. Critical standards—including the writer's own standards—have become more exacting. Publishers' editors are critics of a practical sort, and they make more demands on a manuscript before sending it to the printer. Magazines that pay big fees to their authors expect them to do careful work, with the result that articles, like books, are being produced more slowly. In the 1850s Trollope was learning to write two hundred and fifty words every fifteen minutes, with his eye on the clock; his manuscripts would go to the printer, with little revision, on the dates he had promised to deliver them. Trollope was methodical to a degree that other writers of his time regarded as scandalous, but most of the others counted on producing a thousand words or more each writing day. In the 1950s five hundred words were regarded as a good day's work—except by the authors of big naturalistic novels "disdaining all pretensions to style"—and the words were a first draft that was likely to require another day of revision. Aside from the time they spent in gathering material and making outlines, few of the careful novelists or essayists were producing as many as three thousand words in a writing week.

XI.

A NATURAL HISTORY, CONCLUDED

Their Domestic Habits

The domestic life of writers is a subject for a book, or several books. Instead of trying to present the whole of it, I might simply transcribe my notes on some aspects of the subject, beginning with an attempt to picture the average professional writer. I don't say the normal writer. "Normal" is an honorific word—an *epitheton ornans*, as Dr. Bergler calls it—and its use would involve us in a series of value judgments that have no place in a description of actual persons in their actual homes. Even the term "average" is hard to use in discussing a profession that includes so many special groups and eccentric individuals; possibly there is no such creature as an average writer. But if he did exist, and was established in his calling—

At the age of forty he would probably be living somewhere within a hundred miles of New York, unless he was outstandingly successful. In that case he would have complete freedom of residence and might live anywhere from Arizona to Italy and from Tahiti to Cuba (with a concentration of glitter in Bucks County, Pennsylvania, and Fairfield County, Connecticut), but he wouldn't any longer be an average writer. If less famous, he would have developed some specialty like editing or reading manuscripts or writing some particular type of articles or stories on which he could depend for part of his income. He would spend a day or two a week, or a week each month in the city, carrying out his specialty and conferring with editors. He would also travel more than most Americans, both in this country and abroad. His total income would vary from year to year, but it might average six or eight thousand dollars, after deducting his rather high business expenses.

He would have a wife and one, two, or three children, although there are also many childless marriages. The younger writers who served in World War II have been more philoprogenitive, and some of them will end by having four or five children, but until their time the profession hadn't been reproducing itself biologically. The writer of forty would own his house—probably with a big mortgage —but there will be less than the usual number of domestic appliances because he has developed a high resistance to salesmanship. Among the appliances will be a radio, probably FM, and a phonograph with a large collection of records. If he owns a television set he will explain apologetically that he got it for the children, but now the writer and his wife have taken to watching a few programs. He has no strong religious beliefs, though he sometimes attends a local church, more often in the 1950s than ten years before. Probably he is dissatisfied with his work and his mode of life; forty is a critical age for writers, as for many other people. In politics he is vaguely liberal, disturbed by the excesses of the loyalty crusade, and opposed to communism with an intensity of passion that partly depends on whether he had been entangled with pro-communist fronts in the 1930s; the more entangled once, the more passionately opposed. In 1952 he voted for Stevenson because of his speeches; as a *New Yorker* writer explained, "You can't vote against the English language." He has begun to take part in local activities. Recently his wife was elected to the school board, and he would like to run for office himself, but he has decided that the office, and even the campaign, would take too much time from his writing.

Love and Marriage. Writing, not love or power, is the ruling passion to which everything else in his life has been subordinated. Dr. Bergler insists that writers, by definition, are incapable of love. It is hard to argue about such a broad statement, because it is hard to agree on a definition of love. If you cite an example of a writer in love, the analyst can always say, and often does, "That isn't really love, it's just a fixation." Another word is popular with gossips: they say that Tom or Eunice is "infatuated" when they mean that he or she has fallen in love with somebody too young or old or of a different social background, like an heiress with her riding master. Writers have as many fixations and infatuations as the members of any other professional group. If they don't have many Romeo-and-Juliet affairs, neither do other Americans after the age of twenty. Most of the analysts—beginning with Freud, who thought it wasn't proper for his fiancée to go skating—are old-fashioned in their ideal of the sexual relationship. Apparently the pattern that many of them would like to impose is one of lifelong and unquestioning fidelity, the pattern that Jung—who doesn't agree with his colleagues—describes as the medieval marriage. It can be taken for granted that not many writers or bankers or shipping clerks have marriages of that ideal type. The important question about writers would seem to be whether they can achieve any stable partnership between the sexes that is approved by society.

The divorce rate would be a rough statistical index of their success. It is quite high among young writers living in cities, though not nearly so high as among movie actors. There are also many irregular relationships in this group, more than among movie actors, who have to be careful about being found out. Young writers don't have to be careful and sometimes pretend—less often now than in the past—that their legal wives are mistresses. The divorce rate is very low among older writers in the country, where it is hard to live alone and where divorce not only breaks up a household but also—for one partner and sometimes for both—destroys a way of life. Again the rate is low for the many writers attached to college faculties, as it is among professors as a group. Women writers have more difficulty than men in forming stable relationships, and their divorce rate appears to be higher, at least among those under forty.

One conflict between male writers and their wives is over money and social status. The wife wants the family to get ahead in its immediate world—which may be a small community—while the writer wants to rise in the nebulous world of good literature, where income and expenditure don't matter; he wants to keep up with Hawthorne and Melville, not with the Purvises down the block. He wants to earn only enough to feed and clothe the family, not too well, while he is doing his best work, but the wife says, "It isn't fair to the children," and keeps urging him to write potboilers instead of the great novel he is dreaming about. At least that is a familiar picture of the writer and his wife, and it must be true in many cases, though I have also known writers who wanted to earn money fast, while their wives restrained them, saying, "We'll get along somehow till you finish the book." Those other wives don't often appear in novels, especially if the novels are written by men. And who has paid a tribute in fiction to the wives of struggling young writers? Dressed in cheap clothes, living in cold-water flats or in farmhouses with no water at all, having to put up with their husbands' moods and selfishness, not sustained like the husbands by the thought that they are making objects of enduring beauty, sometimes their reward is to be dropped, ditched, when the husbands have made a reputation and younger women run after them. I have known many such wives, including some who have disappeared from the literary world. "Where's Jennie now?" I have wondered, remembering what an appealing household it was when Jennie was entertaining her husband's friends. After he left her for that society woman did she go back to her parents in Omaha? And what about Marjorie, who also vanished? But there are stories with happier endings and often the marriage is lasting.

A fairly common sexual pattern is for the writer to have many affairs in his youth, to marry a woman older than himself, to watch the marriage break up in quarrels resulting from a conflict of standards—or from professional jealousy, if the wife is a writer too, or simply because she drinks too much—then to marry a woman his own age and stay married, perhaps with minor infidelities. If the second marriage is a failure he either makes the best of it or else tries again, for he can't get along without a wife. In a writer's household the wife discharges a whole group of functions besides the simple one of being his mate. She not only acts as housekeeper, nursemaid, chauffeur, and hostess—like most American wives of the business classes—but also serves, on occasion, as secretary, receptionist, office manager, business consultant, first audience for the writer's work, guardian of his reputation, and partner in what has become a family enterprise. That phrase at the end of the forewords of many scholarly books, ". . . deepest thanks to my wife, without whose devoted patience . . . ," is funny because it recurs so often, but also funny because it is innocently true.

Writers' marriages, if they endure, become much closer partnerships than other American middle-class marriages. One reason is that writers have more sympathy with the woman's point of view; perhaps there is more of the feminine in their natures. They are sensual, unashamed about their instincts, and realistic in their personal relations, as women are also inclined to be. They are likely to display more than the usual masculine interest in clothes, cooking, decoration, and gossip, so that the family has a lot to talk about. Another reason for the closeness of these marriages is that writers, men and women, usually work at home. The husbands of women writers go to their offices, so that the woman has a few free hours, but men writers are self-employed, and their wives must put up with them all day. The partners have twice as much time for quarrels—about meals, the children, cigarette burns in the rug, driving the car, having company for dinner, and that perennial complaint of writers, "How can I work in this madhouse?"—but they also have time to know and respect each other. Instead of being a medieval marriage, their relationship is often like that of mother and wayward son, less often like that of father and daughter, sometimes like that of brother and sister living for years in the same house, knowing each other's weaknesses, divided, inseparable, and completely dependent on each other not merely for happiness but even for getting through the day.

Darling. In every close marriage one partner is the darling. That isn't at all the same as saying that he or she is dominant, or wears the pants. He or she may be obeyed as the darling parent, or may be scolded as the darling child, but in either case he is petted and cherished. A married writer usually manages to be the darling of that household. His wife or her husband says over the telephone, "No, I'd rather you wouldn't come for the chairs this morning, Harry [or Eleanor] will be working." The last word is spoken portentously, as if she were saying, "He will be communing with God." She puts down the receiver, and a moment later Harry disappears into the big room that the children are never allowed to enter, although the rest of the family is rather crowded. For an hour or two nothing is heard from the room, not even the clatter of his typewriter; then Harry reappears in the kitchen, where his wife is drying the last of the breakfast dishes after sending the children to school. It's his indigestion again; he hasn't been able to write a line; he's been lying on the couch and suffering. His wife, the petter and cherisher, puts him to bed.

Or instead of playing the sickly child, darling may be active, a mountain climber, an explorer, always packing for another expedition to South America or Central Africa. His wife stays home with the children, but she does the packing and insists that Harry needs heavy woolens and scarves, which will stay in his tent unworn as a memento: "Dear Eleanor, she takes such good care of me." Darling is the public figure, but don't make the mistake of thinking that he always guides the destinies of the family. It is more often the other, the gray-plumaged cherisher, who manages the household with a quiet feeling of being indispensable. The public and private positions of the partners are revealed by the different fashions in which strangers and intimates refer to them. Strangers say, "I'm going to see Henry Proudfit, you know, the novelist"; the wife doesn't exist for them. Neighbors say, "I saw the Proudfits"—as a household—"in the village this afternoon." Their friends say, "Let's drop in on Harry and Eleanor," or even, with a stricter feeling for their relative importance, ". . . on Eleanor and Harry."

Very young writers are likely to overlook this situation when they try, as some of them do, to get themselves adopted or godfathered by a prominent novelist. On a first visit they talk about his work, make brilliant analyses of its effect on them, go away in a glow of love for the novelist and esteem for themselves, with an invitation to come again, "any time—I'll let you know," but the novelist seldom lets them know.

In the meantime the young man has been discussed in the household. "That young fellow Homer Jones," the novelist says. "Seems to me he has a lot of promise. Let's ask him to dinner with Betty and George."

"They wouldn't like him," says the cherisher. "He's really pretty stupid and—I don't know—pushing."

"Why, I didn't notice that," darling says.

"But you never do. You sat there and listened, taking in that coarse flattery, and didn't notice that he hardly said a word to me all afternoon. I know what Betty would think of him."

Education of the Young. The subject is hotly argued in writers' families, as in other middle-class homes. Most of the mothers believe in progressive education, many of the fathers don't, and the difference of opinion sometimes leads to a compromise by which the children are sent to progressive elementary schools and traditional secondary schools. The progressive secondary schools attract more girls than boys. As fathers, writers are likely to have two principles of education that may prove to be in conflict: they believe that it should be democratic and also believe that children should be taught the fundamentals, including grammar and composition. The first principle makes them send their children to public schools, except in New York, Chicago, and Boston, and is sometimes an argument for moving to the country, where the grade schools are a complete cross-section of the community. "Because the schools are better here" is a writer's one excuse for living in the despised suburbs. The second principle, however, causes many writers to take their older children out of public high schools—sometimes against the wishes of the children, who have a good time there—and send them to private secondary schools, which maintain higher academic standards. Exeter is a popular choice for writers' sons, or rather for the parents, because it has the reputation of being exceptionally thorough; other choices are Andover and, of late years, Groton. The daughters are often sent to Putney, which is coeducational and progressive. Harvard is still the favorite men's college, for academic reasons, but there isn't any outstanding choice among women's colleges.

Social Life. Many European visitors, among them Stephen Spender and Simone de Beauvoir, have been impressed or saddened by the loneliness of American writers, as contrasted with the busy literary life of Paris and London. It is true that writers here don't often form groups after the age of thirty, and that comparatively few of them live in anything that might be called a literary colony. Those who do live in or near such a colony are inclined to be defensive about their choice of residence; either they don't talk much to strangers or else they explain, "Our house is four miles from town, and I don't see much of the other writers"—as if not seeing them were a virtue. In the 1950s towns and places with the reputation of being year-round writers' colonies were Big Sur, on the California coast; Santa Fe; Woodstock, New York, among the painters; the elbow of Cape Cod; and Westport, Connecticut, where the writers and illustrators were pretty well submerged by the influx of suburban residents. Writers were less defensive about going to summer colonies; they seemed to feel that anyone could understand their preference for spending a vacation among friends. Besides the endowed colonies, like MacDowell and Yaddo, there were informal summer groupings of writers at the eastern end of Long Island (the

Hamptons), on Martha's Vineyard, and on the Maine coast. Key West, the great winter colony of the 1930s, had been largely taken over by the Navy. In Europe the younger American writers liked to congregate in Rome, Florence, or Paris, with outriders in Majorca, Tangier, and Positano.

Most of the older writers lived apart from their colleagues, but that isn't the only reason why Spender and others were impressed by their isolation. Among New York writers there was very little coffee-house life of the type familiar in Europe. Such of the life as did exist was pretty well confined to the younger bohemian writers, who patronized a few Italian restaurants, taverns, and *espresso* parlors south and west of Washington Square. Their meeting places changed often, by a sort of predetermined pattern. First a group of young writers would discover a cheap restaurant and sit there every evening; then its reputation would spread and it would be invaded by people the writers didn't like: either by uptowners who spent too much and raised the prices, or else by bands of fairies who shrieked and giggled until a uniformed policeman was stationed at the bar. The writers would look for another meeting place, and it might be months before they found one that pleased them.

There had always been something a little clubby or secret about the literary life in New York; even among the younger writers it didn't flourish when exposed to publicity. As for the established older writers, there was no café to which they could go night after night with the expectation of meeting others in the profession; there was nothing like the Café Flore and the Deux Magots, or the Romanisches Café in Berlin (or Schwanneke's before Hitler), or the Café Central in Vienna, nor was there any restaurant so widely patronized by writers as the Café Royal in London used to be. There was "21," of course, but it was "exclusive" in the sense of being too expensive for most writers. The round table at the Algonquin had been like the *Stammtisch* at Schwanneke's, but the "vicious circle" that surrounded it had dissolved long ago. Establishments on the European model had a hard time surviving in New York, as witness the disappearance of the Lafayette and the Brevoort.

There wasn't as much club life as in London—or, proportionally, as in Boston or Chicago—and there were no social clubs primarily for writers, although many of the older men belonged to the Coffee House, the Players, or the Century. Those who didn't belong to clubs weren't greatly bothered by the lack of them, since the clubs were only for men, while most writers learn to prefer mixed company. A more serious lack was that of literary salons like those which have flourished in Paris since the days of Louis XIV. In nineteenth-century England there were few salons, if any, but there were week-end parties in country houses that served much the same purposes. One of the purposes was serious conversation about literature, art, ideas, and public affairs; another was introducing persons of talent to persons of wealth and social standing, often, but not always, to the profit of both sides. New York society hasn't shown much interest in writers, who, in turn, haven't learned much about society. That may be one of the reasons why society in the old sense has been decaying: it had no minstrels to sing its praises or novelists—except Edith Wharton—to make it tragic or glittering. As for serious conversation about literature, most American writers are ashamed or even afraid of it. They sometimes write about ideas, but seldom talk about them.

Friendships between New York writers or their families are interrupted when one of the families moves to the country. "We'll have you out for a weekend," the wife and the husband tell their friends, and they keep the promise once or twice. But weekends, to be enjoyable, require servants to keep the house in order, and writers scattered over the countryside are even less likely to have servants than their neighbors. The result is that the custom of having people up for the weekend has given way to the custom of having near or distant neighbors in for dinner—since dinners are less strain on the housewife—and the neighbors turn out to be not writers but intelligent and prosperous, often retired people who have chosen to live outside the commuting belt. A sort of society is taking shape, in Bucks and Fairfield Counties and the Litchfield Hills, but it isn't a literary society.

All this explains the comment of literary visitors from Europe, and why it has to be qualified. American writers are somewhat isolated from one another, but they aren't isolated from people. They rather like to be told that they are lonely, but the loneliness, though real, is intellectual or emotional rather than physical. The average writer spends more time by himself than men in other professions, but that's only part of the story; he also spends more time in purely social intercourse with persons of many types who aren't office associates or business clients or members of his immediate family. Hemingway often says, "Writing is the loneliest trade," and that is true as regards the trade itself. It is also true, however, that Hemingway knows more people than most Congressmen or their secretaries and has a great number of devoted friends; not many of these happen to be writers.

Although there are fewer social contacts among the writers themselves than among those of almost any other nation, a sort of literary commonwealth continues to exist. Its members don't see each other daily or weekly, but they write candid letters, they serve together on prize juries, they meet their distant friends on lecture tours, they gather in New York at publishers' cocktail parties—which are their mass rallies and demonstrations—and at the spring "ceremonial" of the National Institute of Arts and Letters, and some of them spend one or two winter months in a New York hotel, to which they invite their literary acquaintances. They read book reviews and literary-gossip columns, and they listen to gossip too—not all of which is malicious; there is such a thing as admiring gossip. One famous author knows what another is doing and is obligated to pass judgment on his latest work

This loose professional world is in some ways as snobbish as the Faubourg Saint-Germain. Individuals are received in it or they are not received. The reasons for rejection are partly personal ("I can't stand him, he talks to me as if I were a meeting"), but chiefly professional ("He can't write"). The fraud is pretty quickly discovered and dropped by his colleagues, even though the public still reads his work. The man of talent is invited to parties for a long time after it is known that he might get drunk and start breaking up the furniture, like Hart Crane. One should add that the talented writer is likely to be more interesting and less objectionable than the untalented. There are all sorts of gradations between them, and a pecking order of talent is quickly established: X can make offensive true remarks to Y, who can make them to Z, but Z can't make them to X. "The literary game—" said my friend George Ollendorf. "Sometimes it's exactly like the boys' game of buckeyes. Two authors bump their heads together, or their reputations, until one of them cracks. The victor moves on to crack another reputation, or be cracked in turn. Finally someone is left as King Buckeye—"

"Yes," I interrupted, "and it's probably someone who stayed out of the game until the last moment."

What They Wear. Among writers in the city, none of the dark-brown corduroy suits that painters like, and no businessmen's blue double-breasted suits with a white handkerchief over the heart. In Connecticut no flowered sport shirts worn outside the belt, no saddle-stitched jackets without lapels, not many shorts or sandals, no two-toned shoes. Most American writers of the 1950s dressed rather conservatively, often in the Eastern collegiate uniform of tweed jacket (most admired if it was of the best material, gone threadbare), button-down Oxford shirt (on the Brooks Brothers pattern), gray flannel slacks, and mahogany-colored brogues or loafers. Some writers preferred gray single-breasted flannel or worsted business suits. In the country they wore denim work shirts, levis or khaki pants, and dirty white sneakers. Usually they asked the barber for a medium haircut; those who had crew cuts or wore their hair long in back and at the sides were suspected, most often wrongly, of belonging to deviant groups. There were some beards among the younger writers who had lived in Europe.

Writers' wives followed a diversity of fashions. Some wore dressmaker suits or woolen or silk dresses, but the general impression at cocktail parties was of flaring, brightly colored cottons: peasant or Mexican blouses—often set off with a piece of Mexican silver jewelry or a Sandy Calder pin—broad belts, dirndls or gipsy skirts, and low-heeled shoes or ballet slippers. At home in the kitchen or garden the wives dressed in slacks (or blue jeans, if they were Bennington girls) and a man's white shirt. They had few occasions for evening gowns and seldom wore hats. Women writers could be distinguished from writers' wives by the fact that they did wear hats, some of which belonged in a costume museum. Most of the women writers seemed to have dressed themselves for one of three roles: they might be Sirens and dangerous, or they might be Sensible Girls with straight hair and loose jackets, or they might be authentic and often entertaining Frumps.

Diversions. Golf and bridge were regarded as the two principal diversions of the professional classes, but not many writers played one or the other. Not many were home mechanics. Not many went to baseball games or even talked baseball; the only fans among my literary acquaintances were Hemingway, Farrell, and John Chamberlain. Some writers played a mean hand of poker, many played tennis or badminton, and more played ping-pong, which was close to being the writer's game. There were enough skiers so that each spring one expected to meet one or two novelists on crutches. There were some theater-goers, though not so many as in former years, and many concert-goers; attendance at the movies was rather less than the average for American households. Many hours were spent listening to recorded music; most of this was classical, but younger writers were likely to be authorities on jazz, with strong feelings for or against bop. Most writers liked to travel, and almost all did a lot of reading, though some stopped reading books by others during the months when they were writing books of their own. Many were gardeners or bird watchers, some were hunters—usually of small upland game—and more were fishermen, especially trout fishermen, who could be alone on a stream. The principal diversion of many writers, perhaps of most, was drinking together.

As an excuse for drinking, the younger writers had parties—which were also an excuse for courting—and older writers had dinner parties. The party was a development out of the "orgy" as celebrated by romantic nineteenth-century poets and students; one of their orgies is described at length in Flaubert's *Sentimental Education*. The party of the 1950s is less self-consciously wicked. It may be planned and scheduled like any other social event, and the guests may dress for it with careful informality, but many of the best parties are given, or thrown, on impulse. Some young writers will be having dinner at a big table in an Italian restaurant; each pays for his own food and more wine than usual, and the girls pay too if they are unattached. Somebody says, "Let's have a party. I'll phone Jerry and Pat." "We'll go to my place," someone else suggests. There will be a great deal of dancing and embracing in corners, some barber-shop singing, and perhaps a public quarrel, but the real characteristic of a party is the feeling that anything can happen or be said. Next morning it turns out that "anything" wasn't very unusual or outrageous, but still there was that feeling of possibility, and afterward there is the absorbing pleasure of going over the details, with comments on how people acted and revealed their characters when they didn't think about how they were acting.

The dinner parties of older writers are much like other such parties in servantless American homes. If she is lucky the hostess has persuaded a neighbor woman to serve the dinner and wash the dishes. There is a noisy conversation over cocktails, mostly about personalities, but the hostess misses a lot of it because she is wondering whether people will think she is serving the right wine and whether the roast will burn. Later she feels relieved when everyone praises the dessert. Most of the guests leave early, explaining that they have work to do, but usually one of them gets launched on a monologue about a famous novelist who, he claims, has never learned to write. At twelve his wife announces that George and Betty are taking her home. At two the last guest is still talking and is in no condition to drive. At three the host gets his own car out of the garage and urges the guest into it, while the guest keeps mumbling, "Goo shent'nsh olluz life." The host, who has heard the formula before, interprets it as, "I could forgive Jack Ribblesdale if he had written one good sentence in all his life. I can't believe that any complete bastard ever wrote a good sentence."

SOME VICES ATTRIBUTED TO WRITERS

Alcoholism. Not all writers drink more than they should, but a great many of them do. I know more writers who don't smoke than who don't drink, and in fact the nondrinkers are regarded as a little eccentric—unless they explain candidly, like a friend of mine, "I can't drink because I'm an alcoholic." That always starts a conversation about Alcoholics Anonymous, an organization that includes a fair number of literary members, as well as many lawyers, locomotive engineers, and a few priests. Writers drink partly for the same reasons as men and women in any other professions; one of the general reasons, often overlooked, is that the heavy drinkers in many professions form an inner group, almost like a Yale senior society, which people want to be considered worthy of joining. They study for the degree of ND, or Noble Drinker, as others study for a doctorate. But writers have special reasons for drinking, and these operate with such force that alcoholism becomes one of their occupational hazards. Among the special reasons, I might mention three:

1. Writers are probably shyer, on the average, than members of other professions—except painters and composers—and at the same time they are more eager to establish direct personal communications. Alcohol serves, or appears to serve, as a bridge between person and person. After a few drinks writers talk, and listen while others talk; they reveal their inner thoughts with calculated indiscretion; they achieve what they feel to be a moment of interpersonal

truth. There is a similar moment after the act of sex, and it helps to explain a good deal of sexual promiscuity.

2. Writing is an activity that involves a high degree of nervous tension, and alcohol is a depressant that helps to soothe the nerves. Sometimes writers get drunk as if they were taking a short vacation; they sleep soundly and feel rested in the morning.

3. For many writers drinking becomes part of the creative process. They drink in order to have visions, or in order to experience the feeling of heightened life that they are trying to convey (like Hart Crane and, I suspect, Dylan Thomas), or in order to get in touch with their subconscious minds—feeling, as many writers do, that these are the source of their best work—or in order to overcome their excessive obedience to the inner censor, or simply in order to start the flow of words—"I'm priming the pump," they say. Years ago one of my friends urged me to write a novel; he had just finished a first novel of his own. I told him that I was afraid I couldn't get started.

"I was afraid of that too," he said. "But I tried sitting down at the typewriter with a tumbler full of alcohol and water"—it was during prohibition—"and it made everything easy. After the first two chapters I didn't need to drink."

The lucky drinkers are those who suffer from gout or ulcers—as this friend did afterward—and have to taper off in time. The unlucky ones are those with iron constitutions who continue drinking until they are told that they must stop or die. Sometimes they find that drinking and writing have become so involved with each other that after they stop drinking they can only go through the gestures of writing, as Booth Tarkington, once a noble drinker, seemed to be doing in his last books. I know two distinguished novelists who have never stopped. One of them is among those true alcoholics who shouldn't take a drink for the rest of their lives. That is the one rule solidly founded on experience: once a man becomes alcoholic he can never resist taking a second drink if he has taken the first. This novelist, however, has an almost inhuman pride and will power. Coming out of a spree that has almost killed him, he takes a drink every two hours, then every four hours (with the sweat standing out on his forehead as the moment approaches, but he doesn't cheat the clock), then in a few days he is back on the schedule that should be impossible for a man in his position: one cocktail before lunch, two before dinner, and not another drink all day. The second novelist has built his daily life around alcohol. After spending the morning at his desk, he starts drinking at twelve o'clock—always the same drink, gin and orange juice, half and half: gin for calories and orange juice for vitamins. He believes that most heavy drinkers suffer from not getting enough vitamins or enough sleep. In the afternoon he reads himself to sleep, then starts drinking again at five and continues until ten, when he sits down to a good dinner—without dessert—takes a vitamin capsule, and goes to bed. According to members of Alcoholics Anonymous, the proof of alcoholism lies in the answers to four questions: Do you drink before breakfast? Do you ever miss a meal? Do you black out? Do you worry about your drinking? The second novelist drinks more gin than any other man I know, and his mark on the test would be zero.

Homosexuality. Dr. Bergler thinks that there is a high incidence of homosexuality among writers. There are no statistics on the subject, except the doctor's clinical notes on his thirty-six patients, who are too specialized a group to provide reliable evidence. My own observations and clinical notes would lead me to an opposite conclusion: it seems to me that there is a smaller proportion of homosexuals among writers than in many other professions. Of course the conclusion depends on one's definition of writers and on whether or not the calling includes everyone with a vague desire to be published. It is quite possible that there may be a high incidence of homosexuality among would-be writers, as opposed to the professionals. Here again there are no statistics available, and I doubt that even Dr. Kinsey could gather them, but one notes that a good many of the hopeless manuscripts that come into a publisher's office either deal with homosexual themes or else reveal, in their depiction of female characters, a special sort of malice or cruelty that seems to be based on sexual aversion.

Several observers have told me that there is more homosexuality among professional writers in England, where the practice would seem to have been encouraged by conditions prevailing at the great endowed boys' schools that most of the writers attended. The situation might change in the future if—as now seems probable—more English writers of the next generation will have been educated in the new coeducational schools supported by the state. At present there also seems to be more homosexuality among German writers than among the Americans, but there is rather less among the Italians and the French—and this in spite of the famous confessions, or half-confessions, made by homosexual authors like Proust, Gide, and Jouhandeau; these men have been exceptions in a literature quite largely devoted to celebrating carnal love between the sexes.

In the American literary world, although the homosexuals are possibly more numerous than in France, they form a relatively small minority; if there were more of them they would have made their presence more obvious. Writers aren't given to concealing their sexual proclivities; in fact they seem to feel a compulsive need for revealing their true inclinations, whatever those may be. In Paris years ago I knew an American writer, now dead, who complained of the handicaps imposed on persons of his special bent. He said querulously, "The fairies have their cafés, the lesbians have their cafés, the pimps have their cafés, but there's no place where we sadists can get together for a quiet talk." The same man confessed or boasted in a book of having eaten human flesh in West Africa, and the book aroused some indignation in literary circles—one or two authors refused to shake his hand after reading it—but I can't remember that anyone did more than laugh at his confession of being a sadist. In the same way homosexuals have to face some ridicule, but they don't suffer from many social disabilities—in the literary world, that is; I am not speaking of the larger world, where the disabilities may be painful or tragic. In New York, as in London and Paris, they have their cafés where they continue to meet as long as they don't act in such a manner as to attract the attention of the police; but meanwhile they do suffer from certain professional and artistic handicaps, and these might help to explain why, among professional writers, there aren't so many homosexuals as one might otherwise expect.

First I should say that the handicaps don't seem to weigh heavily on writers in their early twenties. The homosexuals among them have the great advantage, in most cases, of being freed from family responsibilities; they have no one to support but themselves (unless they may be helping a divorced or widowed mother in South Bend). They have time to write, and they also have a strong motive for writing, in their need to assert themselves against a hostile society. Some of them may have a very early success. In part the success may be due to the encouragement they receive from other homosexuals, who like to discover new persons of talent, especially if the persons are candidates for membership in their own circle of friends.

This inclination to help along others of the same type might lead to the formation of a pressure group, with unfortunate results for literature in general—and for homosexual writers too, since pressures lead to countervailing pressures—except for another strong tendency in the same circles to separate into hostile cliques. The very young writer, however, isn't yet subject to these intramural jealousies, and he may be helped on all sides: his work is talked about admiringly, it is shown to magazine editors and book publishers, and, if the work is even passably good, it is likely to appear without delay.

Sometimes young homosexuals get into print so quickly and their books are so favorably reviewed that a false impression may be created about the tastes and tendencies of a whole generation. Not long after World War II a young novelist began telling people that all the interesting new writers of the postwar generation were homosexuals like himself; he mentioned half a dozen names. He had just published a first book that was freshly written and deeply felt and seemed to promise that he would have a brilliant career. Soon the career was cut short by death, but not before he had published two other novels that were full of obscure grudges and contained no living characters. By that time two of the other new novelists whose names he mentioned had proved that their talents were authentic. A third had become a professional and prolific writer, although he had nothing much to say, while a fourth and a fifth had been forgotten almost as prematurely as they had been published. Several other talented novelists had appeared, at the slower pace of men with wives and children to support, and nobody would have claimed any longer that the generation was homosexual in any marked degree.

The professional and artistic handicaps of which I spoke had begun to make themselves felt. Some of these are simply the opposite face of what had earlier been advantages. For example, a younger writer can do more work if he has no family responsibilities, but an older writer without a wife feels lost and emotionally unstable. Homosexual relationships seem to involve a continual small turmoil that isn't favorable to artistic production. The taste for novelty that prevails in homosexual circles often leads to the discovery of new writers, but it also leads to the neglect of older ones, who become the victims of professional jealousies and simple malice. As for the artistic handicap under which such writers labor, it was explained by Tom Hopkinson in his book, *Love's Apprentice*, where he said in part:

> With the deadly logic which directs our life, the attempt to exclude woman leads to an overfemininity in those making the attempt, an overfemininity of character and manners, but, above all, an overfemininity in the productions of their art; so that it becomes the hallmark, for example, of stage designs by a man who despises and disinherits woman that they should be a perfect outburst of extravagant frivolity, the costumes a mass of elaboration from which no feminine attribute or provocation is omitted. Similarly among writers, the distinguishing marks of the woman-excluder are airy fantasy, a fixed determination to amuse and a malicious wit; nor are these qualities to be despised. The point is that they are feminine qualities, and none but the genius—who will in any case reach the balance of masculine and feminine inside himself and be liable to show attributes and emotions of both sexes—can break through the logic which demands a precise and literal compensation for every task avoided.

The precise and literal compensation, or punishment, may take the form of an inability to present any characters in whom and for whom the reader feels an ordinary human warmth. Sometimes it takes other forms as well: for example, the reader may feel that the sexes have been transposed and that the women in a novel are really boys; or he may feel that the heroine is being hounded to death or insanity for the crime—as it appears to the homosexual author—of having normal passions; or again he may feel that the author, in depicting love between the sexes, has made it seem brutal or even bestial. Walt Whitman tried to depict normal love—or "woman love," as he called it—in his "Children of Adam" poems and gave an impression of forced brutality that contrasts with the appealing tenderness of his homosexual or "Calamus" poems. I don't mean to imply that these characteristics are shared by every homosexual author. Hopkinson is right in saying that artists of exceptional talent aren't subject to the usual rules and often—not always—escape the usual penalties for breaking them. There is no doubt, however, that the homosexual of talent, if he achieves a literary success, does so in spite of handicaps that aren't imposed on other writers.

Play-Acting. Writers are proud of their profession, but at the same time most of them seem to be a little ashamed or protective about it. Instead of saying, "Today I plan to write," they say, "I'll be *working*," as if working were more responsible than writing and entitled them to respect as solid citizens. Once a reporter for the *New Yorker* went through a pile of telephone directories and found that only one man in the metropolitan area listed himself as a writer; he was Brom Weber of Brooklyn, the author of a book about Hart Crane. Partly the other writers, who merely listed their names, were displaying the same sort of delicacy that is practiced by the Yale graduates who don't mention the name of their university among strangers; if they do talk about their college days, they say, "When I was at New Haven." But partly the writers were showing the effect of the years when they were painfully set apart from other boys and girls by the mere fact of having literary ambitions. As grown men and women they seem to feel that if they don't mention their profession they can be more at ease among the neighbors.

A fairly common characteristic of the writing tribe is that they pretend to be something else, adopt a protective coloring, put on masks, and hope to deceive others because, in many cases, they have already deceived themselves. They like to be regarded not as the hard-working professionals they really are, but as amateurs writing successful books in their leisure moments. I know, or my friends have known, writers who pretended to be swells or dandies, brisk executives, clubmen, tough guys, hipsters, great lovers (male and female), explorers, big-game hunters or fishermen, foresters, farmers (dirt, subsistence, or gentleman), hucksters, horsemen, horticulturists (especially cross-breeders of irises and delphiniums), military or naval strategists, radical or reactionary politicians, publishers, public monuments, and businessmen of several types, including steamboat operators and country storekeepers. Sometimes the public figure, or persona, is so distinct from the writer in private life that he falls into the habit of admiring himself in the third person; he doesn't say, "I think," but "John Ribblesdale thinks." Since many writers have a studious turn of mind, they may be highly successful in their assumed roles, to such an extent that they neglect their writing and sometimes abandon it. They betray themselves, if at all, by playing the roles too eagerly, like Hollywood actors riding to hounds. I suspect that the novelist Louis Bromfield is a more passionate farmer than anyone in the United States who earns a living by farming.

Writers in business are a special topic. Kenneth Burke says that he knows many more failed writers who are successful businessmen than failed businessmen who have become successful writers. In business the writer has many advantages, including the habit of looking at things in the large and an imaginative grasp of possibilities. On the other hand, many writers in business have taken too many risks, have neglected practical details, and have put too much trust in their partners, as witness the resounding bankruptcies of Scott, Balzac, and Mark Twain. It is possible that many corporations might profit by having a writer on the board of directors, to suggest new policies, but they might be asking for trouble if they named a writer as president.

On the Incapacity of Writers. We have heard much about the incapacity of writers in general, and poets in particular, for leading successful lives. The archetypical poet of the modern era is supposed to be impractical and weak-willed, a man who wastes his money, lives in poverty and disorder, goes crazy, dies in the gutter, or commits suicide. Hölderlin, Baudelaire, Francis Thompson, and Hart Crane are cited as examples.

One might ask whether the apparently formless lives of such poets weren't connected with the high degree of form, direction, and decision that was displayed in their poems. Form, direction, decision are exhausting qualities, and the man who achieves them in one medium is often left with not enough energy to achieve them in another. Napoleon might be contrasted with these poets; as a very young man he wrote sentimental essays and started a novel. In other circumstances he might have finished the novel and might have followed it with better ones, but then he found that he was able to impose his will on masses of living men; they became his field of decision and, in a sense, his artistic medium. Baudelaire worked with words, made his choices among them as Napoleon chose persons to carry out his orders, and tried to organize the words into a new system of relationships—almost, one might say, a new society. If he showed no talent for organizing his own life, let alone the lives of others, one reason might be that his energy was exhausted in writing the poems.

We might also note that Baudelaire, like many other poets of the modern era, was trying to convey an effect of hallucination. The effect depended on his cultivating a type of intensely personal vision that kept him from being a well-adjusted member of any social group. That is a special disability of subjective and visionary poets, but prose writers also find at times that the mere act of writing makes them less competent to meet the problems of daily life. Sitting at his desk or pacing up and down the room, an author hears his own unspoken voice, but he doesn't properly hear other voices or see what people are doing. Sometimes he is absent-minded and a little helpless for several months while he is writing a book, though at other times he may prove to be a hard-headed man of affairs. After he has finished the book—or even a magazine article—he doesn't want to talk or listen for a while, but merely to be told that what he has done is wonderful and unique.

"I've always thought of myself as a practical person," George Ollendorf told me. "I try to plan ahead, save a little money, and buy nothing I don't need. But the day I finish a story almost anybody could sell me almost anything—especially if he started by reading the story and showing that he liked it. Perhaps it's the way your mind gets to working. Day after day I've been looking for remarkable features in the persons I was writing about. I've been trying to construct something, not tear it down. Then, if a fellow wants to sell me a piece of land or a garden tractor or an idea, I see its remarkable features too and I say, 'Yes, yes, tell me more about it.'

"And another thing," George continued. "I always think of myself as a first-class chauffeur. Gathering material, I often drive fifteen or twenty thousand miles a year, and never an accident. But it's different when I've just finished a story or when I'm thinking hard about what to write—then it's keep away from George Ollendorf, the absent-minded man. Or that's the way it used to be, but now I have better sense and make Betty drive when I can't keep my mind on the road."

I said, "Maybe the highway police should invent a test for absent-minded writers, like the test for drunken drivers."

George sat there stirring the ice in his highball with a square forefinger. At last he said, "It's not a bad life, looking back at it."

"You mean being a writer?"

"It's a good life, and I'd choose it again, but it has some bad years in it, especially around the age of forty. That's the time when writers have to face up to what they've been doing, like everybody else. They are halfway through their active careers, and perhaps they've made a little success, but not the sort they were hoping for, and now the future begins to look like the past and not so interesting. They begin to wish desperately that everything could be changed, starting tomorrow—wives, jobs, friends, places, everything, before the walls close in. It's the forty-year-old crisis that Shaw talked about in one of his letters to Chesterton, who was recovering slowly after a serious illness. Shaw told him that the same sort of thing had happened to most writers in their forties, including himself, although in other cases the illness mightn't be physical. The forties are the time for nervous breakdowns, like mine—" George looked at me sideways— "not to mention writer's block, visits to the psychoanalyst, religious conversions, taking to drink or swearing off, running away with a younger woman, going back to your wife, and maybe, at the end of it all, growing up, or at least coming to terms with yourself. Writers take a long time to grow up, but the good ones wear better than other people do."

He emptied his glass and rose to go. "After fifty it's not so bad," he said as he paused at the door. "You don't expect so much and you work harder, even if you have less energy. In fact there are two things I really enjoy about growing old as a writer, outside of being a free man and having to face new problems each day. I've always been fascinated by the curious patterns that persons make of their lives—billions of lives and no two patterns exactly the same. As the people around me get older, the patterns become more intricate and more distinct, and now I know the end of many stories that I won't ever write, but I won't forget them either. I think about them when I can't sleep, and I think what curious lives we lead in this world."

George opened the door and stood with his bald head shining pink in the late-afternoon sun. "The other pleasant thing about getting older is a personal matter too, but I think you'll understand it. All my life I've been talking to myself, as I suppose most writers do. I've learned a lot in sixty years, and now," he said as he backed away, "the conversation is more interesting."

THEIR PUBLIC STATUS

Writers occupy a peculiar position in the class structure of American society; they compose what sociologists would call an out-group, or rather a collection of such groups. From the economic standpoint they belong to the professional segment of the middle classes and, as a rule, they have no inherited capital except that which was invested in their educations. Their incomes are smaller on the average than those of doctors and attorneys, larger than those of clergy-men, and roughly equal to those of college professors. Socially they don't fit into the middle-class pattern, and their behavior is in some ways like that of the rich, in other ways like that of the urban poor. Their marginal position is typified by their choice of residence. In cities they often live in districts abandoned by the rich and taken over by the poor—like Greenwich Village—or else on the dividing line between rich and poor neighborhoods, as in the far-east Seven-ties of Manhattan, the Near North Side of Chicago, and in Boston on the wrong slope of Beacon Hill. When they move out of cities they go beyond the middle-class suburbs into areas where small farms are interspersed with gentlemen's estates.

Their profession gives them freedom of movement—and of con-duct too—but it confers no luster on its individual members, as medi-cine does to a greater extent than architecture and engineering. Peo-ple don't say, "He's a writer," with the undertone of wonder and distrust that creeps into their voices when they say, "He's a scien-tist"; the distrust is there, but not often the admiration. Such luster—or prestige or mana—as individual writers possess is usually due not to the quality of their work, but to its public acceptance. The quality of the work is praised or condemned by their professional colleagues, but not by the public at large, which is interested chiefly in hearing that the author's last book had a very large sale and earned a great deal of money; in that case he may be admired in the same fashion as the politician who was elected by a very large ma-jority. Alexis de Tocqueville thought that this sort of tribute to pub-licly selected individuals was to be expected in any democratic society. "At periods of equality," he says in the second volume of *Democracy in America*, "men have no faith in one another, by rea-son of their common resemblance; but this very resemblance gives them almost unbounded confidence in the judgment of the public; for it would seem probable that, as they are all endowed with equal means of judging, the greater truth should go with the greater num-ber."

The novelist whose books have sold in the millions, and the dramatist whose last play was reshaped into a successful movie after running two years on Broadway, may both be minor writers, but they are great men by virtue of their public positions; in a democracy the consumers' dollars are ballots, and these authors have received millions of votes. They are besieged by the public as if they possessed a mana that could be transmitted to others not only by personal contact, or by ownership of a book or program that the great man has autographed, but also by a pilgrimage to the house where the book was written. Betty MacDonald's *The Egg and I* described her misadventures on a chicken ranch in a rather unfrequented section of the Olympic Peninsula. After her book had sold a million copies the new owners of the ranch were so besieged with visitors that they put signs on the highway and charged an admission fee. *Anthony Adverse*, that great success of the early 1930s, was written by the late Hervey Allen in a Bermuda house called Felicity Hall. The house was later occupied by friends of James Thurber, who reports that for a year or two, "there was a constant stream of sightseers. They offered fabulous amounts for a harp gate that Allen himself had built and for a large sewing chair he had made for his wife. And they offered as much as a pound or five dollars for any pencil he had used."

The mana of a famous author can be commercialized by others, but the author himself is unable to convert it into cash. If his income is to remain in keeping with his position in the world, he has to write new books as popular as those with which he earned the position, and sometimes the mana itself makes the books harder to write; either he can't spare time from his public appearances, or else the hero-worshipers have given him a false picture of his talent. Victor Hugo suffered from delusions of greatness; "He thought he was Victor Hugo," a younger writer said. Entranced by his reputation as a historical romancer, Hervey Allen came to believe that he could hear his ancestors talking among themselves. If their conversation was what he set down in his later, less popular novels, it was stilted and makes dull reading.

Few writers have to face this problem of dealing with mobs of admiring or merely curious strangers. The others, if they do good work, are plagued with requests for assistance from younger people in their own profession, but the general public lets them alone. At most they are visited by solitary pilgrims, confused but enthusiastic. I was trimming some pine trees at the edge of the town road when a ten-year-old sedan stopped with a shaking of loose fenders. The driver, a middle-aged man, put his head out of the window.

". . . Mathewson?" he said.

"You'll have to speak louder."

"I'm looking for Mr. Mathewson." The fenders started shaking again. ". . . where he lives?"

"There's nobody named Mathewson on this road." Pause. "There's a Josephson." I was thinking of Matthew Josephson, author of *Zola* and *The Robber Barons*.

"Josephson, that's right."

I told him how to find the Josephson house, and the pilgrim put his car into gear. Then he shouted above the clatter of the fenders, "He's a great man!"

As I went back to trimming pine trees I reflected that a double impulse must have led him to make that statement. Partly he was atoning for his mistake, but partly he was scolding the town in my person for its lack of respect to a distinguished resident; at the very least there should have been a signboard with Josephson's name on it, so that strangers and pilgrims wouldn't look for Mathewson. Most towns—I'm not thinking now of ours—don't pay much attention to writers unless they demand attention by some form of eccentric behavior. The writers, in turn, don't often take much part in town activities. As a rule they don't join country clubs or "service" clubs or bridge clubs or reading circles, and they don't belong to church or civic organizations (except the PTA, if they have children). I suspect that the neighbors regard them with distrust, as if they were surrounded with an atmosphere of the dangerous and illicit. Lights burn too late in their houses, where sometimes there is noisy singing behind closed blinds or a burst of laughter from the darkness of the lawn. Writers are rumored to drink too much and to be careless about their marital attachments. The tradespeople aren't certain that they will pay their bills. Often the rumor gets around that they are Communists.

The vague hostility that divides writers and intellectuals from the mass of the American population has a long history behind it. For each new generation it started in grade school, where most of the future intellectuals were poor boys who made high marks. If they weren't poor they had some other social handicap, like being Jews or the children of college professors, and of course the high marks were a handicap in themselves. The future writers were more likely to come from middle-class families with books in the house. They were lonely boys and girls with lots of ability, so the teachers said, but with mixed academic records; they made A's in their favorite subjects, but, unlike the future intellectuals, they often did badly in mathematics or science. Most of them weren't very good at sports, were shy or boisterous in company, and weren't invited to all the parties. It was the same in high school and later in college; on one side was the uneasy feeling of the athletes and class politicians that they weren't being sufficiently admired; on the other side was the shame of the bright boys at not being asked to join fraternities in which, as a matter of fact, they would have been unhappy. Still later in life the division that began by being one of temperament would take the form of opposing caste loyalties, though individuals might move from one caste to another. A few of the boys who belonged to the literary crowd in college afterward became successful business-men or corporation lawyers, but they did so, in some cases, with a sense of having betrayed their own natures. Very few of them went into politics. We have had some literary Presidents, notably the first Roosevelt, but it is seldom and as if by accident that a writer gets elected to Congress.

Politicians as a class aren't friendly to writers, and that helps to explain why the government hasn't made an impressive record for itself as a patron of literature. Except in the years of the Federal Arts Projects [1] (1935–1943), the American republic has done less for its writers, even quantitatively, than some of the smaller European king-doms, including Belgium, Denmark, and Sweden. It has no ministry or bureau or government-sponsored council of the fine arts. It offers no prizes, medals, or honors of any sort, and no financial rewards in the shape of stipends, pensions, or sinecures to writers, artists, or

1. There were four of these federal projects: Theater, Writers', Music, and Graphic Arts. The whole program, designed to bring art to the people on a vast scale, was conceived by Jacob Baker, of the Work Projects Administration, and was carried out by Harry Hopkins, head of the WPA. In other words, it was a creation of the executive branch, which has always been more friendly, or less unfriendly, to the arts than the legislative. The artistic efforts of the four projects were always hampered and confused by the notion that WPA was simply a charitable organization; the best workers were likely to be dismissed, as not being in need, while they were writing a guidebook or painting a mural that nobody else could finish. Moreover, the projects were always under attack by Congress, which suspected that any artist was a Red, and they received only a divided support from the administration. In 1939 the Federal Theater Project, which had been the most enterprising of the four, was voted out of existence. The other projects lingered on unobtrusively until 1943, when the WPA was abolished or, as the President said, was given its "honorable discharge."

musicians. Exactly one government post in about two million is reserved for a practicing artist; it is the privately endowed chair of poetry at the Library of Congress. A succession of poets had been appointed to the chair for one-year terms. In 1954, however, it had been empty for about two years, because the last poet nominated for the position had failed to receive a security clearance.

The picture isn't quite so negative as I have made it seem. In an indirect fashion the government has offered not a little help to the arts in America. Notably its taxation policy has favored the establishment of great endowed institutions like the Ford, Rockefeller, Guggenheim, and Bollingen Foundations, which in turn have subsidized a great number of scholarly projects and a smaller number of literary projects; together the foundations serve almost the same purpose as a European ministry of culture. Besides granting them tax exemption, the government has taken a few measures of its own to encourage the literary trades. It helps to arrange for the exportation of books to Europe and Asia. It maintains the Library of Congress, which is the largest in the country and which offers many services to other libraries. The Army and the Navy have purchased books in quantities for camp and shipboard reading. The United States Information Service has purchased others for distribution abroad, as well as maintaining overseas libraries. A few writers have been granted government fellowships—Fulbrights—after receiving security clearances, and others have been sent abroad on cultural missions by the State Department. On the other hand, there are some respects in which writers, as compared with members of other professions, are penalized by federal laws or administrative practices. To mention a few of these, some old, some new:

There is the obsolete and inadequate copyright law. It offers less protection to American authors than they would receive from their government if they were citizens of almost any other country. It is also unjust to foreign authors, and it is full of traps for the careless and unwary. For years the Authors' League and the publishing industry have been trying to bring it up to date. A modern copyright bill has been introduced at every session of Congress, but it usually fails even to reach the floor.

There are unfair provisions of the income tax. Over a five-year period an author is likely to pay more in taxes than members of other professions whose total incomes were larger than his, but also were more regular. The author may have spent the five years in writing two books, only one of which was a financial success. In that case most of his income has been received in one or two of the years and has been taxed at a much higher rate than he would have paid on his average income for the whole period.

There is the postal regulation which provides that any parcel containing as much as two or three lines of handwritten or typewritten material must pay postage at the letter rate. The corrected galley proofs of a novel are a "letter" weighing several pounds. The manuscript of a novel is also a "letter," and it is doubly expensive to mail, considering that the author should enclose stamps for its return. In many countries manuscripts and corrected proofs can be mailed as "commercial papers" at a lower rate; thus, a Canadian author can submit a manuscript to a New York publisher for about a third of what it would cost in postage if he lived in Connecticut.

Finally there are the restrictions on travel abroad and on employment by the government that have been imposed as a result of the cold war. In theory the restrictions shouldn't bear more heavily on the writing profession than on any other. In theory they are intended to prevent Americans from acting as Communist couriers in Europe or Asia, and to keep untrustworthy persons from being appointed to posts in which they might betray government secrets. In practice the restrictions have extended to a much wider field and many public, private, or endowed institutions have begun to require a modified form of security clearance for work that bears no relation to national security. Appalled by the prospect that a Congressional committee might accuse them of giving money to homosexuals or subversives, some universities and some foundations have hired professional investigators to look for "derogatory information" about applicants for posts or fellowships. In practice, derogatory information about writers is easy to find, or fabricate or misinterpret, if only because of the gossip that circulates at cocktail parties. A writer conducts his education in public, expresses his opinions, and leaves a printed record of his mistakes. Any talented writer likes to associate with other men of talent, who may not always be men of discretion. Trying to be honest, he is certain to offend some people; he is lucky if he makes two friends without making at least one enemy. If an investigator wants to find derogatory information about a book reviewer, for example, he has only to inquire among the authors whose books the reviewer didn't like. One or two of them are pretty certain to believe, sincerely, that the reviewer is either a fascist or a paid agent of the Cominform: how else could he have failed to acknowledge the deep cogency of what they had written?

Investigators are trained as policemen, not as literary critics or evaluators of literary gossip, and they live in a world with different folkways from those of writers. Sometimes their reports contain items of derogatory information, soberly repeated, that sound pretty fantastic to a writer's ears. One rather famous poet, who had often been scolded in the 1930s for his lack of interest in radical movements, was refused a security clearance in 1952 on suspicion of having been a radical. Among the items of derogatory information that weighed against him were (1) that he had once, long ago, written an obscure and ambiguous poem in which the word "Communist" was used with what appeared to be a favorable connotation, though one couldn't be certain, and (2) that he had contributed to *Partisan Review*. The investigator hadn't read *Partisan Review* and didn't know that it was anti-Communist. Another poet—we might call him X—was granted a Fulbright fellowship but also failed to receive his clearance. One derogatory item was that he and his wife had attended a cocktail party given by Y, a distinguished author who was suspected of being homosexual. Afterward Y applied for a Fulbright and received his clearance; the suspicion hadn't been confirmed. Z is a novelist who wanted to spend a year in Europe. He was refused a passport, not because he belonged to any subversive organization—he didn't belong to anything and is a loyal citizen, like all the others I have mentioned—but presumably because he had written and published a statement that the Passport Bureau didn't like. I say "presumably" because the bureau doesn't have to offer any specific reason for its action. It merely cites the McCarran Act, which it interprets in a broad fashion, and the victim, if he is a writer, usually keeps quiet for fear of being branded as a subversive character. There have been many refusals of passports that didn't get into the newspapers. As for positions with the government, very few writers applied for them after 1950, word having gotten around that anyone who had published a book was likely to get into trouble with Congress. Roy M. Cohn, chief counsel for Senator McCarthy's subcommittee, might have been speaking for many Congressmen when he was asked about the choice of speakers for a television program and said, "Any author is out."

Any author was open to political attack because authors as a class had little or no political power. What some of them wrote might influence voters in ten or twenty years, but they were seldom able to help their candidates in a given election. It is even a serious question whether their almost unanimous support of Stevenson in 1952 added to or subtracted from his total vote; other groups may have decided to vote against anyone who aroused such enthusiasm among the eggheads. There is one Congressional district out of 435 where people in the literary professions—including writers, editors, publishers, agents, and book designers—have settled in such numbers that they might conceivably hold the balance of power in a close election. The district is the Fourth Connecticut and at one time, exceptionally, it was represented by a writer, Clare Boothe Luce. Her successor was John Davis Lodge, who is the son of a rather gifted minor poet. In 1954, however, the district was represented by Albert P. Morano of Danbury, who, if he had ever read books or spoken to authors or defended their interests in Congress, had managed to conceal the derelictions.

As I read over these last pages, it seems to me that they might give a false impression of my notions concerning a possibly ideal relationship between American writers and their government. I might appear to be arguing that writers should be exempt from political restrictions and yet should have a great deal of political influence, that many of them should be appointed to government positions, and that Congress should appropriate money to encourage American literature. As a matter of fact I am dubious about all three of these propositions. Writers in politics haven't always or often proved to be wiser than other politicians; sometimes they have been more foolish. Many writers in government have shown themselves to be capable and effective public servants, but the better they were as bureaucrats, the more likely they were to acquire bureaucratic habits of thought, which are fatal to good writing. That Congress should establish a bureau of fine arts, with money to spend for literary prizes and fellowships, is a much more tempting notion, but there are a few serious arguments against it. One is that such a bureau would be involved in politics, with its prizes going to writers whose opinions were politically correct at the time, and to another group of writers in the next administration. Another argument is the increased danger of federal censorship; if Congress were spending money for literature, it would try to encourage some types of literature and might soon decide that other types should be penalized. Still another argument against such a bureau is that it might lead—the more influential it became, the more surely it would lead—to an official school of art and an official theory of writing that all Americans would be expected to follow, as all Russian writers are expected to be socialist realists.

I am a pluralist in questions of literary doctrine as in theories of government. I don't like to see too much power concentrated in one man or place or party or institution. The federal government is our greatest institution, but I should like to see its power counterbalanced by that of smaller institutions, not only state and local governments, but also the churches, the schools, the universities, the newspapers, the magazines, the arts, and the different professions, each with its feeling of separate life, each with customs and standards that have the force of law in its separate domain. The literary profession is one of those domains, and I should like to see it enforce its own standards. In one sense the critics are its courts of law, but it is even more important for them to honor good writing than to condemn cheap and careless writing; also the standards they enforce should be those of quality, not those of method or doctrine or political opinion. There should be many theories of literature and many centers of literary activity. If writers need financial help to do their best work—and many of them do need such help, because the rewards for distinguished writing are not always enough to support them, and also because it takes a long time for a writer to become established—then the help should come from privately endowed institutions, as at present, rather than from the federal government. All that the writers can fairly ask of the government is that it shouldn't discriminate against them. Notably, it shouldn't interfere with the institutions that have been helping them, nor should it try, as some Congressional committees have been doing, to force universities and foundations into a great coordinated —*gleichgeschaltet* was Hitler's word—system of correct mass opinion.

It was in 1831 that Alexis de Tocqueville made his only visit to this country. When he wrote his two volumes on *Democracy in America*, he included a short book or section called "Influence of Democracy on the Action of the Intellect in the United States." Literature and the trade of writing are discussed in that section, but in the brief space that Tocqueville thought they deserved. At the time of his visit our only writers of distinction were Irving,

Bryant, and Cooper. Although he seems to have read and mildly admired them all, he dismissed them as being "English in substance and still more so in form. . . . The inhabitants of the United States have at present," he said, "properly speaking no literature. The only authors whom I acknowledge as American are the journalists. These indeed are not great writers, but they speak the language of the country and make themselves heard." On the basis of American journalism—and also of his general theories about life in a democratic society—he offered a series of predictions about the American literature that was likely to appear. One is surprised to find that a few of the prophecies he made on that basis might serve as descriptions of American writing today. Here are some remarks from his one-page chapter on "The Trade of Literature":

Democracy not only infuses a taste for letters among the trading classes, but introduces a trading spirit into literature. . . .

The ever increasing crowd of readers and their continual craving for something new ensure the sale of books that nobody much esteems.

In democratic times the public frequently treat authors as kings do their courtiers; they enrich and despise them. . . .

Democratic literature is always infested with a tribe of writers who look upon letters as a mere trade; and for some few great authors who adorn it, you may reckon thousands of idea-mongers.

Tocqueville was almost as severe, but much less accurate, when he talked about the style and structure, or lack of structure, that one might expect to find in a democratic literature. He said in part:

Taken as a whole, literature in democratic ages can never present, as it does in the periods of aristocracy, an aspect of order, regularity, science, and art; its form, on the contrary, will ordinarily be slighted, sometimes despised. Style will frequently be fantastic, incorrect, overburdened, and loose, almost always vehement and bold. Authors will aim at rapidity of execution more than at perfection of detail. Small productions will be more common than bulky books; there will be more wit than erudition, more imagination than profundity; and literary performances will bear marks of an untutored and rude vigor of thought, frequently of great variety and singular fecundity.

In 1831 that was what every foreigner expected that American literature would be when it finally appeared; and later there were some American authors—notably Whitman—who tried hard to fulfill the expectation. But neglect of form, a vehement style, and a rude vigor of thought didn't prove to be qualities that would distinguish American authors as a group. On the contrary, most of the good ones, beginning with Washington Irving, were stylists, and a few were great stylists; no aristocrat of letters spent more time in choosing the exactly right word than an apparently untutored author like Mark Twain. Instead of displaying a rude vigor of thought, American writers as a group proved to be careful workmen, even highly skilled technicians; they included a long line of inventors, properly speaking, that runs from Poe and Hawthorne to Pound, Eliot, and Cummings. This passion for clean workmanship and technical research, which also appears in American painting and architecture, doesn't prove that the writers or painters or architects were aliens in their own country. What Tocqueville failed to see was that the American interest in practical science and engineering, which he praises in another connection, would be displayed not only in workshops and factories but also in art and literature.

There are other characteristics of American writing that seem to result partly from social forces and partly from the specific situations in which writers live. Always they are subject to the mass pressures of a democracy—that is, they are constantly being admonished, by looks or gossip, to vote the right ticket, have the right appliances in their kitchens and the right flowers on their lawns, drive the right sort of car, and shape their books to the right pattern. Lately some critics have taken to scolding authors for feeling alienated from society. It seems to me that conformity, not alienation, is the danger to which most authors are likely to succumb. At the very least they are tempted to prove their standing in society by spending and earning more money and thereby sacrificing the quiet and watchful indolence that a talent needs if it is to flower. Tocqueville said of this country in 1831, and might have said of it today, "Everyone is in motion, some in quest of power, others of gain. In the midst of this universal tumult, this incessant conflict of jarring interests, this continual striving of men after fortune, where is that calm to be found which is necessary for the deeper combinations of the intellect?"

American writers have no centers of opinion among themselves that would help them to resist social pressures; I mean, nothing that serves the purpose of French salons and literary schools. Much of their work seems to show that they don't often hear good conversation. Americans in general, including the writers, are story-tellers rather than conversationalists, and an evening in company is likely to hop rather than glide along, in a series of anecdotes each followed by laughter and a silence. Enough cocktails will give the illusion of conversation but not the reality; not the current of words and ideas in which a group is carried forward like swimmers in the same river. One result is that American writing, especially when it deals with ideas, seldom gives the impression of being spoken. Try reading it aloud and some of it seems unpronounceable.

Much of our serious writing, as distinguished from our magazine stories, has always tended to be eccentric or provincial; even Hawthorne and Emerson bear the marks of their isolation from good society and their partial isolation from any society, just as Faulkner and Wolfe would later bear them. In subject matter too, American literature shows the result of isolation, since few of our authors have lived in close contact with financiers or politicians or labor leaders or simple businessmen. If many representative figures are missing from our representative novels, the reason is chiefly that the novelists preferred to write about persons with whom they were familiar. Often they chose exceptional characters who, like themselves, were outside the current of American society.

For the most part our literature has been critical of that society, and we have never produced an official poet like Vergil, who created the myth of the Roman state. Our great authors have scolded the nation more than they praised it. Often their scolding has been eloquent and wholly justified, but often too it has been eccentric or ill-informed. Lacking in most of our fiction have been the qualities that Matthew Arnold praised in Chaucer's poetry, which he described as having a "large, free, simple, clear yet kindly view of human life," and again as having "largeness, freedom, shrewdness, benignity." The qualities are indeed present in Whitman and Mark Twain, but elsewhere in the best American writing they are likely to be replaced by narrowness and intensity, with depth of experience compensating for its want of breadth.

There is a fact-mindedness in American life that has always produced good reporters. One of them, John Bartlow Martin, said in 1954, "I spend at least as much time in leg work as I do in writing. Probably a great deal more. But I've a belief that the important thing in a piece is the cumulative impact of the facts themselves." That belief in "the facts themselves," as distinguished from reflections on the facts, is peculiarly American; but so too is the how-mindedness, the respect for technical skill, that has made our writing almost from the beginning, and certainly from Hawthorne's day, as smooth and efficient as our engines. The skill is best shown in shorter efforts, lyrics and stories and novellas, some of which are unexcelled in any literature of our time; it isn't often combined with the imaginative grasp or the patient meditation that unifies a long novel. In general we do not give our authors the sort of leisure or the sort of recognition that would encourage them to undertake vast constructions. There are no real epics in our poetry and, except for *Moby-Dick*, we have produced very few epics in prose.

XII.

THE NEXT FIFTY YEARS
IN AMERICAN LITERATURE

During the first half of the century, and increasingly after World War II, American life was changing in more fashions than most people realized. Some of the changes were largely quantitative and can be disregarded in a book that deals, as this has dealt, with the folkways of literature. Others were qualitative and had begun to produce new characters with new values and a different sense of life, one that will be reflected in the writing of the next half-century.

The population of the country had doubled in my lifetime; the increase was from 76 million in 1900 to 151 million in 1950. Here was a quantitative change that involved many changes in quality. In proportion to the total population there were more women in 1950, when they first outnumbered the men; there were more persons over sixty and many more white-collar workers, while the number of farmers and miners had decreased absolutely as well as relatively. More of the new Americans were living in Michigan, Florida, Texas, and on the Pacific Coast, where the population had been growing faster than elsewhere in the country; all four regions, but especially California, were playing a larger part in literature. In some of the prairie states, the population wasn't growing at all.

Most of the increase for the country as a whole was in the standard metropolitan areas; by 1950 there were 168 of these, each including one or more cities with at least fifty thousand inhabitants.

In almost all the metropolitan areas the suburbs were growing faster than the cities, many of which were standing still. City dwellers have often been depicted as lonely creatures lost in a crowd of strangers; sometimes they live for years in a big apartment house without speaking to anyone there except the janitor. The new Americans lived outside the city in communities where they knew their neighbors by name and tried to win their approval. "People like people," said William Levitt, "that's been our experience." By acting on that principle, Levitt and Sons—William was one of the sons—became the largest planners and builders of suburban communities.

The new Americans liked to be with other Americans and spent less time by themselves than their parents used to do. They also spent less time at work, more time with their wives or husbands and the younger children, less time with other relatives, and more time with persons of their own age having about the same incomes and many interests in common; to use a sociological term, they depended on "peer groups" for companionship. Living in groups, they learned to cooperate and compromise. They asked advice about their personal affairs more often than in the past, and more of their business decisions were made in conference. Once a man was judged by what he could do with horses, cattle, crops, timber, and money—could he make it breed like his animals?—but after World War II he was judged, in his business life, largely by what he could do with people. More and more of the successful Americans were administrators or—whatever their titles might be—managers of personnel.

The physical type was changing along with the social character. Americans were taller than their parents of the same sex,[1] with broader shoulders, deeper chests, narrower hips, and longer legs. Though quicker and more agile, they seemed to have less physical endurance; they didn't excel in marathon races or cross-country skiing. A doctor in charge of athletes at the University of Virginia complained that football injuries increased by thirty per cent after the introduction of a new rule that kept players in the game for longer periods. "Most boys today," he said, "don't walk as much

1. My son is nine inches taller than my father was; I stand between the two. In World War I, when a company was lined up in order of height I was somewhere near the head of the line, usually in the fourth eight-man squad; in World War II, I would have been demoted to the middle of the company.

as they used to. They usually ride in an auto and consequently their legs and their bodies are weaker." The favorite exercise of many young Americans was a short, fast swim, followed by a sun-broil on the beach. One pictured a new race built like herons, with slender legs not designed for walking or climbing, but merely for standing in shallow water.

The climate was changing, though nobody knew how long the process would continue. Heat instead of cold was becoming the enemy to be outwitted, sometimes by taking long vacations or living near a lake, sometimes by installing air conditioners. As the summers grew hotter, southern plants and animals were spreading northward, like mesquite and sagebrush in the mountain states. The land itself was changing as its inhabitants were redistributed around the metropolitan centers and along the radiating lines of force that were superhighways. Away from the highways and summer resorts, broad sections of the country were poorer and emptier than they had been in 1900. The settled areas were more thickly settled and, with automobiles moving at high speeds in all directions, they seemed uncomfortably crowded. A thousand Americans and their machines took up as much space as fifty thousand Chinese.

Fertile land that would be needed if the population kept growing was destroyed each year: not only was it being washed or blown away, as we read so often, but also, in settled regions, it was being covered with factories and housing developments, paved with concrete and asphalt, condemned for pipe lines, excavated for sand and gravel, buried under rocks and debris, flooded for power dams and lakes with bathing beaches, or converted into airfields, golf links, parking lots, drive-in theaters, and automobile junkyards. Driving through Westchester County, one found it hard to realize that this had been a region of rich farms, like those of Sleepy Hollow, where Ichabod Crane "rolled his great green eyes over the fat meadow lands, the rich fields of wheat, of rye, of buckwheat, and Indian corn, and the orchards burthened with ruddy fruit."

Not only fertile land but other resources were diminishing from year to year; part of the price for winning World War II had been the iron ore of the Mesabi Range. Meanwhile the industrial capacity of the country was growing along with its labor force and its technical skills. The problem of the early 1950s wasn't how to produce wealth—for the moment there was more than enough of almost everything for almost everyone—but how to find consumers for the products. Instead of admiring the heroes of production, says David Riesman, author of *The Lonely Crowd*, people began to emulate the pioneers and heroes of consumption, those who tried to set new fashions in cooking, dressing, reading, and interior decoration, in all the activities that fashion magazines described as "gracious living." Although social position still depended on the money that people earned, it was coming to depend even more on how they spent the money.

The existence of a large standing army was something new in American life and it produced many qualitative changes. For many thousands of young men it prolonged a feeling of dependence on something outside themselves; the Army took the place of their parents. It also solved a financial problem for middle-class parents by supporting the sons during two or more difficult years. It involved the existence of a new bureaucracy, including military intellectuals who were always tempted—though most of them resisted the temptation—to overemphasize the danger of war in order to get more money for their profession. It provided for the national security in two ways: externally as a defense against other nations, and internally by giving work to thousands of factories while taking millions of Americans off the labor market. Security rather than opportunity was becoming the national ideal.

The word "security" was so popular that it came to have different meanings. One of the meanings was safety, or simply insurance. Everybody wanted to be insured against all sorts of disasters, including poverty, unemployment, illness, old age, and acts of God; the government had to enter this new field as a measure of social justice. Another meaning was secrecy in regard to military or administrative decisions. It became high praise of a man to say that he was "security-minded," in other words, able to keep official secrets. The government undertook a determined search for "security risks," beginning with the disloyal or possibly disloyal, but not ending there; soon the term was applied to anyone of unorthodox conduct ("drunks, perverts, nudists"), or given to expressing unorthodox opinions, or having questionable associates. Thousands of agents were employed by scores of government bureaus, Congressional committees, and private or semi-public institutions in tracking down security risks, and the agents tried to justify their continued employment by finding more and more suspects. Many ex-Communists became paid informants and some of them developed fabulous powers of memory or imagination. In spite of the extremes to which it led, the loyalty crusade couldn't be laughed out of existence, as had been the Red scare after World War I; this time there were real secrets and real spies in search of them, if not so many as the public was led to believe.

The need for protecting secrets led to the creation of many restricted areas: military camps, airfields, naval bases, arsenals, atomic installations and proving grounds, artillery ranges, and the land around factories working on secret contracts. As late as 1935 one could go almost anywhere in the country without being stopped by armed guards; the largest forbidden areas were the Vanderbilt estate in North Carolina and the King ranch in Texas. After 1950, traveling by almost any transcontinental railroad or highway, one passed mile after mile of climbproof fences with guarded gates, sometimes without much sign of what lay behind them. Tom Lehrer, the Cambridge minnesinger, had a ballad about Nevada:

> 'Mid the cactus and the thistles,
> I will watch the guided missiles,
> While the old FBI watches me, *yahoo*!
> Yes, I'll soon make my appearance,
> Soon as I can get my clearance,
> 'Cause the Wild West is where I want to be.

Many decisions that would deeply affect the lives of ordinary citizens had to be taken without consulting their representatives in Congress; two examples were the defense of Korea and the adoption of a "crash program" for making hydrogen bombs. In the first case there wasn't time to consult; in the second, as in other questions of atomic warfare, Congress and the public couldn't be given all the information on which the decision was based. One effect of these sudden or secret actions was that ordinary citizens felt themselves to be living at an enormous distance from the guarded rooms in which policies were discussed around a table. Many citizens ceased to regard politics as a struggle for power in which they might personally engage; it was becoming one of their spectator sports, like baseball; they tuned out the Dodgers and listened to the Army-McCarthy hearings. The players were professionals and often the ordinary citizen liked them best if they didn't act like amateurs, but played the game hard and dirty. Just as every American boy chose a favorite baseball team ("I'm a Giant fan, what're you?"), so the grown citizen had his favorite politicians; he was a McCarthy fan (and compared him to Leo Durocher), or a Stevenson fan, or an Eisenhower fan. Meanwhile the games that an average citizen played hard for himself were office politics, leading a successful private life, and trying to be liked in his community.

There was never a time in American history when private life seemed so much more attractive than public life. The quest for privacy was reflected, in fiction, by the new emphasis on the good qualities of individuals and the bad qualities of institutions (or by the pretense, in some of the new-fashioned novels, that institutions didn't exist). In life the same impulse was reflected by the movement of prosperous families into the open countryside and by the popularity among those families of high hedges and close-woven fences, often protected by No Trespass signs. When I first moved to a little New England town in the middle 1920s, there wasn't a No Trespass sign in thirteen thousand acres of woodland and elm-dotted meadows; one could ramble or fish or hunt where one pleased. By 1950 most of the farms had been sold to city people or flooded for a lake, and there were few unposted areas.

Most of the newcomers planned to enjoy themselves with close friends and pursue their own aims in private, whatever the need for conforming to public standards, or simple hypocrisy; but the public had representatives in every household. The radio brought the news of the world at breakfast time, with a hint of the proper opinions to hold about it; the school took over what had been the parents' task, of molding the children into good citizens; and after school the television set imposed its idea of standardized entertainment. What Tocqueville wrote about the citizen of a democratic country had become immensely more true in another century. "The same equality," Tocqueville said, "that renders him independent of each of his fellow citizens, taken severally, exposes him alone and unprotected to the influence of the greater number. The public, therefore, among a democratic people . . . does not persuade others to its beliefs, but imposes them and makes them permeate the thinking of everyone by a sort of enormous pressure of the mind of all upon the individual intelligence."

1.

When discussing the changes in American ways during a single lifetime, one is always tempted to condemn the present and exalt the fresh world of one's boyhood. "That was a better world," one can't help saying, or implying, to those who live in another day. It was indeed a better world in some respects, and notably in its feeling of self-confidence, which later gave way to the fear of impending disaster. In those days there seemed to be no social problem that couldn't be solved in a few years by intelligence and good will. For the private citizen no mistake seemed irretrievable. Even if he was convicted of a crime, he could serve his sentence, then move to the West or Texas and start life over again; many valued citizens of Western towns had curious backgrounds, if anyone had looked into them. That was before the time of the individual and inalterable record that later began with the inked footprint of the newborn child. The record continued with the reports of his schoolteachers, which grew longer year by year, and the files of the dean's office in college; then it expanded with his military service and again with his income-tax returns, and again with his social-security account, and once again with his folder in the personnel files of the corporation for which he worked, and once or many times again with the dossiers compiled by various investigative agencies of the federal government—until any prominent citizen could be buried ten feet deep in the accumulation of papers that would end with his death certificate and his newspaper obituaries, rewritten from still other files. In a sense the future was being buried under the records of the past, and living men were being judged by what they had been, not, as in earlier days, by what they might become.

The first years of the century were a less documented and regimented age, and they seem more spacious too, since we look at them from a distance, but they weren't a better age for the average American. In the 1950s he earned more money, which would buy him better food, clothing, shelter, and more equipment for his home. His children were healthier and spent more years in school. He could look forward to a longer life, with the prospect of being partly supported in his old age, and meanwhile he had more leisure and was finding more entertaining ways of spending it. There was no longer the gulf that had threatened to open in the

1920s between the white-collar classes and men in overalls. Office workers had fallen a little in the social scale—as note the observations of C. Wright Mills in *White Collar*—but it was more significant that manual workers had risen, both socially and economically; often they had moved into the same streets as the white-collar people and were driving bigger cars.[2] There was less racial prejudice, including anti-Semitism, or at least it was being less openly expressed. The Negroes had made great progress, economically, politically, and educationally, and perhaps even greater progress had been made by Catholic immigrants from Eastern and Southern Europe; they had started as pick-and-shovel workers, but their children were playing an important part in the business life of many communities.

All these are measurable changes that have already been reported at length by the sociologists. What interests me more, and has a closer relation to our future literature, is the change in the intimate lives of American families. It seems to me that families were learning to have better times together, that they took more interest in serving a variety of good food, in cooking and eating and playing outdoors, in having pleasantly livable rather than showy houses; more of them owned their homes. Even if the homes were shabby, like mile after mile of wooden one-family dwellings in Chicago, cars stood outside most of them, waiting to take the children to a public beach or a picture palace. There were more children in the average family, and they were receiving more attention. One kept hearing about friends who had planned to spend a year or more in Europe, but hurried home after the first month because they were worried about the children, who weren't doing

2. Anyone who wanted to live again in an earlier American age had only to visit some farming sections of English Canada. There he would find the feeling of space and freedom, the lack of No Trespass signs, the greater self-reliance—but also the uglier, less comfortable houses, the briefer schooling, and the abundant but monotonous food, with everything fried or baked. Prince Edward Island, where I spent a month in 1940, seemed almost exactly like Cambria County, Pennsylvania, in 1910. I loved the island, but was driven away by indigestion.

By contrast I spent the early months of 1950 in Seattle, where everything was modern, including the excellent food in private houses. Everyone seemed to be middle class and literate, no matter what his trade. We lived on a street lined with picture-windowed houses that were owned, not rented, by business people, skilled mechanics, and college professors. The milkman, the dry cleaner for the neighborhood, and the cleaner's wife were college graduates, as were many of the taxi drivers.

well without their pediatricians, dentists, and child psychologists, their certified milk, frozen orange juice, and streptomycin. In the days when pediatricians were known as child specialists and were likely to be homeopaths, Mrs. Malaprop used to say that homeopathy was good for infantry, but allopaths, or conventional physicians, were better for adultery. In the 1950s Europe was a continent for visiting adults, and sometimes for their adulteries, but America was the children's paradise. American society, instead of being matriarchal, was becoming filiarchal or pedocratic.

Voices—except for those of high-school students—were less shrill than I remembered them from a Western Pennsylvania boyhood. A mood of gentleness seemed to be spreading over the country; half a century before, the older families in the seaboard states were almost the only ones who tried to be gentle people. As servants disappeared from middle-class households, the family itself became a closer group, with more shared tasks. These were lightened by a variety of mechanical servants; one businessman I know counted twenty-three electric motors in his household, as well as five internal-combustion engines (two cars, an outboard motor, a lawnmower, and a garden tractor). Among the most popular household appliances were entertainment machines reduced to a family scale. Public facilities like railroads, streetcars, buses, theaters, concert halls, stadiums, and coliseums all suffered from competition with private facilities like television sets and passenger cars. Mass-transportation systems noted a special decline in evening traffic and concluded that families were staying at home. On Wednesday evenings, when boxing matches were televised, buses in Pittsburgh ran almost empty.

Husbands and wives not only spent more time together but had more interests in common than at any earlier period. They talked more frankly about their sexual problems, and the frigid wife, instead of being proud in her virtue, began to feel ashamed and inferior. Except in a few cities, houses of prostitution were no longer tolerated; most of the remaining houses in New York and Los Angeles were merely telephone numbers, and the wires were likely to be tapped by the police. The relation between the sexes had changed immensely for the better at all age levels, beginning with the seventh or eighth grade in grammar school. When I was that age, girls were an alien race, plainly inferior, but gifted with a mysterious self-possession that made boys feel awkward in their presence. One speculated about them ("Does she?"—"Jimmy says she did it with him"), but one never had much to say to them. By the 1950s boys in the seventh grade were making dates and wondering how soon they could go steady.

The institution of "going steady" was something new in American life; at least it was new for lower-teen-age boys and girls of the middle classes. Until the First World War a middle-class girl was at least eighteen before she consented to make all her dates with one beau—as the "steady" was called in those days—and then she was likely to regard herself as informally engaged. In the 1950s "going steady" had ceased to imply an engagement; it was an institution that existed for its own sake as much as for the future. Its popularity seems to have been connected with the general demand for security: girls said, and boys too, "If I didn't have a steady I might have to go to parties alone," and they hesitated to run that minor risk. "Can we—c'n we go steady?" the boy plucked up his courage to say, as if he were making a proposal of marriage. Often the "steadies" got married when they finished high school, if that was the end of their education, but they were likely to separate if one or both of them went on to college, or sometimes when the boy went into the Army. In the meantime the relationship had involved some degree of sexual intimacy—if usually no more than heavy petting—together with daily companionship, so that it had come to be a sort of trial marriage. There was reason to believe that it might prepare young people for real marriages, often with other partners.

Relations between parents and children were better than they had been in the teens and twenties of this century. There were fewer attempts at dictation by the parents, who had been advised to be "permissive," and also fewer rebellions by the children, with a little more frankness on both sides. The gulf between generations had seemed to be widest in the years after World War I; at that time young people avoided the company of their elders, who were thought to be stuffy, conventional, and unprepared to hear the jokes that young people told among themselves; also the parents didn't know what the children wanted out of life. "Mother and I don't see why you insist on going to New York [or Chicago or Paris]," they would say in the 1920s, and the children would try to explain, but with a feeling that they wouldn't be understood. Usually they ended by going, and afterward they saw the parents only once or twice a year. In the 1950s the older children saw their parents oftener and sometimes took their advice, so that the two generations seemed to be closer together. There was, however, merely an appearance of understanding, based on the absence of scoldings and rebellions, and the parents were as far from the children as they had been from their own fathers and mothers; perhaps the real gulf was even wider. That too might be a subject for novels in the future.

The young writers of this age—I am thinking of those born after 1920—belonged to the first generation that really grew up with the automobile, the first for which driving three or four thousand pounds of steel at sixty miles an hour became as instinctive as walking and more habitual; nobody liked to walk any more. They were also the first to grow up with radio, the jukebox, and talking pictures—that is, with omnipresent voices and music—just as still younger persons, born after 1940, would be the first to grow up with television. The effect on both groups was to make them more ear-minded and picture-minded and to occupy much of the time they might have spent in reading. On the average they had probably read fewer books than their elders at the same age—or it might be more accurate to say that the reading, even for future writers, began later in life, when they were in college rather than when they were in high school. They were the first generation to attend new high schools at a time when secondary education had become almost universal and teen-age boys and girls composed an independent society, resentful of interference by older people. The education they received was different, with more stress laid on adjustment to the group and less on competitive achievement in their studies; in high school there were also fewer themes to write, less homework, less study of foreign languages, and a less thorough grounding in English. They were being prepared to get along with people rather than to manipulate words or ideas.

The new writers were children during the depression, which most of them later seemed to have forgotten, although there were signs that the fear of poverty was still embedded in their minds. They served in the Second World War if they were old enough; many of them spent five or six years in uniform. They learned much about warfare, somewhat less about foreign countries, and more about Americans of all types, while they also acquired the habit of looking to the government for food, clothing, and answers to the question, "What shall I do next?" The habit continued for many after their discharge from the armed forces, since the government sent them checks to pay for their education, with a few dollars extra for wives and children; most of them had married young. Meanwhile still younger writers were also having their share of military life—some with assignments in Korea—and were being taught to hold a similar attitude toward an impersonal, all-powerful, and all-nourishing state. In civilian life both groups would benefit from the longest period of prosperity this country has known—the state was also responsible for that, through its military spending— and both would learn to fear a sudden disaster in which their world might go down to ruin.

The two groups together were sometimes called "the silent generation," though I don't know why—unless it is because they had published fewer books and magazine articles about themselves than their predecessors had published at the same ages. That was largely the fault of publishers and editors, or rather of the public they serve, which seemed to be less interested in hearing new voices than it had been in the 1920s, with the result that more novels than ever before remained in manuscript. But the word "silent" may also have referred to the fact that young writers were expressing very few political opinions. Once I thought that the failure to express opinions was due to caution, but later I came to believe that they didn't want to "sound off" about questions they weren't qualified to answer; they didn't like people who sounded off. The young writers and their friends were not at all silent in sympathetic company; in fact they were fond of explaining themselves, simply and candidly. Some of them said—I have heard the phrase several times —that they felt as if they were standing at the edge of a cliff; soon they might be pushed off, or the cliff might crumble.

Not many of them—or only one group—displayed the personal recklessness of their predecessors, who had believed that the ground was stable underfoot and that they could, if they so desired, assume wild postures without losing their balance. In these later days when society itself was endangered, many young people began to appreciate the solid satisfactions it offered, including love, marriage, and children. They wanted to fall in love, get married, and have children while there was still time. If they were apprentice writers, most of them wanted to study the technique of literature, defend its traditions, and learn to enjoy its pleasures; they weren't quite so eager to rush into print. The generation as a whole seemed to have no such hunger for social distinction as had been felt by young men in the 1920s—by Scott Fitzgerald, for example, who wanted to make the best eating club at Princeton and marry "the most beautiful girl in Alabama *and* Georgia," as he boasted that he was doing. At Princeton forty years later every junior was elected to an eating club; the student body had decided that no one should be left out. At Yale the *News* stopped printing the names of men pledged to the senior societies on Tap Day, so as not to discriminate against those who had been overlooked.

Young men didn't try so hard to get their names in the papers or even to rise in the business world. "Why kill yourself earning a big income," they asked, "when the government takes most of it in taxes?" Comparatively few of them wanted to work for themselves or for somebody else's small business in which advancement might be rapid if the business prospered; as a rule they didn't like "ifs." They said, making fun of their modest ambitions, "A steady job, a little house near the golf links, and a big family." Again they said, "We want to be unmolested," and most of them conformed to social rules in order to be molested as little as possible.

There was one fairly large group that refused to conform and waged a dogged sort of rebellion—against what it is hard to say, because the group had no program, but possibly against the whole body of laws, customs, fears, habits of thought, and literary standards that had been accepted by other members of the generation. The rebellion was individual and nihilistic; each of the rebels simply refused to accept any model, in literature or life, that older people asked him to emulate. Some made a cult out of heavy drinking, promiscuity, smoking marijuana, or almost any other forbidden pleasure, but their real delights were driving fast—if they could get hold of automobiles—and listening to cool jazz. They liked to be "cool," that is, withdrawn. Often they talked about being "underground" and called themselves "the beat generation"; it was John Kerouac who invented the second phrase, and his unpublished long narrative, *On the Road*, is the best record of their lives. In two respects they were like the more conventional majority of young people: they had no interest in politics, even as a spectator sport, and they were looking for something to believe, an essentially religious faith that would permit them to live at peace with their world.

Whatever course of action the new writers followed—whether they were conformists or thought of themselves as a rebellious underground—they seemed to be a new race of Americans, with a new relation to the state, a new picture of the world overseas, a new attitude toward love and the family, and generally with new values, even though they bewailed the lack of them. They had a new consciousness and a new subconscious too, one that led to dreams of being unmolested and violent nightmares of destruction. When among themselves they seemed to be speaking a new language. Their realism about the world they lived in and their level-eyed candor both held a promise for the future. Even the nihilists among them, by rejecting everything old, seemed to be clearing the ground for new structures. I liked and respected the new writers as a group. My one complaint against them would be that they weren't yet producing new works of literature. They weren't expressing their new sense of life. They weren't coming forward with myths and heroes—that is, with archetypical stories and characters—for the new age in which they lived.

2.

What I am recommending to the younger writers isn't merely that they should treat new subjects taken from the private and public lives of Americans today. That would be a simple course of action, but they could follow it without producing a literature of their own. The fact is that new subject matter has appeared pretty widely in recent fiction. It can be found even—or perhaps one should say especially—in the lower reaches of fiction, that is, in confessional stories ("Mother Is Bugged at Me") and in chain-store and supermarket monthlies, which make a special effort to deal with contemporary problems. There is also new material, though rather less of it, in some of the serious novels by younger writers. One notes, however, that the style and structure of the novels, like the formulas of the magazine stories, are almost always traditional; some of the wine is new, but the wineskins have been used before. In order to express a new sense of life, something more is needed than new melodies in a familiar mode; there must also be new signatures and tempos. In literature there must be new rhythms of speech, new images, new characters, and new methods of telling stories.

It is of course possible that we have reached a wintry time at which our civilization has become incapable of creating new literary forms. Here I am thinking of Spengler, who told us that Western art was losing its vitality, like Roman art under the twelve Caesars. Others have pointed out that *The Decline of the West* contains many errors and misinterpretations, so that we can hardly accept Spengler as a prophet. Still, his two-volume work is full of sidelights on historical events and stimulating figures of speech, and some of the figures might cast light on the situation in American literature.

Reading the second volume, I came across a long metaphor that suggests what was happening to young writers in the 1950s. Spengler is about to discuss the Arabian or Magian culture, which, he says, originated in Syria and Mesopotamia and spread westward across the Roman Empire in the first centuries of the Christian era. It was completely new in spirit, but, as it moved westward, it accepted the forms of the declining Classical civilization, so that there was a conflict between the forms and the new sense of life that was struggling for self-expression. To describe that conflict, Spengler uses the term "pseudomorphism," which he then explains:

In a rock stratum are embedded crystals of a mineral. Clefts and cracks occur, water filters in, and the crystals are gradually washed out, so that in due course only their hollow mold remains. Then come volcanic outbursts which explode the mountain; molten masses pour in, stiffen, and crystalize out in their turn. But these are not free to do so in their own special forms. They must fill up the spaces that they find available. Thus there arise distorted forms, crystals whose inner structure contradicts their external shape, stones of one kind presenting the appearance of stones of another kind. The mineralogists call this phenomenon *pseudomorphosis*.

By the term "historical pseudomorphosis" I propose to designate those cases in which an older alien Culture lies so massively over the land that a young Culture, born in this land, cannot get its breath and fails not only to achieve pure and specific expression forms, but even to develop fully its own self-consciousness. All that wells up from the depths of the young soul is cast in the old molds, young feelings stiffen in senile works, and instead of rearing itself up in its own creative power, it can only hate the distant power with a hate that grows to be monstrous.

It seems to me that a good deal of American writing after World War II, including most of the serious novels and not a little of the poetry, was essentially pseudomorphic. One thinks of all the novels about the second war that were written in Hemingway's early style, so that the authors seemed to picture themselves as part of a beaten army falling back from the Isonzo. One thinks of the other war novels—but sometimes they are the same books—that have utilized Dos Passos' many devices for presenting a collective experience. He was using them to show that individuals are helplessly crushed by society, where most of the new novelists wanted to emphasize the resistance of good men to social pressures; often the borrowed devices ended by defeating the authors' purpose. Again one thinks of the elegant novels about Cleveland and Princeton and Long Island that were written under the shadow of Henry James and in the asthmatic, comma-dotted style of his later years—as if the authors were tired expatriates who had to pause for breath after speaking two or three words, instead of being young stay-at-homes bursting with energy. One thinks of the new avant-garde and its bold experiments, which were bolder when the Paris avant-garde performed them in 1920 or even 1910. One thinks of all the new poets in the tradition of T. S. Eliot, who himself started writing in the tradition of the forgotten Harvard poets of the 1890s, with their Greek learning, their mixture of paganism and Catholicism, their desire to achieve French worldliness, and their belief that poetic dramas are the highest form of literature. Eliot wrote the poems they had all tried to write; he even mastered the poetic drama, in which they had all failed. In the 1950s a battalion or two of little Eliots were trying to realize, for a second time, the frustrated dreams of Philip Henry Savage, Cabot Lodge, and Trumbull Stickney, whose names they had scarcely heard.

Yet the poets, and the novelists too, were more than imitators and epigoni. Underneath the old forms and methods was a new sense of life and perhaps the beginnings of a new culture, born in this land, but—as Spengler said of the Magian culture—it had failed not only "to achieve pure and specific expression forms, but even to develop fully its own self-consciousness." Spengler was thinking of a longer historical period, but, on a greatly reduced scale, his remarks might apply to our own times. In the 1950s, as in Alexandria under the Ptolemys and Rome under the Caesars, young emotions had stiffened in senile works, and I am sure that many young writers felt an unconscious hatred for the great figures of another day, who were forcing them into molds that kept them from breathing.

Not being a Spenglerian fatalist, I believe that the new expression forms will appear before it is too late, but I don't know what they will be; there are all sorts of possibilities. The novel, for example, has shown signs of becoming a frozen form resembling architecture rather than music. The form might decongeal and, instead of novels like funerary monuments, we might have loosely conceived narratives that carried one or many heroes through a variety of adventures. The subconscious feelings of the age have revealed themselves more freely in so-called interplanetary fiction, and perhaps in hard-boiled detective stories, than in any conventional novels. Perhaps the visions of the interplanetary writers might be brought down to earth, or they might be treated by men of greater talent. Poets might write more folksongs and ballads, as W. H. Auden did at one stage of his career; there are new and simple emotions waiting to be expressed in a new language. The search for a religious faith to guide us through this time of troubles might lead to apocalyptic works, like those which appeared in such numbers at the beginning of the Christian era.

Today it seems possible that the whole subjective and introspective tendency that has dominated the modern movement in literature—beginning with Baudelaire or Dostoevski or whatever great name we choose—is drawing to its end. The new literature might be concerned not with personal feelings on the deepest level, but with interpersonal relations. That would be a logical result of the new educational system, which is teaching children to get along with other children and be extraverts. The new system is failing—it hasn't even made a serious effort—to teach the elements of good reading and writing to the millions. A final possibility must be considered that printed literature, in the future, will be written for and read only by scholars. For the public at large it might give way to picture books, or to spoken and tape-recorded stories, or else to dramas and serials composed for television or the new medium that will come after it.

Whatever the new forms may be, I am not at all sure that I shall like them when they do appear. They won't be my forms and won't express my spirit, but I know they are needed if the new age is to become fully conscious of its own spirit. I can think of one way in which their appearance might possibly be hastened. Some of the new writers—not all of them, for literature is a broad field that permits many simultaneous efforts in many directions—but at least a few might abandon the study of advanced techniques and hidden symbols, along with the effort to reproduce what has already been written. Most writers of the age have started by learning the traditional forms, into which they have tried to mold their subject matter; I am suggesting that some of them might reverse the process. Faulkner said in his courtly way, "I was coeval with the time when one could escape an education." A higher education is good for most writers—the higher the better—but a few might try to escape it, like Faulkner, instead of studying his methods in postgraduate courses and trying to tell a story in his manner. They might start with the simplest things, as Hemingway did when he was learning to be a writer. They might tell what really happened, and to whom, and how they truly felt about it, not how they had been taught to feel or were expected to feel. Then the form of their writing would be determined by the subject matter and it might—in one case out of ten or a thousand—be as new as the sense of life it was intended to express.

The recent period in American literature has been a sort of interval or interregnum. One is impressed by the generally high technical level of writing in all fields. The poets have been erudite and generally honest, the novelists have been skilled and sensitive, but only the critics have seemed to know where they were going; most of the others wrote as if they were waiting for something or someone to give their work a more definite direction. Mere talent has been relatively common; it was conviction and character that were needed. The result has been a fluid situation in which the influence of a single great writer might prove to be decisive, in the fashion that Hemingway was decisive for the 1920s and Faulkner for a whole group of Southern novelists. If such another great writer appears and creates new forms, new myths and heroes that speak for this age, then the lesser but talented men and women surrounding him will arrange themselves into a new configuration, like iron filings around a magnet, and perhaps we shall have another great period in American writing.

Sherman, Connecticut, July 1954

INDEX

INDEX